# Inbound Marketing

## FOR DUMMIES®

A Wiley Brand

## by Scott Anderson Miller

**Inbound Marketing For Dummies**®

Published by: **John Wiley & Sons, Inc.,** 111 River Street, Hoboken, NJ 07030-5774, www.wiley.com

Copyright © 2015 by John Wiley & Sons, Inc., Hoboken, New Jersey

Media and software compilation copyright © 2015 by John Wiley & Sons, Inc. All rights reserved.

Published simultaneously in Canada

No part of this publication may be reproduced, stored in a retrieval system or transmitted in any form or by any means, electronic, mechanical, photocopying, recording, scanning or otherwise, except as permitted under Sections 107 or 108 of the 1976 United States Copyright Act, without the prior written permission of the Publisher. Requests to the Publisher for permission should be addressed to the Permissions Department, John Wiley & Sons, Inc., 111 River Street, Hoboken, NJ 07030, (201) 748-6011, fax (201) 748-6008, or online at www.wiley.com/go/permissions.

**Trademarks:** Wiley, For Dummies, the Dummies Man logo, Dummies.com, Making Everything Easier, and related trade dress are trademarks or registered trademarks of John Wiley & Sons, Inc. and may not be used without written permission. All other trademarks are the property of their respective owners. John Wiley & Sons, Inc. is not associated with any product or vendor mentioned in this book.

LIMIT OF LIABILITY/DISCLAIMER OF WARRANTY: THE PUBLISHER AND THE AUTHOR MAKE NO REPRESENTATIONS OR WARRANTIES WITH RESPECT TO THE ACCURACY OR COMPLETENESS OF THE CONTENTS OF THIS WORK AND SPECIFICALLY DISCLAIM ALL WARRANTIES, INCLUDING WITHOUT LIMITATION WARRANTIES OF FITNESS FOR A PARTICULAR PURPOSE. NO WARRANTY MAY BE CREATED OR EXTENDED BY SALES OR PROMOTIONAL MATERIALS. THE ADVICE AND STRATEGIES CONTAINED HEREIN MAY NOT BE SUITABLE FOR EVERY SITUATION. THIS WORK IS SOLD WITH THE UNDERSTANDING THAT THE PUBLISHER IS NOT ENGAGED IN RENDERING LEGAL, ACCOUNTING, OR OTHER PROFESSIONAL SERVICES. IF PROFESSIONAL ASSISTANCE IS REQUIRED, THE SERVICES OF A COMPETENT PROFESSIONAL PERSON SHOULD BE SOUGHT. NEITHER THE PUBLISHER NOR THE AUTHOR SHALL BE LIABLE FOR DAMAGES ARISING HEREFROM. THE FACT THAT AN ORGANIZATION OR WEBSITE IS REFERRED TO IN THIS WORK AS A CITATION AND/OR A POTENTIAL SOURCE OF FURTHER INFORMATION DOES NOT MEAN THAT THE AUTHOR OR THE PUBLISHER ENDORSES THE INFORMATION THE ORGANIZATION OR WEBSITE MAY PROVIDE OR RECOMMENDATIONS IT MAY MAKE. FURTHER, READERS SHOULD BE AWARE THAT INTERNET WEBSITES LISTED IN THIS WORK MAY HAVE CHANGED OR DISAPPEARED BETWEEN WHEN THIS WORK WAS WRITTEN AND WHEN IT IS READ.

For general information on our other products and services, please contact our Customer Care Department within the U.S. at 877-762-2974, outside the U.S. at 317-572-3993, or fax 317-572-4002. For technical support, please visit www.wiley.com/techsupport.

Wiley publishes in a variety of print and electronic formats and by print-on-demand. Some material included with standard print versions of this book may not be included in e-books or in print-on-demand. If this book refers to media such as a CD or DVD that is not included in the version you purchased, you may download this material at http://booksupport.wiley.com. For more information about Wiley products, visit www.wiley.com.

Library of Congress Control Number: 2015947762

ISBN 978-1-119-12050-6 (pbk); ISBN 978-1-119-12052-0 (ebk); ISBN 978-1-119-12051-3 (ebk)

Manufactured in the United States of America

10 9 8 7 6 5 4 3 2 1

# Contents at a Glance

# Table of Contents

# Introduction

· · · · · · · · · · · · · · · · · · · · · · · · · · · · · · · · · · · · · · · · · · · · · · · · · · · ·

*T*raditional marketing methods don't work anymore. With over three billion people accessing the Internet, over half of them via mobile devices, you are living in the connected "global village" predicted by Marshall McLuhan in 1968. Power is shifting from company brands to individual consumers armed with influence and currency. Consumers research, shop, and purchase when and where they want, on their own schedules. Does this mean you should give up marketing for good?

Meet *inbound marketing,* a holistic system that creates meaningful connections between organizations and people. The ultimate inbound-marketing goal is marketing to a customer as an individual, creating a connection that culminates in a desired end — an action in the form of a sale, donation, or subscription.

This book teaches the principles of connecting with consumers on *their* terms, not on the marketer's terms. My aim is to clarify inbound marketing best practices so marketers succeed in connecting products with people. This book is a guide for you as an inbound marketing strategist and practitioner.

Inbound marketing is attractive because it creates timely, relevant, and contextual connections. When executed properly, inbound marketing results in an end purchase, donation, or engagement that appears natural to the user because the consumer proceeds at his or her own pace and stays in control throughout the process. All you have to do is communicate an authentic message that resonates and attracts consumers. Better connections result in better conversions. This customer attraction and conversion process is the essence of inbound marketing.

## About This Book

Inbound marketing is a hot topic. It's more than a trendy fad or a buzzword. Inbound marketing's foundation is attraction over interruption messaging. Inbound marketing integrates messaging that is contextual, relevant, and timely for the intended recipient, and integrates into your target consumer's purchasing behavior. Interruptive messaging (such as a TV ad), on the other hand, unnaturally disrupts your consumer's behavior. Integrating your marketing based on your target customers' needs is a fundamental paradigm shift from "push" marketing to "pull" marketing.

In this new paradigm, traditional marketers are quickly becoming dinosaurs. Their old methods of marketing don't apply in the new digital age. They need a primer to adapt and evolve. By connecting with consumers early in the purchase process and by serving up content that is relevant and timely, marketers can achieve a higher level of success. Anyone new to this paradigm needs a guidebook to correctly implement inbound marketing in his or her organization. That's where this book comes in. *Inbound Marketing For Dummies* teaches marketers and business owners how to succeed in this new, dynamic environment.

# Foolish Assumptions

The book clarifies the principles and processes of inbound marketing to aspiring and seasoned marketing professionals alike. It teaches how to attract, convert, and keep customers for life. As such, it's a good resource for any of the following:

- Marketing directors
- Marketing coordinators
- Marketing consultants
- Ad agency owners
- PR firms
- Small-business owners
- In-house marketing personnel
- Bloggers/content producers
- Users of marketing automation software or sales customer-relationship management software

This book assumes you have a basic working knowledge of marketing from which you are looking to expand and grow. It also assumes your company has Google Analytics connected to your website.

# Icons Used in This Book

In this book, material of interest is sometimes indicated by icons in the margins. This section briefly describes each icon in this book.

Sometimes the volume of inbound marketing information can be overwhelming. You'll see this icon to help you easily scan important inbound marketing information.

 Whenever there's a simpler or better way to make complex information simple, you'll see this icon.

 There's a lot that can go wrong with inbound marketing. Believe me, I've made my share of mistakes. Paying attention to this icon helps you avoid common inbound marketing pitfalls.

 Used sparingly, this icon designates information beyond the basics of inbound marketing. When you see this icon, don't freak out! Just knowing the basics of inbound marketing elevates your knowledge base above the typical marketer.

# Beyond This Book

A lot of extra content that you won't find in this book is available at www.dummies.com. Go online to find the following:

✔ **Online articles covering additional topics at**

> www.dummies.com/extras/inboundmarketing

Here you'll find out how to create three-dimensional content that connects with consumers, learn ten steps to creating an inbound marketing campaign, and ten criteria for choosing marketing automation software, among other details to aid you in your inbound-marketing journey.

✔ **The Cheat Sheet for this book is at**

> www.dummies.com/cheatsheet/inboundmarketing

Here you'll find additional helpful inbound marketing resources online and on my inbound marketing tech e-cheat sheet.

✔ **Updates to this book, if we have any, are also available at**

> www.dummies.com/extras/inboundmarketing

# *Where to Go from Here*

This book makes the new marketing paradigm clear to you. Although it's important to remember inbound marketing is a process, and even small pieces contribute to the whole, feel free to scan the table of contents or the index to find topics helpful to your particular marketing situation. Additionally, I've provided a glossary of useful inbound-marketing terminology at the back of the book.

# Part I
# Getting Started with Inbound Marketing

getting started

with

Inbound

Marketing

web extras

Visit www.dummies.com for great *For Dummies* content online.

# In this part . . .

- ✔ Learning the difference between inbound marketing and traditional marketing.
- ✔ Understanding the positive impact inbound marketing will have on your organization.
- ✔ Learning the four objectives of inbound marketing.
- ✔ Introducing the three-step inbound process to your organization.
- ✔ Discovering components of an organized, systematic inbound marketing plan.

# Chapter 1

# What Is Inbound Marketing, Anyway?

*W*elcome to the world of inbound marketing. If you're a marketer who believes in authenticity, thrives on achieving goals, and embraces measurable success, you're in the right place. Inbound marketing is more than just marketing; it's a business practice. The inbound philosophy can create meaningful change in organizations large and small. Many times, this business evolution transcends financial metrics, affecting the very culture of an organization. The resulting productivity and achievement often surprises even top leadership. The metamorphosis from traditional marketing to inbound marketing attracts better customers and better employees. The outcome is usually expressed as higher revenues and profits. Inbound marketing has improved the businesses of my clients and of my own two marketing firms. I trust that by instituting an inbound philosophy within your organization you'll realize positive change, too. Just remember, inbound is not something you do, it's something you live.

## Knowing the Basics of Inbound Marketing

Inbound marketing is both a science and an art. Inbound marketing involves the science of measuring connections and making data-driven decisions, and the art of dissecting, analyzing, applying, and testing initiatives that connect in a meaningful way. Specifically, inbound marketing measures:

- ✔ Connections between companies and customers
- ✔ Connections between sales and marketing
- ✔ Connections between marketing investments and meaningful, measured financial results defined in terms of return-on-investment (ROI)

Inbound marketing causes actions and reactions. At its most basic level, inbound marketing consists of:

- ✔ Attracting visitors to your website
- ✔ Nurturing those visitors, on their terms, within a structurally planned dynamic environment (your website) that facilitates action
- ✔ Converting those visitors into leads and, in turn, leads into customers through mutual exchange of valuable data (content for customer data) via a systematic process
- ✔ Reconverting prior customers into loyal, lifelong customers

Some other assumptions under the inbound marketing philosophy:

- ✔ Consumers engage with companies on their own terms and on their personal timeline.
- ✔ Information empowers consumers to make smarter shopping and purchase decisions.
- ✔ Online authenticity is rewarded with high customer satisfaction and positive online consumer reviews.
- ✔ Openly sharing information and content creates trust.
- ✔ Content connects products with people, the marketing department with the sales department, and marketing initiatives with measurable business results.
- ✔ Data-driven decisions increase the odds of success.
- ✔ Measuring what matters improves performance.
- ✔ Customers' needs dictate product features and service offerings.
- ✔ Marketing automation facilitates efficient business practices.
- ✔ Relationships between brands and consumers are possible in the digital world.

# Understanding Inbound as a Philosophy and as a Marketing System

You've heard plenty of buzz about it. You're pretty sure you should be doing it. But what — exactly — is inbound marketing?

Inbound marketing is a holistic, fully integrated approach to building your business via the Internet, based on the law of attraction — the belief that like attracts like. Inbound marketing is also both a business philosophy and a business practice.

## Inbound as a philosophy

Philosophically, the term "inbound" goes beyond the marketing function, though the scope of this book is limited to marketing strategy and initiatives. Inbound as a business philosophy, and specifically as a marketing philosophy, refers to a complex customer-centric business model.

In particular, inbound marketing is a paradigm shift from the belief and practice of interruptive "push" marketing methods to a philosophy of attractive "pull" marketing. Inbound marketing isn't solely about great creative campaigns, beautiful graphic design, or logos. Although these things may represent characteristics of inbound marketing, a truly attractive inbound marketing campaign dives deeper than sleek advertising whose main intention is to seek attention.

Does your organization believe in the inbound philosophy? Here are some traits of the inbound methodology:

- ✔ Your company innovates based on satisfying unfulfilled consumer needs.
- ✔ Your customer relationship extends beyond the transactional.
- ✔ Your company connects with customers at multiple levels at multiple points in time.
- ✔ Your focus is beyond making the first sale, extending to creating a customer for life.
- ✔ You encourage customer interaction, listen to feedback, and respond accordingly.

## Is your company ready for inbound?

Answer these questions to determine whether your company is ready to try inbound marketing:

- ✔ Does your company actively interact with prospective customers before the first purchase?

- ✔ Does your company interact with its customers with non-sales messaging before the first purchase?

- ✔ Does your company know the lifetime value of its customers, expressed in terms of dollars and influence?

- ✔ Does your company use content to create meaningful connections before, during, and after a sale?

- ✔ Does your company know its customers beyond the first purchase?

- ✔ Does your company create consumer value beyond a transaction?

- ✔ Is your public messaging customer-centric or product-centric?

- ✔ Is your private internal messaging customer-centric or product-centric?

- ✔ Does your company solve customer problems?

- ✔ Do you communicate with prospects at both the emotional and rational level?

If you answered yes to most of these questions, your company is primed and ready to begin implementing inbound marketing.

The inbound philosophy thrives upon mutual trust, meaningful relationships, and two-way communication. Inbound marketing creates shared connections between consumer and company based on mutually beneficial connective points. The most successful companies create value beyond the product or service they're selling to enhance a consumer's lifestyle. Brands like Starbucks and Red Bull have a value that extends well beyond the customer's need for a beverage; they represent an aspirational lifestyle to which their customers connect on such a deep level they actually "live" the brand.

## Inbound marketing as a system of attraction and conversion

In practice, inbound marketing is a connected system of online customer attraction and conversion. When a stranger becomes a lead, a lead becomes a customer, and that customer lives and advocates your brand . . . *that* is the flawless execution of inbound marketing. This powerful conversion process is why more and more organizations are practicing inbound marketing. Of companies that practice inbound marketing, 93 percent see an increase in lead generation.

Using this principle, inbound marketing specifically aims to attract those potential customers who have signaled or demonstrated an interest in what your organization has to offer. You have a valuable product or service consumers want or need — something they're searching for online. Inbound marketing speaks directly to that need by creating conversations that connect with prospective customers, then facilitating a positive conversion action. By the way, these conversions are not always measured by the items in the online shopping cart. Your desired conversion action may certainly be a purchase, but it also may be any derived action, including:

- ✔ Donations
- ✔ Reviews
- ✔ Shares or Likes on Facebook
- ✔ Retweets on Twitter
- ✔ Downloads
- ✔ Demos
- ✔ Free trials
- ✔ Webinars
- ✔ Newsletters

By offering value and facilitating connections, inbound marketing "pulls" in customers based on their specific expressed needs. This attractive "pull" method is a key approach that defines inbound marketing.

Simply put, the practice of inbound marketing can be defined as:

$$\text{Attraction} + \text{Conversions} = \text{Customers}$$

# Learning Why Inbound Marketing Is Important to Your Organization

Massive change is occurring in the business ecosystem. This is true in the business-to-consumer and business-to-business sectors. Inbound marketing doesn't just address this change; it embraces it.

There is an unprecedented shift of power from the giant corporate conglomerate brands to individual consumers. Never in history has the individual consumer wielded so much power, currency, and influence. You and your brand have lost control. And that's okay . . .

Today, the individual consumer decides:

- ✔ What information to consume
- ✔ Where to consume information online
- ✔ When to consume information online
- ✔ When to engage with your company
- ✔ Whether to perform an online conversion like downloading, purchasing, donating, or signing up for a service or newsletter
- ✔ When to buy
- ✔ Whether or not to leave a positive/negative review of your business or product

Each consumer's online action affects your business. The aggregate consumer behavior may have profound effects on whether or not you're able to attract visitors and convert those visitors into leads or customers. Individual actions affect your overall ability to succeed in business.

Inbound marketing is at the heart of this change in power from brand to individual. Inbound marketing embraces this change by communicating to an individual's specific needs. When your website greets visitors and customers on *their* terms, on *their* timeline, at *their* pace of content and product consumption, you're practicing inbound marketing. Interrupting this flow disconnects you and your brand from your website users. That means you're disconnecting yourself from potential business.

The shift in power from brand to consumer is good news for the savvy, adaptable marketer. It's bad news for traditionalists who keep shouting louder at smaller audiences, barking up the wrong trees.

# Exploring the Benefits of Inbound Marketing

Here are the benefits your organization will see upon embracing the inbound marketing philosophy and implementing an inbound marketing system:

- ✔ Measurable marketing that connects initiatives with business ROI
- ✔ Better communication between your marketing and sales departments
- ✔ Earlier access to the consumer purchase path

- ✔ Increased customer engagement with your brand and products
- ✔ Internal accountability and ownership of results
- ✔ Business growth in dollars, units sold, and market share

# Defining the Differences between Traditional and Inbound Marketing

Traditional media isn't dead, but it's dying. The traditional marketing methodology of interruptive "push" messaging is dying at an even quicker rate. This is due to the ability of the individual to dictate purchase patterns.

Here are some major changes occurring as you read this:

- ✔ 2014 marked the first year in history that total search engine marketing (SEM) spending surpassed total broadcast TV spending in the U.S.
- ✔ Two out of three marketers have moved at least 30 percent of their budgets from traditional media to digital media in the past three years.
- ✔ Print ad revenues are now the lowest they've been since 1950.
- ✔ Nearly half of consumers say they won't return to a website if it doesn't load properly on their mobile devices.
- ✔ In 2015 mobile searches (85.9 billion) overtook desktop-based searches (84 billion) for the first time ever.

## Traditional marketing

Traditional marketing was designed with good intentions, but it was limited by the medium. Before the advent of the Internet and the resulting proliferation of information and data, control of information rested in the hands of a few powerful media outlets. If you wanted to know the weather forecast, for example, you stayed up late to watch the evening news. Remember when TiVo was considered cool because you could watch your favorite show whenever you wanted?

Traditional marketing worked, and it can still work, but traditional marketing, by definition, is a one-way message from brand to consumer. Traditional marketing was founded on interruptive, product-centric messaging, and it relies on massive message broadcasting that's not conducive to developing meaningful, personalized consumer relationships. Further, more media choices means more fragmentation. Consumers accessing multiple screens simultaneously (TV, desktop, mobile devices) results in divided consumer attention, eroding the impact of your commercial message. Individual media consumption and behavior is migrating away from broadcast messaging. So although traditional marketing consumption is still great when measured in terms of hours spent with traditional media, it is becoming less relevant and less effective.

## Inbound marketing

Inbound marketing works for the very reason that traditional marketing doesn't. Inbound marketing meets a previously undiscovered or unfulfilled need: creating meaningful conversations based on individual actions.

By definition, inbound marketing systems create opportunities through bidirectional messaging between brand and consumer. This two-way messaging is attractive to individual consumers who wish to engage on *their* terms and based on *their* perceived needs.

Although traditional and inbound marketing campaigns may be combined, they are quite frequently misused, such as TV ads with QR codes or the annoying pop-up ads on websites. It's too easy for online searchers to bounce from your website by clicking somewhere else, leaving your site and engaging elsewhere with another brand, maybe your competitors. Knowing that traditional marketing practices do not apply to your inbound marketing success helps you avoid costly mistakes, lost revenues, and negative reviews. (Table 1-1 compares the features of inbound and traditional marketing.)

**Table 1-1      Traditional Marketing vs. Inbound Marketing**

| *Traditional marketing* | *Inbound marketing* |
| --- | --- |
| Product-centric | Customer-centric |
| "Push" messaging | "Pull" messaging |
| Interruptive | Attractive |
| One-way communication | Two-way conversation |
| Transactional | Relationship-based |
| Defined start and finish | Ongoing loop |
| Linear | Multi-faceted |
| Static | Dynamic |
| Brand power | Consumer power |

# Understanding the Four Objectives of a High-Performance Conversion System

A high-performance inbound conversion system is designed to attract and convert. A well-designed system facilitates action and reaction. This conversion system acknowledges the multiple conversion points along the purchase path and facilitates a conversion at each point.

Your inbound marketing system's four primary objectives are:

- Inbound marketing attracts visitors to you where you greet the prospective customer on *their* terms.
- Inbound marketing engages your website visitors through meaningful, relevant content so visitors become leads.
- Inbound marketing encourages a lead to take actions that can eventually be monetized (purchase/donation/referrals/and so on).
- Inbound marketing reengages previous customers, causing reactions (additional purchases/reviews/and so on) resulting in repeat customers while fostering a loyal fan base. These loyal fans are sometimes called brand evangelists, fanatics, or advocates. I call them *Lifestylers*.

The type of visitor you attract depends on your customer profile. Conversion time and buyer paths also vary by individual business model. The time it take for a visitor to become a customer and, in turn, a loyal customer, varies greatly for a business-to-consumer e-commerce retailer with an average purchase of $2.00 as opposed to a business-to-business manufacturing company whose average sale is $200,000.

## Attracting interest with inbound marketing

What is inbound marketing if it does not address the needs of your prospective customers? Nothing. So, give customers what they want. Period.

The first tenet of inbound marketing is attraction, search engine marketing (SEM). SEM consists of various methods of attracting people to your website. The various forms of SEM that attract include:

- Pay-per-click (PPC) campaigns through Google AdWords re-targeting campaigns
- Bing ads in the U.S. and Baidu in China

- Online paid display advertising
- Paid listings
- Search retargeting and remarketing
- Search engine optimization (SEO) to be found in organic rankings
- Content marketing
- Social media campaigns on Twitter, Facebook, LinkedIn, Pinterest, and so on
- Email marketing

Purists contend that paid search and online banner advertising are not part of the inbound family. I disagree because SEM practiced under the inbound philosophy is attractive marketing, meaning it serves up relevant results that satisfy consumer needs, based on your understanding of those needs. PPC is a subcategory of SEM and inbound SEM helps attract visitors to your website. Your website content should be relevant, timely, and well-organized regardless of whether it is earned or paid media that attracts the prospective buyer.

## Creating internal and external connections with inbound marketing

Effective inbound processes systematically track visitor and customer onsite behaviors. A well-designed inbound system delivers timely, relevant, and contextual information. We call this *content*.

So, ideally, you'll be able to deliver the information your prospects and customers want when they want it. That's determined by:

- The customer's location in the Purchase Funnel/Buyer's Journey/ Lifestyle Loop
- The buyer profile/persona with whom you're attempting to create a conversation
- The product/service/conversion you're encouraging the customer to seek and buy

## Causing customer conversions with inbound marketing

Customer conversion is a process rather than a single end event. As you can see in Figure 1-1, customer conversions are a series of progressive, connected events. There are key conversion events that can be measured and should be. Each of these key conversions is a link in the Customer Conversion Chain.

The customer conversion process and the Customer Conversion Chain are covered more in-depth in Chapter 19.

**Customer Conversion Chain**

CUSTOMER
LTV
(Lifetime Value)

CUSTOMERS

DEMONSTRATED
INTEREST

SQLs
(Sales Qualified Leads)

MQLs
(Marketing
Qualified Leads)

LEADS

VISITS

IMPRESSIONS

**Figure 1-1:**
The
Customer
Conversion
Chain.

# Introducing the Three-Step Inbound Process

At both of the marketing firms I've owned, we practice a process I learned from Blair Enns, author of "Win Without Pitching" and a consultant to marketing firms. It's deceptively simple because it's only three steps — although I've modified the language a bit. Here it is:

1. Diagnose the business problem.

2. Prescribe strategic marketing solutions.

3. Apply marketing solutions to solve business problem.

Although this message is designed for marketing firms, it has far greater application because it exemplifies the inbound process. In fact, it's a great way to approach any problem because it helps frame and define your situation first. Knowing the problem you're trying to solve may sound like common sense, but how many times have you begun marketing initiatives before fully understanding the business problem at hand? Statements like "We need to do Social Media" or "Let's hire an SEO expert" are usually off-base or premature because they assume an incorrect starting point. Beginning campaigns with tactics is why so many marketers never earn the respect of their business peers. Start with your desired end business result — that is, your ideal business outcome.

## Diagnosing with a baseline assessment/audit

Imagine this scenario: You walk into your doctor's office after twisting your ankle, and he says, "Don't bother sitting down. You look sick. I'm going to get you on chemotherapy right away. Come back and see me next year if you don't get better." You'd leave, wouldn't you? Any sane person would.

 Physicians are trained to diagnose before they prescribe. Marketers should do the same. Like a good physician, you should begin by asking questions of your organization:

- How do you know where you're trying to go if you don't know where you are?

- Do you know your consumer profiles?

- Have you written target buyer personas?

✔ Do you know what motivates your prospective customers?

✔ Do you know and measure your website and page visits, conversion rates, and track leads from marketing to sales?

✔ Are you able to source those leads?

✔ What's the value of your customers?

✔ Can you connect this data, reporting it as meaningful business ratios?

Diagnosing your current marketing situation will help you see where your organization is as opposed to where you want to be. You'll discover there is a gap. Don't worry, there's always a gap. If there wasn't, you couldn't grow.

Unless you are a panicked marketer or an irresponsible marketer, or unless you just like to leave you or your clients' success up to the whims of Lady Luck, performing a marketing diagnostic is the best starting point.

## Prescribing business solutions through strategy

Strategy is a written prescription. Effective inbound marketers start with a strategic assessment (diagnosis) and a formal, written strategic document. This strategic document is your inbound strategy prescription. The best inbound strategies

✔ Define your current state with highly defined metrics

✔ Identify your organization's desired end business results

✔ Define future success, usually in dollars

✔ Perform a SWOT analysis — strengths, weaknesses, opportunities, and threats

✔ Include SMART goals — specific, measurable, actionable, realistic, and timebound

✔ Use keyword research to uncover consumer needs

✔ Connect your current state to your desired future state with a series of well-planned marketing initiatives

✔ Outline a prioritized set of initiatives to most efficiently reach goals and objectives

✔ Include a content strategy

✔ Assign ownership and accountability

✔ Define meaningful metrics by which your success will be gauged

The idea of including a SWOT analysis and articulating SMART goals is not a revolutionary one. It should be standard practice for marketers, but it's not. It's time inbound marketers incorporate a common business practice into their actions and language. So, start with strategy based on a solid audit or assessment or don't start at all. Anything else is just a sophisticated form of gambling.

## Applying solutions with inbound initiatives

The third step is to apply solutions. Remember, the inbound marketer is solving customer problems and business problems, not mere marketing problems. The marketing is the connection between product and persona, and there is no singular path to achieving success. With inbound marketing, there is rarely a "right" or "wrong" initiative. The world is too complicated, the competition too sophisticated, and the consumer too dynamic to predict everything. So even though you're attempting to satisfy a successful desired end result, the path may be twisting with some blind spots along the way. Your end destination is the same, but your method of getting there may change as you uncover new information.

You're here to solve business problems. This is where the marketing expertise of yourself, your team, and your professional marketing partners converge. Knowing your organization's strengths and weaknesses and knowing when to ask for help is as important as the inbound marketing initiatives themselves.

## Things You Can Do Now

- ✔ Read more about inbound marketing so you familiarize yourself with the inbound concept.
- ✔ Research inbound marketing online to further expand your knowledge.
- ✔ Attend a webinar or a conference to fully immerse yourself with other inbound marketers and learn from them.

# Chapter 2

# Introducing the Inbound Philosophy into Your Organization

*In This Chapter*

▶ Understanding inbound marketing as a philosophy

▶ Understanding inbound marketing as a connected system

▶ Learning whether inbound marketing makes sense for your organization

▶ Overcoming internal resistance to change

*W*hether you're the CEO of an enterprise organization or a marketing intern tasked with checking out "this inbound marketing thing," you may face forces that interfere with instituting inbound marketing in your organization. It's easy for old habits and the temptation of others to reinforce a traditional mindset derailing the implementation process.

So, to the CEO I say: Be bold and courageous in leading your company into the forefront of the digital age. Inbound marketing is a proven process and it works. To the marketing person whose pleas for change fall on deaf ears I say: Follow the steps outlined in this chapter — create a case for inbound marketing as a business solution and in doing so you'll create more value for yourself as an employee and for the marketing department as a whole. If you're unable to create change within your organization, you can always consider employment elsewhere at a company who appreciates progressive marketing techniques.

## Creating Satisfaction within Your Organization

Your CFO is satisfied when the bottom line exceeds expectations. Your sales manager is satisfied when he meets goals and makes his bonus. Marketers are satisfied knowing their input has a meaningful impact on the business, and are rewarded for that impact. When your customers are satisfied, everyone in your organization should be satisfied. Inbound marketing facilitates satisfied customers (and their positive online reviews that follow), so perhaps that's reason enough to implement it in any organization. The bottom line is, satisfying (some would say *delighting*) customers creates satisfaction within your organization, and it does so in the following ways:

- **By satisfying your marketing needs:** Whether you're a sole marketer or an enterprise team, inbound marketing and the marketing automation software tools associated with it satisfy your need to capture and analyze data, allowing you to save time and produce better results.

- **By satisfying the needs of your customers:** When performed correctly, inbound marketing connects customers with what they want, when they want it, and at their own pace. Talk about customer satisfaction!

- **By satisfying the needs of the sole marketer:** Inbound marketing allows the sole marketer to scale marketing initiatives beyond a single individual's efforts. Your marketing tactics are multiplied and scalable.

- **By satisfying the needs of the marketing team:** Inbound marketing facilitates sharing and collaborating. The resulting accountability and efficiency creates maximum marketing output for your team. Who doesn't want to work with a bunch of superstars?

- **By satisfying the needs of the chief marketing officer (CMO):** CMOs need data to decide which strategic and tactical initiatives to approve. Access to real-time data and historical data improves a CMO's ability to choose wisely and attain corporate goals and objectives.

- **By satisfying the needs of your CEO:** Innovation and marketing drive many successful companies. But traditional marketing's impact on this success was fuzzy and difficult to measure. Inbound marketing, however, connects marketing investments with real revenue results. So instead of applauding a great marketing idea, your CEO is giving a standing ovation to the CMO who connects those brilliant ideas with measurable results. CEOs, meet your new best friend . . . inbound marketing.

- **By satisfying the needs of the enterprise organization:** When implemented faithfully, inbound marketing creates the sort of nimble, spry marketing effort that in the past has been noticeably absent from large corporations. For those enterprise organizations that embrace independence within structure, inbound marketing is a gold mine for product sales and product innovation.

# Overcoming Internal Resistance to Inbound Marketing

In your attempt to implement inbound marketing in your organization, you will inevitably meet resistance from the nay-sayers. For you, the courageous marketer advocating change, the first step is the hardest. This is because inbound marketing is not a silver bullet that immediately solves your marketing and business problems. It takes time to introduce inbound marketing, to build your inbound Conversion Machine, and to initiate inbound campaigns. Like anything worth doing, inbound marketing requires an investment of resources: time, money, and hard work. For this reason, it's best to view Phase I of inbound marketing as the building-the-infrastructure phase, much as a brick-and-mortar structure is built before opening up shop for business.

The good news is that once you begin implementing inbound marketing and the inbound philosophy, the results usually speak for themselves. When your marketers discover better ways to engage and track prospects . . . when your salespeople begin to close more business . . . when management begins to see real change occurring and business goals being met . . . that's when business becomes fun. When business initiatives work — and, when implemented properly, inbound marketing works — funding for new marketing initiatives will follow, at least for as long as there continues to be a return-on-investment for the company.

But, first things first. You may believe inbound marketing is right for your marketing department and your company, but for inbound to maximize its impact, you certainly must gain the trust and approval from others inside your company.

## Making your case for inbound marketing

Implementing inbound marketing in your company means change, and we all know change isn't always embraced with open arms. If you work at a progressive company that operates with transparency and clearly defined accountability, you may find that inbound marketing is warmly welcomed. Likewise, if you're part of an customer-centric organization that values its people as much as profits, your road to introducing inbound marketing most likely will be easier. So that you're prepared, here are some common objections you may encounter when introducing inbound into your company:

- ✔ **"That's not the way we've always done it."** Exactly. That's why inbound marketing is a positive change.

- ✔ **"Our current marketing is working just fine."** What is "just fine"? Companies are either growing or dying. Inbound marketing compels growth.

✔ **"We don't have the budget for a new system."** Can you afford *not* to invest in a measurable system with proven ROI?

✔ **"I don't understand what inbound marketing is so we're not really interested in pursuing it."** You may not understand inbound marketing, but don't you want to understand your customers better so we can create better marketing?

✔ **"Our website's not broken; it was just re-built by great designers."** That may be true, but is the website built on conversion architecture? If the website is a streamlined Conversion Machine, that's great — because inbound marketing is about more than your website. It's about attracting and converting prospects into customers.

✔ **"We don't have the personnel to create enough content for inbound marketing"** Maybe we should re-think our initiatives if we want to have a meaningful presence with our digital marketing. We know content is king so perhaps we should re-allocate resources to create value for our target customers.

## *Benefits of introducing inbound into your organization*

Inbound marketing offers any organization a number of great benefits. When transitioning to inbound marketing, it's important to communicate these benefits to everyone affected by this change. Even if there is company-wide acceptance that introducing inbound marketing into your organization is the right thing to do, clear communication of the benefits helps people come to terms with the change. By clearly communicating inbound marketing's benefits to your internal colleagues up-front you may later need to refer back to these conversations and presentations when it comes time for marketing to delegate ownership and accountability of the various inbound tasks within marketing and other departments.

By introducing inbound marketing, your organization stands to benefit in a number of ways. The following list breaks down some of these benefits by department:

✔ **Marketing:** Your marketing department benefits in the following ways:

  • As the correlation between marketing and revenue increases, so does the value for marketers and marketing.

  • Instead of being evaluated on fuzzy metrics, marketing can now operate transparently, sharing key marketing performance indicators.

- Better connectivity and communications between the marketing and sales departments results in higher success in achieving your business goals.

- Marketing delivers higher quality leads to salespeople.

✔ **Sales:** Your sales staff benefits in the following ways:

- Inbound marketing gives them the ability to integrate marketing leads with sales CRM.

- Contact with prospects earlier in the decision-making process helps you take the lead position, positively influencing sales outcomes.

- Salespeople are granted the ability for real-time follow-up with prospects via marketing automation software, which increases close ratios dramatically.

- Implementing a lead scoring system provides higher quality leads so your salespeople are talking to better qualified prospects.

✔ **Operations:** Your business operations staff benefits in the following ways:

- Integration of marketing with customer service results in higher customer satisfaction.

- Better predictive metrics for sales means more reliable budget planning for your accounting department.

✔ **Leadership:** Upper management benefits in the following ways:

- Company leadership has better marketing and sales data to allocate resources more efficiently.

- Management has better metrics to measure meaningful performance.

- Your company is better able to make data-driven business decisions instead of emotional decisions.

# Gathering support for the change

Different people will come to support inbound marketing for different reasons and that's okay. As you work to gather support for your organization's change to inbound marketing, you should know your audience inside your company, presenting your case for inbound marketing as you would a creative brief of a client campaign, or an internal marketing campaign. The difference here is that your "customers" are your associates, colleagues, bosses, and fellow employees. Understand their needs and speak to those needs when building support for instituting inbound marketing

Different groups within your organization will require different motivations to make the change. Depending on the group, try using these approaches:

- ✔ **Upper management:** Your company executives will most likely offer their support for the change based on whether your inbound marketing proposal provides a meaningful return-on-investment. Connect with your "C-Suite" by showing inbound case studies and applying likely business results for your company before and after inbound implementation.

- ✔ **Sales:** The sales department will most likely support the change based on the answers to two questions:

  - Does it make salesperson's life easier?

  - Will it increase sales, allowing salespeople to earn more money?

  The answer to both of these questions is yes. It's your job as a marketer to connect those dots for sales personnel in a meaningful way.

- ✔ **Finance:** Because this department is usually characterized by managing expenses rather than creating opportunities, focus on the efficiencies created through inbound marketing. (For example, show your accounting team how inbound marketing allows your company to reach twice the number of prospects with the same staff and same investment level.) For those financial types that value opportunity as much as expense-control, inbound is a rational, planned, trackable expense that is also scalable.

Treat the introduction of inbound marketing into your organization in much the same way you would treat an online stranger you wish to attract and convert into a lifelong brand advocate. Introduce inbound incrementally. Share the big picture pay-off, but get incremental support. Even a hike to the summit of Mt. Everest is made of small steps.

## Understanding the negative consequences of not changing at all

It's no accident that online marketing investment has exploded. Dollars follow customers and customers are on the Internet. So the question of whether to invest in digital marketing is moot. The only questions that remain are: How much of your budget should be invested? In what manner? Getting answers to these questions is why you perform an assessment before you make any recommendations.

One thing is clear: For viable businesses, the cost of doing nothing will eventually be more devastating than any perceived risk of investing in new digital media and inbound marketing.

# Presenting your case for inbound

If you're charged with introducing inbound marketing into your company, there are plenty of resources at your disposal. Here are a few:

- **Education:** Begin educating yourself about inbound marketing. Here are just a few resources beyond this book:

  - Content Marketing Institute (`http://contentmarketing institute.com`)

  - HubSpot (`www.hubspot.com`)

  - Inbound.org (`http://inbound.org`)

  - KISSmetrics (`www.kissmetrics.com`)

  - Marketo (`www.marketo.com`)

  - Moz Academy (`https://moz.com/academy`) and Moz Community (`https://moz.com/community`)

  - Pardot (`www.pardot.com`)

  - Search Engine Land (`http://searchengineland.com`)

I also created a "What is Inbound" video you can reach at `www.marketing mattersinbound.com/what-is-inbound-marketing` and an e-book called "Beginner's Guide to Inbound Marketing" you can download at `http://info.marketingmattersinbound.com/beginners-guide-to-inbound-marketing`.

- **Engagement:** Seek out any internal advocates who will immediately see the value in what you're trying to do. Enlist their engagement to make your case for inbound. If it makes sense, get help from an inbound professional.

- **Embrace:** After doing your research, create a vision of what your company's marketing will look like after you've implemented inbound marketing. Don't be overly optimistic. Paint a realistic picture, and use numbers that connect your marketing efforts with business results. Begin sharing your findings with key management to gauge interest, seek input, and eventually gain acceptance.

- **Encouragement:** After you've instituted inbound marketing, make sure you touch base with key decision-makers on a regular basis, reporting your successes and creating continued value. When you're performing well and attaining goals and objectives, the results will speak for themselves; however, it's always a good idea to remind key internal people why you've instituted inbound marketing and to update them with the results you're tracking.

## Things You Can Do Now

- ✔ Identify stakeholders in your organization who benefit from inbound marketing.

- ✔ Take the temperature of management and peers as to familiarity and openness to change. Identify internal advocates and potential early adopters.

- ✔ List potential internal roadblocks to acceptance and solutions to overcome those roadblocks.

# Chapter 3

# Diagnosing Your Current Inbound Marketing Performance

*T*he first strategic step in implementing inbound marketing at your organization is to understand your current digital marketing position. Your starting point is to perform an *inbound marketing assessment (IMA),* which is sometimes called a *digital marketing audit.* An IMA is a well-written, comprehensive overview document that measures your current digital marketing performance versus key performance indicators (KPIs) and your digital marketing goals. These KPIs include metrics such as your attraction factor (that is, your ability to be found online), your ability to engage with your website visitors, connecting your content with your website visitors, and onsite structure facilitating Visitors to Leads conversions.

In this chapter, you learn the importance of beginning your inbound implementation with an assessment. I cover the differences between a website grader and an inbound marketing assessment (IMA). Additionally, you can use this chapter to determine if you should perform an inbound marketing assessment internally or outsource. By asking certain questions about your current state of marketing, you establish a starting baseline from which you may grow. I cover several questions for you to consider when assessing your website and your digital marketing efforts.

# Performing an Inbound Marketing Assessment

An IMA may measure your technical website problems and your digital marketing efforts. It may also evaluate your ability to connect your marketing with sales. A comprehensive IMA includes an executive summary that outlines gaps in your marketing efficiencies, opportunities for online marketing initiatives and roadblocks to successful implementation. Reporting forms vary, but when performed to best practices, your IMA serves as the basis for your strategic marketing plan document. An IMA identifies past marketing tactics that didn't directly correlate to any marketing success. It also uncovers digital marketing initiative omissions that may have hurt your past performance. Performing an IMA is the map for your marketing plan. When you don't perform an IMA, it's like taking a trip without knowing your final destination. Without it, you'll move in random directions, and you'll never know if you arrived.

So, before you get too excited about jumping into the *tactics* of inbound marketing, perform an IMA. Marketers are often overwhelmed by the sheer volume of online marketing options, each with its own trendy approaches and buzzwords, that it's hard to choose which initiatives to implement first. You may be in the same predicament.

When you perform an inbound marketing assessment as your first strategic step, you can share initiatives internally, provide a rationale for your recommendations, and maintain focus on your desired end result. This assessment report can be created internally or outsourced. Regardless of the source, an inbound assessment provides a set of baseline metrics from which you can choose future digital marketing efforts. Measuring your current status provides baseline attraction and conversion factors so you can adjust your digital marketing initiatives faster and gauge your future success. You can also refer to the IMA later to determine whether future ideas make sense to pursue, basing your decisions on facts that support your end objectives, rather than simply following the trendiest initiatives at the time.

# Understanding Why You Should Perform an Inbound Assessment

Performing an IMA is your strategic starting point. It serves as the foundation for the next step, your strategic inbound plan. In other words, with inbound marketing, you need to learn your starting point before you determine where you're going. Simply put, you want to start with an inbound assessment because:

✔ You'll begin with the end in mind.

✔ You'll have baseline metrics from which you can measure future digital and inbound marketing initiatives.

✔ You'll provide a framework to fail fast allowing you to fix negative influences more quickly.

✔ You'll see digital marketing opportunities more clearly.

✔ You'll identify roadblocks to achieving your marketing objectives.

✔ You'll know where to focus your efforts.

✔ You'll be able to prioritize initiatives based on projected contribution to the marketing goals.

✔ You'll have a document from which you can formulate better inbound and digital marketing strategies.

# Knowing What to Assess

The inbound assessment serves as a diagnosis of your current digital assets and initiatives. You can begin by using online tools to diagnose your current state, or you can hire a consultant to create an assessment for you. When performed properly, an IMA identifies gaps between where you are and where you wish to be.

Additionally, an inbound assessment identifies opportunities that can elevate and improve your digital marketing efforts and the resulting outcomes while identifying online problems that need fixing. Lastly, the inbound assessment can help you organize and prioritize your digital initiatives in order to serve as a basis for marketing strategy. Not everything that can be measured should be measured. You'll get brain freeze from data overload.

Here's what you need to assess:

✔ Your website's technical performance

✔ Your attraction factors from paid search advertising, search engine optimization (SEO), and social media

✔ Your website's mobile capability and functionality

✔ Your onsite conversion factors like conversion forms or call-to-action (CTA) buttons

✔ Your website's unique visits as it correlates with onsite lead conversions

✔ Your website visitor engagement in terms of time on site and depth of navigation

✔ Your content; classified by content type and function

✔ Your lead-generation numbers as they correlate with converted customers

✔ Your customer purchase paths

✔ Your remarketing and retargeting efforts

Some of these questions are relatively easy to answer on your own. Others may require the help of an inbound marketing professional whose experience and access to inbound tools may provide a more in-depth analysis.

## Asking the right questions

I strongly advise you to perform a formal IMA for your inbound marketing efforts. Knowing your baseline marketing and conversion metrics and prioritizing your tactics to achieve your objectives will save you time and money down the road. At the very least, ask yourself these questions:

✔ What are your online business goals and objectives? Are they measurable and are you achieving those goals?

✔ Is your website built to attract? How many unique website visitors do you attract each month?

✔ Is your site built to convert prospects into sales?

✔ What sources contribute to your business getting found online? Do you use tracking URLs for each of your digital attraction methods?

✔ Do you attract visitors by sharing your content through Facebook, LinkedIn, Twitter, Pinterest, and other social networks?

✔ Do you invest in paid search, SEO, and content marketing? Do you measure each digital media's contribution to achieving your digital goals?

✔ On which pages do visitors enter into and exit from your website?

✔ Do you have a written content strategy shared with others in your organization?

✔ What keyword research have you performed? How are you applying that keyword research?

✔ Have you identified your target buyer profiles? Have you created individual personas for those profiles?

✔ Do you understand and measure your target profile's purchase path?

✔ Do you offer content for each step of the customer purchase path?

✔ How many leads does your website generate each month?

✔ Does your website include conversion forms that visitors can use to leave email addresses in exchange for content? Do you use landing pages and measure the conversion rates?

✔ What percentage of your website pages include call-to-action (CTA) buttons and forms?

✔ How do you follow up with leads your website has generated?

✔ Do you send a monthly email newsletter?

✔ Have you created automated email messages, drip campaigns, or workflows?

✔ Do you use Google Analytics to analyze and report meaningful, actionable data?

✔ Do you use marketing automation software effectively? Is it connected to any sales customer relationship management (CRM) software?

✔ Do you perform user testing on a regular basis?

## Distinguishing between a website grader assessment and an IMA

Recently, a popular trend is for marketers to grade their websites through various website grader tools. Although it's not as comprehensive as an IMA, a website grader is a good starting point for assessment because your website functions as the powerful engine behind inbound marketing. Figure 3-1 shows a website grade from HubSpot's marketing grader (`https://marketing.grader.com`). A website grader in itself should not, however, be the end game in your baseline assessment.

Your website is only one part of the inbound marketing process, so after you measure the effectiveness of your website as the hub of online connecting, you should look beyond your website to make connections between your efforts to attract and convert. You can do that with an IMA, which should include a diagnostic report of your website performance.

The difference between a website grader and an inbound marketing assessment is a bit like the difference between a written repair estimate for the engine in your car and a certified diagnosis done on your entire automobile. The website grader assesses only your website, whereas the IMA assesses all your inbound marketing efforts. The first gives you valuable and useful information about one part of your vehicle, but the second tells you in-depth information about every aspect of it. For more about this, see Table 3-1.

When your inbound marketing is firing on all cylinders, it can become what I call a Conversion Machine — because a well-designed inbound marketing program acts like a well-oiled machine. A Conversion Machine powers sales through an automated system that attracts visitors to your website and provides a frictionless navigation path for visitors to become leads and eventually to become customers.

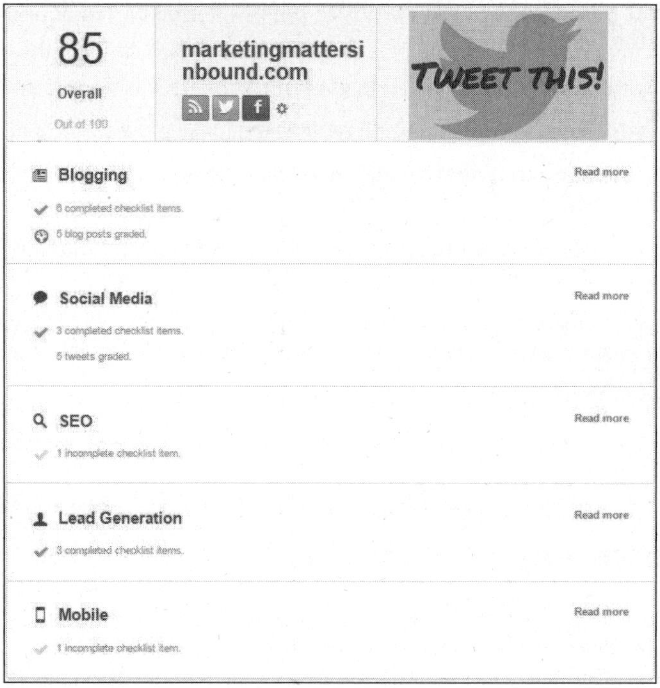

*Courtesy of HubSpot*

**Figure 3-1:**
An example of HubSpot's website grader.

## Table 3-1 Comparing the assessments of website graders and IMAs

| Website Grader | Inbound Marketing Assessment |
|---|---|
| Tactical | Strategic |
| Grades your website | Grades your digital marketing and your website |
| Singular in focus | Holistic focus |
| Reports website statistics | Reports attraction and conversion statistics |
| Focuses on technological metrics | Focuses on business metrics |
| Company-centric (usually) | Customer-centric |

This machine is powered by an inbound engine, also known as your properly designed inbound-purposed website. But this machine also consists of other parts, including all of your Internet-related activities, such as blogging, social media, and email marketing. Each of these parts, or *input factors,* affect your conversion factors in the purchase path. Each of your digital marketing initiatives, offsite and onsite, is a link in your Customer Conversion Chain.

Because all these initiatives are interrelated, each of your digital marketing efforts affect not only each other, but also the end conversion result, which, in most cases, is defined as a sale. Any marketing initiative that causes a positive input factor positively affects the other links in the Customer Conversion Chain as well as the outcome, or end result. Likewise, a marketing initiative that causes a negative input factor negatively affects the other links in the Customer Conversion Chain and the outcome.

When all of these efforts are coordinated and documented within a highly organized and integrated attraction and conversion methodology, the result is your strategic inbound plan. Your IMA is the first part of your strategic plan.

So you can start by looking under your digital hood with a website grading tool. Diagnose your website "engine" because it powers your online activity and is the hub of all the rest of the moving parts. After you've fine-tuned your website, you can look at an IMA performance report. Performing an inbound marketing assessment looks at the engine, too, but it also looks at the transmission, the exhaust, the brakes, the tires . . . you get the idea. Your IMA is a full-service diagnostic and anyone wishing to build a Conversion Machine needs one.

## *Using a website grader*

Because your website is the engine powering your online attraction and conversion, let's start there. Before you get into the nuts and bolts of grading your website, ask yourself some higher-level questions like:

- ✔ Why do you have a website?
- ✔ What is the main interactive function of your website?
- ✔ Is your website built to attract?
- ✔ Is your website built to convert prospects into sales?
- ✔ Are your interactive initiatives connected to your website?
- ✔ Does your website encourage revisits and repurchases?

The purpose of a website grader is to let you know how well your website is set up for inbound marketing. It follows that a website grader should be part of any IMA you perform. At the minimum, your website grader should include:

- ✔ Onsite website metrics such as:
  - • Website traffic
  - • Website bounce rate
  - • Time spent on site

- • Inbound and links
- • Broken links
- • SEO metrics
- ✔ Competitors' standard website metrics
- ✔ Diagnoses of both your website and your existing inbound marketing

At some point, you should also measure your website user flow, and later, when you decide to perform testing, you can measure onsite user experience (UX). If you're not overwhelmed by the basic reporting outlined here, you can choose to include these analyses as part of your website grader report or IMA. The objective is to identify where you can reduce customer *friction*. User friction is any impediment to conversions and sales, so it's key to know where any roadblocks exist on your site that cause visitor bounces, exits, and non-conversions.

Provided you have access to the information, be sure to report conversion factors like the volume of leads generated, the quality of those leads, and the total number of customers generated. This helps facilitate future inbound marketing initiatives. These reports help you create a customer Conversion Machine consisting of your website, your digital marketing efforts to attract visitors, and your conversion and reconversion efforts. A well-designed Conversion Machine helps create a customer for life. And that's something you and your marketing department can take to the bank!

## The components of a basic inbound assessment

Because an IMA provides a deeper, more thorough assessment than a website grader, it is more actionable. It also requires more effort. In addition to grading and analyzing your website, it defines a baseline for most or all of your current digital marketing connected to your website from which you may measure your future inbound marketing success.

An IMA measures your inbound marketing efforts against key performance indicators (KPIs). Your IMA measures differences between inbound marketing strategies and conversion metrics in greater depth so you'll know where to best focus your inbound marketing activities.

At its core, inbound marketing is about forming connections. An IMA reports how well your marketing connects at multiple levels. This includes:

- ✔ **Technological connections** such as Google Analytics, marketing automation software, and sales CRM connections

- ✔ **Internal connections** such as combined marketing/sales reporting and measurable return-on-investment (ROI) from marketing efforts.

- ✔ **Consumer connections** such as unique visits generated, leads captured, and customers won.

A basic IMA may be performed internally and outlines gaps between how your marketing connects with prospects and customers at each stage of the Purchase Funnel. It measures your strengths and weaknesses in connecting with prospective customers at several points in their purchase path:

- ✔ Top-of-funnel gaps — where consumers research

- ✔ Middle-of-funnel gaps — where consumers shop

- ✔ Bottom-of-funnel gaps — where consumers buy

You can perform a basic IMA yourself; however, a comprehensive IMA performed by a professional provides deeper insight into any inbound marketing performance gaps. Many marketing firms even provide a limited basic IMA for free as an introduction to their more robust IMA paid offering. At any rate, a proper professional IMA provides actionable marketing discoveries, and the resulting recommended marketing tactics may be executed by the firm performing the IMA, by a different marketing firm, or by you.

Many inbound marketing firms also provide an IMA score or grade that includes the following metrics:

- ✔ **Attraction gaps and recommendations:** Are your paid search, Google rankings, and content marketing attracting the ideal prospects?

- ✔ **Nurturing gaps and recommendations:** Is your website organized for easy navigation, providing content that form an inviting, intuitive path to conversion toward a purchase?

- ✔ **Conversion gaps and recommendations:** Does your website have enough onsite and landing page conversion point opportunities?

- ✔ **Analytics and reconversion gaps and recommendations:** Are you effectively measuring inputs that directly and positively affect your ability to create your ultimate end conversion?

- ✔ **Composite score for four components of inbound marketing:** How does your inbound marketing rate compare versus your competitors and against KPIs?

Most organizations don't have the in-house tools to perform an objective IMA on themselves. So, if you're considering hiring a professional firm to perform a comprehensive paid IMA, check first to see if that firm will perform a basic free IMA. Even though the results aren't as comprehensive, you'll glean useful information while gauging the professionalism of the firm providing the initial IMA. (See Figure 3-2.) A multitude of marketing firms offer this service. The results from even a free IMA require explanation, so there's usually a 30-minute telephone consultation associated with a free IMA to explain the results. You can find my free IMA that scores your efforts on a 100-point scale here: `http://hubs.ly/y0Krhk0`.

**Figure 3-2:**
An example
of a basic
IMA report.

## The components of a comprehensive inbound assessment

An inbound marketing assessment helps you discover gaps between what your website can achieve and your online marketing initiatives. Use your final report as a basis for your inbound marketing strategy and to prioritize objectives. Then you can address and improve your online and inbound marketing efforts.

For a deeper dive into your online marketing efforts, a more comprehensive IMA provides more attraction and conversion metrics, is more detailed in its scope, and investigates more complex factors, connecting your marketing efforts with online business results. A comprehensive inbound marketing assessment measures:

✔ Your online and business goals

✔ Your inbound visitor sources

✔ Your search engine marketing (SEM)

✔ Your keywords for search engine optimization (SEO)

✔ Your customer conversion ratios

✔ Your remarketing efforts

✔ Your onsite and online marketing gaps

✔ Your website statistics vs. your competitors'

✔ Your customer conversion ratios vs. conversion KPIs

✔ Your email workflow gaps

✔ Your on-page and blog content

✔ Your ROI

✔ Your website user experience flow

Here's a breakdown of a more comprehensive IMA report:

✔ **Website analytics:** Much of the information found in a website grader is reported as one part of the IMA. Here you can get the answers to questions like: What's your website rank compared to all other websites — and in particular, your competitors. Beyond ranking, what is the relative strength, or "juice" of your site?

✔ **Digital marketing assessment:** A digital marketing assessment examines your ability to attract visitors and convert them into leads and customers. A digital marketing assessment does the following:

- It measures your marketing's ability to attract.

- It measures visitor sourcing and charts conversion contribution by attraction type (SEO, content, PPC, blog posts, and so on).

- It measures user flow, content connections, and your ability to nurture leads.

- It measures the multiple points of your customer conversion.

- It looks at your automation, your analytics, and your ability to reconvert customers.

- It tracks your content inventory by profile and assigns content pieces to a customer's place in the purchase path (is it educational, engagement-oriented, encouragement-oriented, and so on).

✔ **Keyword research:** Keyword research assesses keywords in order to determine their market potential to attract website visitors. By measuring relevant keyword search volume it provides a target list of rankable keyword phrases and including the following data:

- Which keywords are effective at attracting visitors, leads, and customers

- Your keywords rank according to search engine results page (SERP) position

- Your keywords' industry opportunity and market potential

- Keyword segmentation (that is, organizing them into subcategories) through association with consumer's place in the purchase paths (that is, are they researching, shopping, or ready to buy?)

- Your keyword's volume and traffic for both your company's branded ("Coke") and non-branded ("cola") search terms

✔ **Conversion metrics:** Conversion metrics measure the key points in the customer purchase path, discovering opportunities to increase consumer engagement. This assessment does the following:

- It measures multiple points of conversion via custom conversion chain or a similar tool.

- It calculates the number of onsite conversion opportunities.

- It calculates landing page conversions.

- It computes the popularity of your downloadable content's rank by number and percentage of leads captured.

- It compares your conversion metric ratios against KPIs. (For more on this, see Chapter 22.)

- It performs conversion gap analysis and recommends action points.

- It conducts return-on-investment (ROI) and/or return-on-advertising-spend (ROAS) analysis.

✔ **Analytics:** The analytics report in a comprehensive IMA evaluates whether you are using analytics and marketing automation software effectively. Data here include the following:

- A report on your Google Analytics statistics

- Use and connectivity of marketing automation software and a customer relationship management (CRM) systems for lead and sales data

- A measure of the efficiencies and prospect reengagement from your automated email campaigns efforts

- Examines lead quality statistics for future lead classification, and higher lead quality hand-off from marketing to sales

- Looks at any lead scoring system with recommendations on how to best score prospective customers' onsite activities.

## *Measuring customer conversion points*

In addition to grading your website, you can assess and analyze consumer conversion points along their path to purchase. There are multiple conversion points in a path; it's not just the end sale that counts. Each of these steps in the purchase path is a link in a chain (refer back to Chapter 1). From a business metrics perspective, one of the most beneficial evaluations you can make is an analysis of your conversion metrics with respect to conversion KPIs. This includes sequential conversion metrics for each step in the customer purchase path (shown here in sequence):

1. Impressions

2. Click-thru-rates (CTR)-to-visitors ratio

3. Visitors-to-leads ratio

4. Leads-to-marketing-qualified-leads (MQLs) ratio

5. MQLs-to-sales-qualified-leads (SQLs) ratio

6. SQLs-to-presentation (demo, trial, sales meeting, and so on) ratio

7. Presentation-to-customer ratio (close ratio)

8. Customer-to-reconversion ratio

Certainly, additional customized inputs and conversion metrics (such as shopping-cart abandonment for e-commerce) may be measured depending on your business model. The ratios outlined here are the basics and are therefore the ones that serve most organizations well in evaluating their digital marketing efforts and connecting those efforts to sales and ROI. The Customer Conversion Chain and its associated ratio metrics are covered fully in Chapter 22.

# *Determining Who Should Perform Your Inbound Assessment*

You have a choice when you assess the current state of your digital marketing. You can perform an internal assessment or you can hire a professional to perform your IMA. I usually recommend retaining an objective outside expert because doing so gives you an alternative perspective, a less biased lens on your digital marketing data. You and your team can use the outside party's findings to apply solutions and write your own prescriptive strategy. I usually recommend this, as I say, but because marketers often have limited resources, I'm including the necessary information here for you to perform an in-house IMA yourself.

# The benefits and drawbacks of self-diagnosing

Sometimes it makes sense for you to perform your own IMA. This is usually because of a business's size or budget limitations. No worries. Your needs are more basic, so you can take an IMA as far as your time and learning ability allow. Self-diagnosing your current digital marketing state is beneficial when:

- You need a quick look at how you're website is performing.
- You have the technical skills to fix coding and back-end problems.
- You need to determine the extent of any website issues in order to determine if you need help.
- You are a one-person marketing department or you are the owner/manager of a small company.
- You have no budget.
- You want to get the lay of the land before you consider outsourcing a formal paid assessment with a marketing firm or consultant.

Performing an actual website grade is in itself a useful activity and mostly harmless. But it doesn't take long for many marketers to get in over their heads. Here are some pitfalls about self-diagnosing:

- Your reported results are less objective.
- Your report, other than the automated graders, may be shaded by opinion rather than fact.
- Your organization may not possess the expertise to assess, analyze, and interpret your findings.
- Your discoveries may be discredited by others in the organization who have a different agenda.
- You must be extra cautious to form a conclusion and build the data to support that conclusion.

# Self-diagnosing

It's possible to perform an inbound marketing assessment on your own. Doing so takes a bit more work and, if you're unfamiliar with inbound marketing in general, there is a high learning curve. At the very least, ask yourself these questions:

- How attractive is your website to a potential customer?
- How does your website measure up to that of your competition?

✔ What are your conversion rates for visitors, leads, and customers?

✔ What is your return-on-investment?

✔ Where are most of your visitors coming from?

✔ Which social media channel offers you the most traffic?

✔ Where do most of your contacts come from?

✔ Which of your website pages are the most influential for lead generation?

✔ Which pages are the least influential?

✔ Which email was most successful in your last marketing campaign?

✔ How much traffic did your website see last month?

## Using online tools for self-diagnosis

There are some great tools for self-diagnosing your current state. The following list describes a few. In fact, even if you decide to retain a paid professional, I recommend you start by checking out some of these tools on your own:

✔ **Store Grader** (`https://ecommerce.shopify.com/grader`): If you run and maintain an ecommerce site, Shopify's Store Grader is a good place to grade your efforts in website usability, site performance, SEO, content marketing, and social marketing. Grade your e-commerce site here.

✔ **Alexa** (`www.alexa.com`): For a quick snapshot of your website performance, go to Alexa and type in your home page URL. The free version provides an estimated ranking for your country and the world based on a couple of factors. (Your ranking is not solely based on traffic.) While Alexa has its limitations, it's quick and it's easy and you can delve even deeper with their paid version to achieve more accurate data.

✔ **Moz Rank Tracker** (`https://moz.com/tools/rank-tracker`): Moz has been a leader in SEO initiatives for years and they provide a different look at your website. Moz ranks your site from 0 (no value) to 9.99 (highest value) based primarily on "link juice" — that is, the number of backlinks to your website as well as the quality of those links. Like the Richter scale for earthquakes, the ranking is logarithmic.

✔ **HubSpot Marketing Grader** (`https://marketing.grader.com`): HubSpot's transition from a website grader to a marketing grader is indicative of the increasing demand for tools to measure more than just a website. HubSpot's innovative grader runs quickly and provides useful actionable information to help you identify gaps in performance. Marketing Grader includes your Alexa and Moz ranks and much, much more. This tool is comprehensive, offering actionable points that you can begin working on today.

✔ **Nibbler Grader** (`http://nibbler.silktide.com/`): Nibbler has a grader that scores your overall efforts on a ten-point scale, including accessibility, experience, marketing, and technology. Sub-categories are broken down into individual scores, too. Nibbler also looks at social media page connections and grades your mobile site. Like HubSpot's Marketing Grader, it provides an interesting dashboard, a customized word cloud for your website, and useful, actionable points for you to improve your efforts.

✔ **Woorank Grader** (`www.woorank.com`): Woorank grades your social media, SEO, conversions, and your mobile site. Delivering quick results, Woorank outlines critical areas that need immediate attention and points out the areas where you are performing well. The action points are outlined under each of the initiatives graded with an easy-to-read actionable list.

✔ **Quick Sprout** (`www.quicksprout.com`): Quick Sprout's website analyzer grades your SEO based on a letter grade (like school) while measuring and displaying your mobile site. The SEO breakdown is quite detailed with easy-to-read tables, clearly displaying your results. Website Analyzer breaks down your factors into High, Medium, and Low priorities so at least you know where to focus on improvements even if you don't plan on doing the work yourself.

✔ **WRC Validator** (`https://valaidator.w3.org`): The World Wide Web Consortium (W3C) developed their Validator that's geared more toward the Internet-technology set than toward marketers. Although it doesn't have the fancy dashboards and easy-to-read action points, it does specifically identify potential problems.

## *The benefits and drawbacks of outsourcing IMAs*

Educating yourself by performing some self-diagnosis is generally recommended. Doing so moves your engagement point further along with prospective consultants and helps you make an informed decision as to which IMA provider best suits your needs.

Here are some benefits to hiring a pro to perform your IMA:

✔ A professional IMA provides an independent, objective analysis.

✔ Outsourcing saves you time so you can assess more quickly and go to market with your recommended initiatives earlier.

✔ Sometimes an IMA will support what you know to be true but your message is falling upon deaf ears. In other words, it can serve as an independent proof that positive change needs to occur.

✔ A true pro provides a written document or playbook, which can be immediately shared, and referenced in the future.

✔ Reputable marketing firms and consultants provide sound, factual data to enable collective data-driven decision-making.

Unfortunately, even when you invest money in an IMA there are possible pitfalls. Here are some pitfalls to outsourcing your IMA:

✔ Hiring a pro costs money. Many times it's an investment of thousands of dollars.

✔ Usually, the IMA is only the first of a two-step strategic plan and, guess what? Someone has to write the inbound strategic plan, too! Unless you write the strategic plan yourself, that's an additional investment.

✔ All IMAs are not created equally. Research your options and choose a provider you feel comfortably matches your needs in a professional manner.

✔ Some individuals in your company (maybe even you!) value action over planning. That is dangerous! By not immediately "doing" your inbound initiatives you could be derailed by these people before you even get started.

## Outsourcing your assessment

Self-diagnosis is a good start to understanding which marketing efforts are contributing to your online success. For smaller companies, an in-house assessment may be all you need; however, such assessments are self-limiting by definition. For a more sophisticated approach to measuring your online marketing efforts and how you can best connect with prospective customers, it may make sense to hire a consultant or marketing firm to perform your inbound marketing assessment.

If you choose to outsource your IMA, make sure you understand up front what your report will cover and how much it will cost. The pricing and associated deliverables vary greatly. My marketing firms have performed IMAs that range from basic $1,500 conversion-chain analyses to $60,000 full-blown enterprise assessments. Chances are, you can outsource your IMA for between $2,000 and $10,000. Plenty of inbound marketing firms and consultants perform IMAs. Many IMAs are a snapshot of *what* is happening and not *how* to fix the problems identified. That's okay, because at this point you're trying to identify and frame problems, not solve them. Later, you'll write a strategic inbound plan based on your IMA discoveries — to connect the "why" of your inbound marketing with the "what" and the "how."

At the least, your paid professional assessor should identify the following:

✔ Online goals

✔ Current inbound attraction efforts

✔ Base keywords for search engine optimization (SEO)

✔ Current search engine marketing (SEM) metrics

✔ Current remarketing efforts

✔ Conversions

It's fair to expect a paid inbound marketing assessment to include a broader measurement than a website grader. The best IMAs view your website as a hub that connects your online marketing efforts and will report findings based on the dynamic interaction between those efforts and your hub.

A proper inbound marketing assessment is holistic in nature, measuring the purchase path that connects people with your product or service — the Customer Conversion Chain. A professional inbound marketing assessment should reflect the complexity of your prospects' purchase path by measuring each link, or conversion point in this process. The IMA may report data simply for clarity, but the underlying complexity of interactions require a look at each input and factor that affects your desired outcome. As such, your paid professional IMA should identify where your online marketing efforts are paying off as well as where you're falling short. After performing your IMA, you will have actionable improvements that can directly affect your inbound marketing's ability to attract and convert.

So now is the time for action. Take the first steps in elevating your inbound marketing by gauging your baseline metrics through a website grader and IMA.

# Things You Can Do Now

✔ Search for free online inbound assessments and take them so you get a few opinions on your current efforts.

✔ Choose an assessment path: Self-diagnosis or hire a pro? Self-diagnosis is free, but limited in scope and objectivity. Assessing with a professional consultant may reveal issues you wouldn't discover on your own while providing focus and direction.

✔ Go ahead and perform your formal assessment. Starting with a website grader and/or IMA now may put you one step ahead of your competitors.

# Chapter 4

# Prescribing Strategic Inbound Marketing Solutions

*In This Chapter*

▶ Documenting your inbound marketing plan

▶ Creating a strategic roadmap to success

▶ Establishing goals and objectives

▶ Reverse-engineering your inbound plan

▶ Sharing your inbound plan

▶ Mapping successful inbound marketing

*A*fter diagnosing the current state of your inbound marketing, you must think about which solutions to prescribe to fix your impediments to online marketing success. Prescribing solutions through strategy is the second step for instituting inbound marketing at your company. That's what this chapter covers. Here you'll see that inbound strategy is, in many ways, created the same way business strategy is.

In this chapter, I cover the basic components of inbound strategy and how to create a strategy that connects your marketing initiatives with business results. You learn the importance of creating strategy before you deploy your tactical marketing efforts. By formulating a plan based on goals and objectives, your path to achieving those goals will be clearer, enabling you to share the future direction of that marketing path with others in your company. I include some guidelines on choosing a starting point — either an attraction plan or a conversion plan — and, near the end of the chapter, include some examples.

Let's strategize!

# Strategizing Business Solutions

If you were sailing from San Diego to Honolulu, you wouldn't just buy a boat and shove off. If you did, you would literally be leaving your chances of arriving at your destination to the winds. Being a smart sailor, you would buy charts and maps. You'd check the forecast for winds, tides, and currents. You'd plan a route and timeline. And you'd have milestones of achievement along the way. Then you would craft a Plan "B" and a Plan "C." You might even have a crisis plan in place to account for an unplanned hurricane or a capsized boat.

As a savvy sailor, you'd monitor the wind and currents, adjusting your sails and rudder to stay on course. The weather forecast may be wrong, unexpected storms may temporarily blow you off course, and you may not reach your destination on time, but at least you've armed yourself with the right tools and information to increase your chances of a successful outcome. The same is true for any business goal, including inbound marketing.

As an inbound marketer, you're sailing in the sea of the uncertain marketplace, populated by dynamic consumers whose unpredictable and sometimes whimsical behavior can blow your marketing efforts off course. However, because you've documented your inbound marketing plan, you are prepared to reach your final destination . . . achieving your business goals and objectives.

You completed Step One by performing an assessment. Now it's time to identify your desired successful outcomes (business and goals) and to document a path that charts your success markers (objectives) and the tools you'll use to achieve those goals. To simplify, I prefer to use the G.O.S.T. (goals, objectives, strategy, tactics) model outlined by Rich Horwath in his book, *Deep Dive*.

## Starting with a Strategic Inbound Plan

You have probably heard the saying, "Plan the work and work the plan." Everything worth doing in business deserves to start with a plan. Online marketing and inbound marketing are no exceptions. Your inbound marketing strategy answers why, what, and how: *Why* you're doing what you're doing, *what* you're aiming to do, and *how* to get it done.

Big successes come from big plans that are written and executed with business objectives in mind. Your strategic plan provides solid, data-driven rationales for choosing your marketing recommendations while identifying and outlining how to achieve your goals and objectives. The objectives you set forth in your plan include specific, measurable success markers and identify the tactical tools you will use to attain these milestones.

As with any successful business strategy, your inbound marketing strategy

- ✔ Begins with desired business outcomes/results in mind
- ✔ Answers why you're performing your recommended marketing initiatives
- ✔ Provides written direction for future initiatives
- ✔ Prioritizes initiatives so your team differentiates the critical ones from the optional ones
- ✔ Provides a documented, shared performance platform for measuring and reporting marketing success as it pertains to achieving business outcomes
- ✔ Results in more efficient allocation of time and resources
- ✔ Connects financial budgets with revenue/profit goals

Inbound marketing strategy was rarely discussed on the Internet or in marketing circles until a few years ago. Today, exceptional online success *requires* an inbound marketing strategy. The shift to attracting new clients and customers through inbound means (as opposed to outbound ones) is a genuine one. A documented strategy can help you compete by garnering a larger market share and growing sales on- and offline. Your inbound strategy is a plan to connect with those people early and often.

Often, companies buy in to a strategy based on creative ideas which is backwards. Strategy occurs for the wrong reason with little or no measurable business metrics so the business problems at hand go unsolved. Approaching strategy from the point of creative tactics rather than overarching business goals is a fallacy and one reason many in the C-suite maintain a certain mistrust of marketing types and why the average ad agency/client relationship is less than two years.

As a marketer, you can diminish this mistrust by applying inbound marketing to solve *business* problems rather than marketing problems. Inbound marketing's inherent accountability, transparency, and ongoing measurement of success factors elevates the position of marketing within a company.

So why is it that so many organizations fail to begin with inbound strategy? A formal written strategic inbound plan takes time to develop and implement. Some organizations lack the capacity or the expertise to write their own plans. More often, they have a culture of "doing" rather than "thinking." Typically, these companies reward production and the completion of tasks, regardless of those tasks' contribution to the goal. It's easier and quicker just to start doing something. You look like you're busy, and you are, but you're probably working on the wrong tasks, tasks that won't affect the business goals in any meaningful way.

Some organizations, especially small- to mid-sized companies, fail to allocate budgets for strategic planning. It's not cheap to engage the help of a qualified, objective professional. Plus, it takes time to find a viable consultant or inbound marketing firm partner to complement your team and to satisfy your unique needs.

Commonly, the short answers I hear for why organizations don't have an inbound marketing plan are time and money. Nonsense. I've identified some common culprits for the absence of a strategic inbound plan at companies:

- ✔ Short-term vision and culture
- ✔ Lack of organization
- ✔ Lack of accountability
- ✔ Lack of responsibility
- ✔ Lack of transparency
- ✔ *Perceived* lack of time

## Understanding the benefits of a strategic inbound plan

An effective inbound marketing strategy creates conversations between your prospect and your company. Creating this two-way communication is no longer a luxury; it's mandatory to stay atop your industry today and to remain competitive tomorrow. Why? It's what customers want. It's what today's customer demands.

Because of the nature of the Internet, your chances of success in today's competitive, data-driven online economic model are driven by attracting visitors to your site from search engine marketing (SEM), social media sites, and referrals, and converting through great content. Removing (or failing to add) just one of these components from your strategic marketing plan substantially decreases the chances that your company's marketing efforts will succeed over the next few years. At the very least, your marketing efforts won't be maximized. Your organization's lack of investing in business and content strategy compounds the chance of failure. Regardless, your company will never reach its full sales and earning potential without a sound strategic inbound marketing plan in place — unless you're just plain lucky. And, in my experience, Lady Luck tends to perform inconsistently.

If you're not playing the marketing game with a formal written inbound marketing strategy on your side, you're not even in the game at this point. So don't just get in the game, own it. Go ahead and reallocate some of your budgeted funds from traditional marketing into digital marketing. But before you jump headlong into implementing inbound marketing tactics, invest in an inbound marketing strategy.

# Knowing the Components of Your Strategic Inbound Plan

At the most basic level, there are five steps to creating an effective inbound marketing strategy. You should expand upon these basic steps because a comprehensive inbound plan serves you and your organization better.

However, if you're pressed for time or have very limited resources, invest time toward these five steps. They are:

1. Set goals and objectives

2. Establish your inbound analytic metrics

3. Develop your attraction and conversion plans

4. Formulate your opportunity analysis

5. Create content strategy

Following these steps sets the stage for attracting and converting new clients/customers through inbound marketing. It helps you attract visitors to your website, convert visitors to leads, turn leads into customers, and customers into repeat customers — maybe even fanatic, loyal customers who live to promote your brand! These customers are known as *Lifestylers*.

## Setting goals and objectives based on your baseline assessment

Establish high-level goals and measurable objectives for your inbound marketing. You do this by balancing your company revenue and profit needs with your target customers' needs.

You may already understand the customer types your business attracts. Formalize those customers into groups, segmenting them by demographics, lifestyle, title/position, and shared purchasing habits. These groups are commonly called customer *personas*, although I prefer the broader term *profiles*. In this book, I use both terms interchangeably.

Is your first point of contact with prospects at the product research phase? Do you know that your best customers are women age 25 to 29 who have two kids and drive a domestic minivan? Do you understand the different buying motivations for an end user of your product as opposed to a procurement agent purchasing your product for a company? Understand your target customer and his or her needs. Structure your online goals and objectives with these needs in mind.

Think of *goals* as paths and *objectives* as the steps to walk down that path. Here's an example:

Goal: Dominate rankings on Google and Yahoo search-engine result pages (SERPs) for your top industry keyword terms within 18 months.

Objective #1: Outrank your top three competitors on Google over the next 18 months by achieving a SERP rank between 1 and 4 for the 20 most highly searched industry keywords.

Objective #2: Own all ten organic rankings for your branded keyword terms on page one of SERPs and maintain that for the next year.

So you see, it may take multiple objectives to achieve a broad-based goal.

As with business strategy, your inbound strategy is most effective when you follow the SMART acronym. That is, your objectives should be:

- ✔ **S**pecific
- ✔ **M**easurable
- ✔ **A**ttainable
- ✔ **R**elevant
- ✔ **T**ime-bound

If you don't set goals and objectives in the beginning, you'll have no way of measuring success. Being SMART with your objectives results in a more finely tuned inbound marketing strategy.

# Do you believe in G.O.S.T.s?

When I consult for companies large and small, there often seems to be an invisible negative force at work. It's called strategy, and its presence (or lack thereof) seems to be as visible as a phantom. In other words, most companies do not truly have a documented, formal strategy. The company vision is invisible. That's why I believe in G.O.S.T.s.

G.O.S.T. was developed by Rich Horwath, author of *Deep Dive* and *Elevate*, and here's how he describes the acronym:

**G**oals: What you're generally trying to achieve.

**O**bjectives: Specifically what you're trying to achieve.

**S**trategy: How you're going to achieve your goals.

**T**actics: Specifically how you're going to achieve your objectives

## Developing your attraction and conversion plan

Good inbound marketing strategy starts with knowing your product/service offerings and your customers' motivations for purchase. You can then design easy access to purchase. Create customer attraction for your products through search engine optimization (SEO) and search engine marketing (SEM) best practices outside of your website. By understanding your prospects' needs and their place in the purchase path, you can direct prospects to the appropriate content on your website based on the words prospects use in their search queries.

Of course, this requires you to create onsite content that fulfills the need of your prospects at their points of entry to your website. Interesting blog content attracts prospects and facilitates their ease of entry to your website. A well-designed online tool that promises to uniquely solve a prospect's problem (such as a mortgage calculator) is a valuable offering that engages visitors. Gating content by requiring customer form completion begins the conversion process.

Once visitors find and land on your site, it's time to engage. A Call-to-Action (CTA) Map (see Chapter 11) delivers your website content in a manner that appears fluid and intuitive to visitors. Ideally, your website CTA Map provides a frictionless path to conversion. A *conversion* is defined as the meaningful exchange of valuable information between a prospective customer and your company. This could be a customer email address in exchange for an e-book or a customer's credit card number in exchange for a product purchase. The ultimate conversion for a business is usually considered a sale.

Business-to-consumer (B2C) and business-to-business (B2B) conversion paths look much different. The B2C purchase path is usually quicker due to relatively low-cost purchase prices that can be made online. Many B2B purchase paths are much longer, especially those that are high-dollar purchases. Because these sales are usually made offline, it's especially important to collect buyer data early and often. Doing so will allow your business development team to engage earlier in the purchase, guiding prospects with meaningful, relevant conversations.

## Establishing inbound analytics

What's your current customer worth in dollars and cents? What's your average sales transaction? What percentage of your business is repeat business?

Know the answers to these questions before you begin by looking at Google Analytics. Why? Because it's not only about numbers; it's about people. Prospects and customers create these numbers. Success comes from satisfying customers. Positive numbers based on consumer behavior on your site will demonstrate this satisfaction.

When you visit your website, interact with it as if *you're* the prospect. Note possible navigation, conversion, and sales barriers to achieving your ideal onsite conversion (sale, demo, trial, sign-up, and so on). Look for user-flow dead-ends. Only when you've gotten a sense of these dead-ends should you look at your numbers.

In addition to Google, you're going to want to invest in marketing automation software. You're ready to track visitor behavior, track conversions of visitors to leads, and track online and offline sales.

A professionally written inbound marketing strategy defines baseline analytics for you based on the above criteria and the goals and objectives outlined in the earlier part of the plan.

## Formulating your opportunity analysis

When you attract website traffic, you want to keep it coming. Now it's time to attract more visitors and discover and break down barriers to entry and sales. Your visitor, lead, and customer habits provide numbers that expose gaps in performance. The best ways to fix and fine-tune your content, CTA Maps, site design, and paid search and landing pages are dictated by the gaps that are preventing you from achieving your goals and objectives.

Developing an inbound marketing strategy can be daunting, but you don't have to go at it alone. There are inbound marketing companies and consultants who can help your company migrate to attraction marketing from traditional interruption marketing methods such as TV and radio ads.

Outbound marketing certainly has a place in any business, especially for creating consumer awareness. Inbound often circumvents the need to start with customer awareness. Prospective customers may search for products and land on your site before they're even aware your company exists. Although it's certainly possible that they'll check you out to affirm you are a legitimate company, the online search and purchase process isn't necessarily linear. By creating engaging online content, designing and implementing an inbound marketing strategy in tandem with your outbound efforts creates efficiency in your marketing budget.

If you're still committed to traditional media, take a portion of your budget (30-80 percent) and reallocate it to inbound marketing. This reallocation results in better ROI when measured dollar-for-dollar invested. Your marketing message will reach Internet shoppers who have never heard your traditional marketing message, attracting new customers.

## Creating content strategy

Content strategy is your plan for the sum of your online content marketing efforts. Because content fuels the inbound marketing machine, a content strategy is imperative. Two major components are:

- ✔ **Connective content:** This is written and visual content that is created and delivered in a manner that is relevant, timely, and contextual to your buyer persona needs at any given place in the purchase path.
- ✔ **Call-to-Action Maps:** This is a conversion-based map designed to create a frictionless Buyer's Journey from initial consumer contact through first customer contract (purchase). I cover this topic more fully in Chapter 11.

Content strategy delivers relevant answers to prospects' questions. CTA Maps make it easy for visitors to convert.

Your content strategy should include an inventory of your current content to identify connective gaps and opportunities. You can create a thorough content strategy by:

- ✔ Taking inventory of all your content
- ✔ Classifying your content by form (written, video, infographic, and so on)
- ✔ Assigning your content to key points along the consumer purchase path (Educational content during the research phase, Engagement content during the shopping phase, Encouragement content during the purchase phase, and Embracing content for current customer reengagement)
- ✔ Assigning your content to a product pyramid/purchase path so that you're connecting people with your products, creating relevancy, and increasing content engagement
- ✔ Prioritizing content needs by inbound campaign importance
- ✔ Looking for gaps at key conversion points, especially for the most important inbound campaigns

# Building Your Strategic Inbound Plan

Now you're ready to define where you want your business to be. Your strategic inbound plan bridges the gap between your present state and your desired future state. Using your IMA as a foundation to begin building that bridge, you may now take the next steps toward creating a strategic inbound marketing plan.

## Using your assessment to prioritize initiatives

If you completed your diagnosis in Chapter 3 with an inbound marketing assessment, you have a better understanding of where your current marketing efforts and metrics are. If you think in terms of a SWOT analysis, your assessment was the first snapshot of your **S**trengths, **W**eaknesses, **O**pportunities, and **T**hreats.

Now it's time to prioritize because you probably don't have the resources to complete every single initiative, capitalize on every opportunity, or fix every problem. Start with these steps:

1. **List the goals that are most important to achieve, including an estimated timeline.**

2. Create a list of objectives that must occur to achieve each of these goals.

3. Identify through your Customer Conversion Chain metrics which goals are most attainable. Write down the dollar contribution of achieving that goal as well as successfully achieving each objective under that goal.

4. Prioritize your objectives by focusing first on those objectives that are easily monetized and that help you reach your goals more quickly.

5. Determine which of your goals and objectives result in the biggest payout in the shortest amount of time. This is probably your biggest opportunity. Share with other stakeholders within your organization.

6. Assess the cost in time, money, and energy to achieve each objective. Specifically list barriers to achieving objectives and the cost to bridge the gap.

7. If you have the resources to bridge the gap for any significant objective, proceed with any given inbound marketing initiative. If not, seek additional resources or focus on another goal; one that is more attainable.

By thoughtfully going through this process and sharing your progress with your company team members, superiors, procurement, sales, and other key internal stakeholders, you'll have meaningful business conversations. Sometimes these are tough conversations because you may need an increase in budget or you may need to hire people. That's okay. You're setting yourself up for failure if you don't communicate honestly, objectively, and factually to paint a realistic picture for everyone in your company to see.

## Identifying tactical tools to activate success

With inbound marketing, you have an arsenal of attraction and conversion tools. In fact, there are so many options it can quickly become overwhelming to decide which initiatives are the most important. Should you attract traffic via organic rankings or paid search? Where in the Lifestyle Loop purchase path should you attract? Should you create more forms or A/B test your landing pages? Here's an ordered check list to serve as a basic guideline. Feel free to customize it for your needs.

### 1. Fix your website.

Because your website is your Conversion Machine engine, start there. It doesn't make sense to attract prospects to a broken site. Your IMA identified the technical, UX, and conversion path gaps. Based on these findings, decide if you:

- Need to build an entire new site

- Can use existing pages and content to redirect visitor on-site flow based on a conversion-based CTA Map blueprint

- Need to optimize the conversion path by offering more onsite conversion opportunities to engagement content, specifically with buttons, forms, and landing pages.

2. **Determine your first focus: attraction or conversion.** Here's how:

   a. If you have enough traffic to achieve your objective with standard minimum key performance indicators (KPIs) — Traffic × Conversion KPI = >Objective — start with a conversion focus.

   Here's an example. Let's say your organization is currently tracking these numbers:

   Sales objective: $100,000/month

   Average sale: $1,000, or 100 units/month

   Current traffic: 5,000 visitors/month

   Current traffic-to-end-sale conversion rate: 1 percent

   Maximum conversion rate (hypothesized based on your industry standard): 2 percent

   With these values, you can calculate the current state as follows:

   Current state: 5,000 visitors × .01 (1 percent) = 50 units or $50,000

   And the hypothesized state as:

   Maximum state (hypothesized): 5,000 visitors × .02 (2 percent) = 100 units or $100,000

   From this you can conclude: You have enough website traffic to succeed if you increase your conversion rate, so focus on that first. Work to increase overall conversion rate from 1 percent to 2 percent.

   b. If your sales objective is unattainable, even with high-performing conversion percentages, start with an attraction focus. You need more website visitors.

   Here's an example. Let's say your organization is currently tracking these numbers:

   Sales objective: $100,000/month

   Average sale: $1,000 so 100 units/month

Current traffic: 2,500 visitors/month

Current traffic-to-end-sale conversion rate: 1 percent

Maximum conversion rate (hypothesized): 2 percent

With these values, you can calculate the current state as follows:

Current state: 2,500 visitors $\times$ .01 (1 percent) = 25 units or $25,000

Maximum conversion state (hypothesized): 2,500 visitors $\times$ .02 (2 percent) = 50 units or $50,000

From this you can conclude: You cannot achieve your objective even at the maximum conversion rate. Your primary focus, then, should be on increasing traffic from 2,500 to 5,000 (and from there to 10,000) because that's the minimum number of visitors needed to convert at the maximum conversion rate in order to meet your goal. Your secondary focus should be on increasing the conversion rate from one to two percent.

c. If you're not sure, start with onsite conversion. Unless your website traffic is very anemic or your sales goals are unrealistic, it's usually a quicker route to achieving objectives.

**3. Choose tactical tools based on your IMA results.**

a. Identify which attraction sources (SEO, PPC, Referrals, Direct Traffic, etc.) drive the most traffic to your site.

b. If you have automation software, measure which attraction inputs convert at the highest ratios.

c. Segment traffic and conversion percentages by product to estimate total conversions. Usually, you'll start with the biggest profit opportunity that can be achieved in the shortest period of time.

d. Identify your content gaps and decide whether you have the resources to produce new content to fill those gaps as well as a timeline to complete.

e. Perform a Customer Conversion Chain analysis (see Chapter 22) based on your desired business outcome.

f. Form a hypothesis as to which mix would perform optimally to achieve your business outcome.

g. Allocate your resources of time, money, and energy on those tactics that achieve your objectives most effectively and most quickly.

h. Initiate your inbound tactical campaign with a very specific timeline.

i. Measure as you go. Adjust in real time.

j. Compare your results with your hypothesis. Replicate success. Adjust non-performing or negative inputs.

## Mapping future success today

Your strategy is simply a map connecting your current status with your future objectives. You create your inbound map based on the Customer Conversion Chain that links the purchaser with your product. So, once again, begin with the end in mind.

Map your plan as follows:

1. Understand your company's stated goals and objectives.

2. Assess the competitive landscape looking at competitors' websites, their content, and the keywords they're using to attract and convert customers.

3. Identify your target purchasing profiles and associate an average unit sale and average dollar sale with each profile.

4. Use historical data to determine for each profile the average length from first contact to first contract and the percentage of repeat purchases.

5. Examine your visitor and conversion data and apply those metrics to the Customer Conversion Chain model.

6. Outline your attraction and conversion plan, taking into consideration the different inputs that will affect your metrics.

7. Form a business outcome hypothesis, based on your anticipated conversion rate and, defined in dollars and cents. Then choose the most efficient method to market based on whether increased attraction or increased conversions have a greater positive impact on your ROI.

8. Build your creative assets.

9. Implement your inbound campaign.

10. Measure your campaign against success metrics and adjust accordingly.

## Remapping success along the way

You've formed a conversion hypothesis. You've implemented your inbound campaign. Now it's time to plug in your actual numbers and compare them to your original hypothesis.

No one ever said your inbound hypothesis was written in stone. Sometimes you'll rock out and other times you'll fall flat. Access your data on a regular basis, and you can tweak your digital initiatives along the way. Evaluating real-time data means you can fail fast.

When you access data during the process rather than measure after a campaign is complete, you can identify which parts of the campaign are not working. If too many parts are unworkable in achieving your objectives pull the plug on the campaign. Failing fast ultimately saves your company time and money.

Likewise as you discover small successes in one campaign, you can apply similar tactics to another campaign, raising your overall marketing success.

Try leveraging the success you've had with one inbound product campaign by applying it to another product campaign. You may look for:

- ✔ Identifying successful engagement content for one product funnel and creating similar content for other purchase paths increasing your data collection and ensuring conversion rate

- ✔ Successfully converting form and buttons to apply to additional campaigns

- ✔ Checking blog posts that attract higher visitor volume and creating similar topics

- ✔ Replicating high-conversion landing pages and applying them in additional inbound campaigns

- ✔ Measuring attraction sources and testing the highest converting sources in other campaigns

- ✔ Creating side-portal entryways (any pages, other than the website's home page, that help consumers get the information they're seeking more quickly)

- ✔ Building tools for one campaign similar to those that have a proven high-engagement factor

Eventually, you'll replicate successes by modeling premium customers, examining those customers' path to purchase, and facilitating that path to a sale by attracting more of the same type of customers into that proven path. In other words, you create attractive messaging to people similar to your customers and streamline their path to purchase.

# *Things You Can Do Now*

✔ Collect and document sales goals for current year so you know the target you're trying to hit.

✔ Plug your numbers into the Customer Conversion Chain so you can begin reverse-engineering a strategy that applies a methodical approach to achieving your objectives and, eventually, your end goal.

✔ Research strategic consultants/inbound firms to see which may be a good fit to help you write inbound strategy for your business.

# Chapter 5

# Applying Inbound Solutions: Executing Your Plan

. . . . . . . . . . . . . . . . . . . . . . . . . . . . . . . . . . . . . . . . . . . . . . . .

*In This Chapter*

▶ Developing a timeline for your inbound plan

▶ Deciding who should do your inbound work

▶ Delegating inbound marketing initiatives

▶ Determining whether or not to outsource

▶ Establishing and measuring milestones

. . . . . . . . . . . . . . . . . . . . . . . . . . . . . . . . . . . . . . . . . . . . . . . .

*T*he third inbound marketing step is applying your tactical inbound solutions. This follows the diagnosis you made in Chapter 3 and the strategic inbound plan you developed in Chapter 4. In this chapter, I cover the basics of applied solutions. You learn about developing a timeline, delegating your inbound initiatives, and establishing a method for choosing the most impactful inbound marketing applications.

I also introduce an important concept, the Shared Strategic Blueprint (SSB). SSBs are mini-marketing plans that break down a long-term strategy into pieces, usually into pieces that cover short, three-month periods. Implementing SSBs means you get better feedback and you'll get it more quickly. SSBs help you focus on the important marketing attraction and conversion initiatives acting as inputs and affecting your ability to achieving your business objectives. You also learn about milestones and metrics and how your measurements contribute to optimal inbound marketing.

# Implementing Your Strategic Inbound Plan

You've performed your initial assessment. You've written a plan. Now it's time to execute. If you're following my methodology of reverse-engineering your marketing initiatives from the objectives you're attempting to achieve, the execution will be more clearly organized. By documenting your inbound strategy, you're able to answer *why* you're implementing certain inbound marketing efforts providing your team with context and meaning. Now you can drill down to the *how* — as in *how* you're going to achieve your objectives.

Now it's time to break down your inbound strategy into manageable pieces. First, outline your timeline. You can begin with a 12-month plan and break it down into 3-month marketing sprints by using our Shared Strategic Blueprints. By segmenting your timeline into shorter periods, you'll have the flexibility to make adjustments as you collect and analyze your measurement data.

After you've set forth your timeline, it's time to delegate. You'll need to make an honest assessment as to what your organization has to offer in terms of time, talent, and budget. You may need to outsource to experts in order to avoid steep learning curves while shortening your time to achieve objectives.

Many of your milestones are outlined in your strategy. Now you'll break those down into multiple metrics. By measuring, sharing, and reporting analytics on a regular and ongoing basis, you keep focused on your objectives and can make real-time adjustments if necessary.

# Developing Your Inbound Timeline

In your inbound marketing plan, you've written a timeline overview that can be broken up into manageable segments. By breaking your annual plan into 3-month sprints and then working backward from your 12-month objectives, your inbound marketing efforts will be more nimble.

Here's a simple way to break down your objectives:

- **Annual:** What objectives does your inbound marketing plan need to achieve in the next 12 months?
- **Quarterly:** Shared Strategic Blueprints (SSBs) — these three-month mini-plans are actually the most important components of your plan. What marketing milestones do you need to achieve in order to successfully achieve your annual goal?

✔ **Monthly:** Are you on track to achieve your three-month objectives? Which of your inbound marketing efforts are performing and which are under-achieving? Monitor the under-achievers to spot trends and adjust accordingly.

✔ **Weekly:** Develop a weekly report to track progress on each of your inbound efforts. Stay in front of any delays so you can substitute alternative initiatives if so required.

✔ **Daily:** Depending on your size, some inbound metrics should be tracked daily. At the very least, look at your inbound dashboard to see if your visitors, leads, and other conversion metrics are on course. Inbound initiatives like PPC should be monitored on a daily basis to track input.

# Creating a Shared Strategic Blueprint (SSB)

In 2012, my team at Marketing Matters Inbound set out to simplify the inbound process. We discovered that proactively creating a flexible inbound plan actually reduced the traditional reactive nature of marketing. The way in which our team provides marketing solutions and communications for our clients changed and so did our digital marketing success. This restructuring of our internal processes gave rise to what we've coined as the Shared Strategic Blueprint (SSB).

An SSB is a mini three-month plan that helps you focus on achieving your business and marketing goals by breaking down your overall strategic plan into manageable parts. My business partner, Nathaniel Davidson, invented the SSB while working at Marketing Matters Inbound. It's a method of mapping out your measurable action plan in short sprints. SSBs:

✔ Are written three-month action plans in which inbound initiatives are determined by their individual contribution to the milestone objectives

✔ Operate off the same SMART goals that you wrote in your inbound strategy

✔ Are usually specific to inbound campaigns but can also be applied to your other initiatives

✔ Can be used internally and externally when you're working with outside consultants or inbound marketing firm

The SSB focuses on and brings to light not only what it is that we're doing, but also forces us always to state why we're doing it.

The SSB process revolves around four key meetings each year, one meeting every 90 days. During these meetings, your internal team collaborates with all key contributors (including your outsourced marketing team) to answer the following questions or address the following points (arranged here by topic):

- ✔ Reporting

  - What does your IMA tell you are the critical, necessary, and "wish-list" priorities?

  - Establish the metrics you'll need to hit in order to successfully complete each quarterly SSB.

- ✔ Objectives

  - When you break down your annual plan into concurrent three-month sections, what milestones do you need to achieve at the end of each quarter?

  - Are each of your objectives SMART (specific, measurable, attainable, relevant, time-bound)?

  - Establish the milestones that help you achieve each quarterly objective to ensure you've created a realistic plan to success.

  - What tools and services do you need to help achieve these business goals?

- ✔ Ideation

  - What creative campaigns are best at connecting with your target customers?

  - Brainstorm and document the creative content you need to populate your campaigns?

  - Which marketing initiatives best achieve your objectives? Think beyond the obvious.

  - Consider which personas will be most responsive to your efforts, testing several ideas for bringing your message to market.

  - What types of inbound marketing campaigns will contribute the most to successfully achieving your objectives?

- ✔ Measurement

  - What constitutes success?

  - How will you measure your success against quarterly and annual objectives?

  - How will you determine if your choices from the "Ideation" phase impacted the business in the manner desired?

> • Are the ideal marketing initiatives affordable?
>
> • What adjustments need to be made?

After each SSB meeting, you'd ideally create a 30/60/90 SSB plan as to how your team will roll out the next set of initiatives to meet the shared objectives. You can see a sample summary in Figure 5-1. Effectively, this type of SSB creates an ongoing, monthly schedule to touch base and report back to stakeholders while allowing for larger, more in-depth meetings each year.

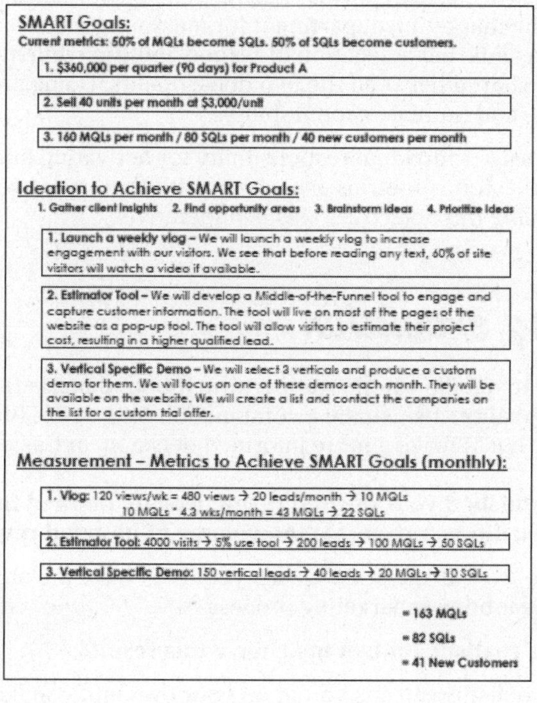

**SMART Goals:**
Current metrics: 50% of MQLs become SQLs. 50% of SQLs become customers.

1. $360,000 per quarter (90 days) for Product A

2. Sell 40 units per month at $3,000/unit

3. 160 MQLs per month / 80 SQLs per month / 40 new customers per month

**Ideation to Achieve SMART Goals:**
1. Gather client insights   2. Find opportunity areas   3. Brainstorm ideas   4. Prioritize Ideas

1. **Launch a weekly vlog** – We will launch a weekly vlog to increase engagement with our visitors. We see that before reading any text, 60% of site visitors will watch a video if available.

2. **Estimator Tool** – We will develop a Middle-of-the-Funnel tool to engage and capture customer information. The tool will live on most of the pages of the website as a pop-up tool. The tool will allow visitors to estimate their project cost, resulting in a higher qualified lead.

3. **Vertical Specific Demo** – We will select 3 verticals and produce a custom demo for them. We will focus on one of these demos each month. They will be available on the website. We will create a list and contact the companies on the list for a custom trial offer.

**Measurement – Metrics to Achieve SMART Goals (monthly):**

1. **Vlog:** 120 views/wk = 480 views → 20 leads/month → 10 MQLs
   10 MQLs * 4.3 wks/month → 43 MQLs → 22 SQLs

2. **Estimator Tool:** 4000 visits → 5% use tool → 200 leads → 100 MQLs → 50 SQLs

3. **Vertical Specific Demo:** 150 vertical leads → 40 leads → 20 MQLs → 10 SQLs

= 163 MQLs

= 82 SQLs

= 41 New Customers

**Figure 5-1:**
A sample SSB summary.

Your quarterly SSB breaks down tasks that contribute to a desired result after three months. If any task doesn't contribute to the result, eliminate it. Be brutal in whittling away tasks that don't contribute; they waste time, energy, and money, and detract from achieving your inbound marketing goals.

# Delegating Ownership of the Work

You're probably starting to realize that embracing inbound marketing within your organization can be quite an undertaking. Take a deep breath. Don't worry. The inbound life is the good life; it just takes some time and hard work to get things started.

Now that you've performed a digital or inbound assessment and written a plan (or at least a plan outline with timeline), how are you going to get everything done? Who's going to do all the work?

Now that you know your workload, it's time to assign ownership. This is done on several levels, as follows:

- ✔ **Organizational:** Should you outsource or perform the work in-house? (Read below.)
- ✔ **Departmental:** The sales department is responsible for sales conversion metrics, and the marketing department for marketing metrics. So, each department has internal delegation of responsibilities while the common objectives are shared between the two departments. Doing so creates a common cause and mutual accountability.
- ✔ **Individuals:** Assign individual responsibility for activating initiatives, tracking the milestones/metrics associated with that initiative, and actually achieving the objective. This is imperative.

## Outsourcing execution

Here's a quick way to decide whether to perform inbound marketing in-house or to outsource. In reality, it's usually a combination of the two, but this may help you (and your boss) make a more informed decision, in this order:

1. **Have you established your desired result, usually defined in currency? In other words, did you generate the volume of planned revenues?**

   Answering "No" to this question means you don't have a plan; go back to that step in the inbound-marketing process.

2. **Do you have a realistic budget to achieve this result?**

   A "No" to this question means you're on your own and you'll need to invest a lot of time to achieve your results. Or it means you need to seek the budget you need to get the job done.

3. **Do you have the resources to achieve your desired result in the allotted timeframe?**

4. **Does your organization have the available personnel to get the job done?**

5. **Do you, or does your internal team, have the expertise to get the job done?**

   Answering "Yes" to questions 3–5 means you can perform inbound marketing on your own. A "No" means you need to outsource.

## In-house execution

The "R" in SMART refers to "relevant." Your company's desired outcome may be an ideal outcome. That's fine, as long as you now apply the "A" which is "Attainable."

It is your job as a marketer to determine whether or not the objectives created are achievable, no matter whether those objectives originated in your department, or they were handed to you. I may want to fly to the moon, but if I don't have the time, money, and expertise to build a rocket ship, I'm not going to get there. It's okay to shoot for the moon, but you're going to need resources and expertise to get there. NASA has that; you don't.

When executing a strategy to achieve your business goals, take an honest assessment of your in-house team so you don't commit to unattainable objectives. Know your strengths and fill in identifiable gaps. You can do this by referring to gaps identified in your IMA and matching up your in-house skillset, determining where you may need to outsource. This will be easy if you're a one-person marketer; less so for larger organizations and marketing teams.

# Establishing Your Inbound Metrics and Milestones

*Milestones* are significant points along the path of achieving your overall objective. *Metrics* are the important contributing factors to hitting milestones and eventually actualizing your objectives.

Let's say you're a B2B company whose annual objective is to sell 100 units in a year. In this case, your milestone might be 25 units per quarter. Your SSB plan might be to attract 2,500 visitors that convert to customers at a 1 percent rate each quarter via content marketing (1,000 visitors), organic traffic (1,000 visitors), and event marketing (500 visitors).

Your *objective* is to sell 100 units annually.

Your *milestones* are 25 units each quarter.

Your *metrics* are:

- Total visitors (2,500 visitors)
- Visitors by attraction source (1,000 by content marketing; 1,000 by organic traffic; and 500 by event marketing)

✔ Total customer conversion percentage (one percent)

✔ Conversion by attraction source (10 units by content marketing; 10 by organic traffic; and 5 by event marketing)

The numbers above are just a simple example. Of course there are other contributing factors to consider, such as:

✔ Time spent on purchase path from first visit to first purchase by source (for example, if trade show website leads take three months to convert whereas leads derived from organic search take six months)

✔ Content and offers that convert at a higher or lower percentage

✔ Cost-per-lead by source

✔ Cost-per-acquisition by source

You could break the metrics down even further by looking at each of these contributing factors. Based on historical data, for example, you might change your metrics to 833 organic visitors per quarter converting overall at 3 percent (contributing 25 units sold).

# Measuring Your Success

Success isn't defined by how much you report or even how many hours you worked. So, how do you measure success? The first question you need to answer is whether or not you achieved the business milestones set forth in your plan. Seek insight as to why you achieved success and solutions for the areas that underperformed.

Thick reports filled with detailed minutiae and graphs too complicated to digest encourage confusion rather than clarity. Be very clear as to what the important contributing metrics are and seek agreement up front on those metrics with all involved. Then build custom dashboards or use marketing automation software that report those KPIs.

## Sharing your analytics

When sharing your analytics, do everyone involved a favor. Build your metrics dashboard based on what everyone collectively agrees are the important contributing factors to achieving success. Include the Customer Conversion Chain metrics. Don't simply report by reading back the numbers that everyone in the room can clearly see. Be prepared to provide a more detailed analysis by doing your homework *before the meeting* as to the make-up of the dashboard numbers you're reporting. In other words, report *what* happened through the dashboard metrics, but be prepared to answer *why* the numbers appear as they are.

When you uncover inconsistencies, or your inbound efforts are not measuring up to your hypothesis, be prepared to state openly what you've discovered as the likely or possible cause. Remember not to act evasive or defensive. Next, provide one to three thoughtful solutions to improve.

Lastly, when someone asks you to report on a metric other than the pre-defined contributing inputs, be prepared to ask how that metric contributes to successfully attaining your objective. Sometimes this leads to an insightful breakthrough. Most times, it is just noise. Stay focused on the inputs that matter; however, remain open to additional inputs that had not been previously considered.

## Communicating your activity

You are responsible for how you allocate your marketing resources and should be willing to be held accountable. More importantly, the true value you bring to the table as a marketer is in streamlining activities so that you achieve your inbound goals and objectives efficiently, with as few resources as it takes to achieve success. You also create value when you overachieve milestones within acceptable costs of your company's time and money. You're most valuable when those streamlined activities are scalable because you can now replicate and communicate activity that has a more predictable outcome.

Activity alone doesn't equal success. Just because you and your team are busy doesn't mean you're working on activities that contribute efficiently to the end goal. Don't let your ad agency masquerade their "doing" as productivity, either. Instead, focus on the value your activities bring to achieving stated objectives. The marketing activities you and your team perform must be meaningful. In other words, there should be a measurable correlation between your inbound marketing activities and the end result.

## Reporting your results

In an optimized inbound marketing program, the marketing and sales departments share goals and objectives up-front. Each department works together to achieve the end sales result. These goals should be shared with management and approved up-front. It follows that the marketing and sales departments are each held accountable for achieving their respective metrics and milestones and then report back on a regular basis.

The process of sharing and reporting objectives aligns your internal and external team towards achieving the overall *business* goals, clearly outlining expectations and accountability for both parties to achieve said goals.

Reporting your results based on the timeline outlined in the SSB portion of this chapter provides regular feedback allowing you time to make any necessary adjustments to your inbound marketing plans.

## Tweaking links in your Customer Conversion Chain

The reason for accountability between marketing and sales isn't so they each play the blame game. You're trying to solve business problems here, not find who is at fault. So, when things aren't quite going to plan, the aim is to fix the broken parts. The best method of discovering this is by evaluating the Customer Conversion Chain links.

By analyzing each conversion point in the customer purchase path and comparing your resulting metrics with the hypothesis that marketing and sales formed together before execution of tactics, you report and act on facts rather than blame and emotion.

So if the sales staff says the leads are weak, don't get defensive. Review your company's definition of a marketing qualified lead, check your lead scoring to see if there are some incorrect assumptions as to what constitutes a qualified lead, and model your premium customers in order to attract and convert.

## Things You Can Do Now

✔ Estimate a realistic timeline to begin implementing inbound initiatives so you can share with others in your organization and manage expectations.

✔ Set your milestones and metrics for a 12-month period so it's clear which marketing factors need to be measured and which marketing initiatives are important to implement first.

✔ Attempt to populate your first SSB so you have a clear understanding as to what marketing needs to accomplish in the next three months.

# Part II
# The Art and Science of Consumer Connections

For a discussion about the benefits of user testing, check out www.dummies.com/
extras/inboundmarketing.

# In this part . . .

- ✔ Understanding Lewis's Purchase Funnel, whose path every buyer follows, as well as some newer purchase models like the Buyer's Journey and the Lifestyle Loop.

- ✔ Understanding the hidden meanings of keywords.

- ✔ Segmenting keywords for relevant connections.

- ✔ Learning the new 4 P's of Inbound Marketing.

- ✔ Connecting consumer needs with content and your products/ services with customers.

# Chapter 6

# Mapping Your Customers' Purchase Paths

Mapping the consumer purchase path helps marketers identify key points in the decision-making process that connects people with products. As a marketer, you've probably heard of the *Purchase Funnel,* a concept developed at the advent of marketing in the late 1800s. In this chapter, I use the Purchase Funnel as a basis for explaining new marketing models that better reflect the complex interaction between customer and company.

Marketing itself is actually a relatively young field. St. Elmo Lewis's Purchase Funnel was developed in 1898 and its linear map reflects the simpler consumer times of yesteryear. It's interesting that a sophisticated enhancement wasn't presented until 2003 when Hugh Macfarlane wrote *The Leaky Funnel.*

Now that the world has changed, marketing must change with it. It must be able to rise to the demands of the new needs, habits, and purchase patterns of today's sophisticated, multi-dimensional, digital economy.

# In the Beginning: Lewis's Purchase Funnel

For most businesses, the ultimate conversion is a sale. Making a sale sounds simple, but the consumer purchase process gets complicated very quickly.

For a sale to occur, every consumer must take the same steps toward a purchase. No matter what the product; no matter who the person is, the journey is the same. This idea isn't new to marketers. It originated from Elias St. Elmo Lewis in 1898 and was called the *Purchase Funnel*.

Lewis's Purchase Funnel was revolutionary because he was one of the first to map a consumer's purchase path. The Purchase Funnel consists of four steps taken in sequence, which lead the consumer down a path toward a purchase:

1. Awareness

2. Interest

3. Desire

4. Action (Purchase/Donation/Subscription)

Here's an example: Let's say you're at the grocery store waiting in line to check out. You notice a point-of-sale rack filled with different brands of chewing gum (*awareness*). You think to yourself that you'd like some gum (*interest*). You usually buy the green spearmint sticks but today you notice an oddly-shaped package with cubes of gum. Although it's not the brand you normally buy, you think it looks good and wonder if it will taste as good as the packaging makes it look (*desire*). The price for the new gum is the same as your regular brand, you notice, and so, *what the heck* . . . You hand it to the check-out clerk to scan with your other groceries (*action* — in this case, a *purchase*).

The original Purchase Funnel, as seen in Figure 6-1, is functional in that it helps marketers understand the basic steps that connects a person with a product. It accurately maps a simple, quick commoditized purchase for which the market presents limited options.

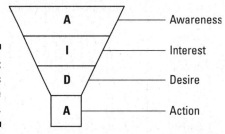

**Figure 6-1:**
Lewis's
Purchase
Funnel.

A — Awareness

I — Interest

D — Desire

A — Action

So, Lewis's Purchase Funnel is a useful starting point. Every one of your customers became aware of your existence. At some point they demonstrated interest; they shopped based on a desired option that you offered, and ultimately they purchased from you.

Numerous variations on this concept have cropped up since Lewis's time. A popular variation breaks the steps down even further — into sub-steps such as Top of Funnel (ToFu), Middle of Funnel (MoFu), and Bottom of Funnel (BoFu). (See Figure 6-2.) These substeps are as follows:

1. Awareness (ToFu)

2. Opinion (ToFu)

3. Consideration (MoFu)

4. Preference (MoFu)

5. Shopping (BoFu)

6. Purchase (BoFu)

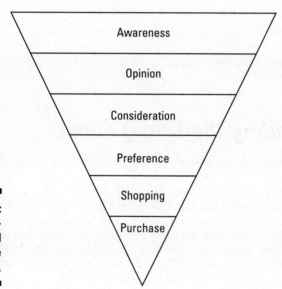

**Figure 6-2:**
The slightly-
evolved
Purchase
Funnel.

The steps shown in Figure 6-2 accounts for more steps in a consumer purchase, but it still assumes a linear, logical path. Additionally, there is a definitive termination with the end purchase. Because the Purchase Funnel is common language for so many marketers, I will continue to make reference to Lewis's Purchase Funnel.

# *Welcome to Today: The Buyer's Journey*

*The Buyer's Journey* is the next evolution from the product Purchase Funnel. Even the first word in this concept is revolutionary. Including the word *buyer* denotes a radical shift from product-based marketing to consumer-centric purchase paths. The term *journey* connotes a more thoughtful, deliberate movement over time than the mindless, gravitational free-fall suggested by *funnel*.

The concept of the Buyers' Journey was coined by Hugh Macfarlane in his 2003 book, *The Leaky Funnel*. Mcfarlane's model is characterized by:

✔ Customer-centric selling

✔ Sales and marketing units

✔ Mapping and measuring your sales pipeline

✔ Identifying and managing prospect leaking from the Buyer's Journey

The following sections discuss some of my key Buyer's Journey takeaways from *The Leaky Funnel*.

## *Understanding the Leaky Funnel*

Hugh Macfarlane summarizes his original Leaky Funnel concept as follows:

*The main idea that a sales funnel has a smooth progression from top to bottom and no leakage was a flawed metaphor. Is this just picky? Maybe, but the issue isn't so much that some leak from your funnel, but what you do about that. For example, do all buyers leak from the same point in your funnel? Perhaps not. And do they leak at the same rate regardless of how they got there? Almost definitely not. And finally, the idea of 'leakage' from your funnel invites another kind of big question: "What do I do with the leaked buyers?"*

*The Leaky Funnel* refers to a simple methodology for building your sales and marketing plan, and here's the essence: Recognize that *everything* is about the buyer, not you (the seller). So, start by making your strategy buyer-centric. This means proceeding according to the following steps:

1. Work out what problem you want to solve for buyers.

2. Master solving that problem. Do your best to become the best in the world at solving it.

3. Work out who most has that problem and make them your focus — even ignore all other buyers unless they show you they have this same problem.

4. Work out the journey each individual buyer takes from *hello* to *thank you*.

5. Figure out how many buyers need to move to each stage every month for you to meet your plan. (Ideally for three years, but you can cheat and make it shorter.)

6. Choose your tactics so that they're good enough to move those buyers at that rate through your funnel, and back into the funnel when they leak (as most will at some point).

7. Measure progress. Don't measure how many times *you* do something (send, call) but how many times *the buyer* moves (clicks, reads, downloads, calls).

Inbound marketing is designed to attract and reattract based on customer needs, rather than on a product's features and benefits. *The Leaky Funnel* provides direction in planning your outcomes mathematically. This involves examining trend data of the percentages of prospective target customers that convert to customers and identifying those prospects that "leak," or do not convert. Understanding that not everyone is your customer is an important first step. And further, not everyone who fits your target customer profile is going to complete the entire journey down the purchase path. This is okay. It actually provides freedom to attract those most likely to buy, resulting in messaging clarity designed to attract those most likely to become your ideal customer.

# Evolving into the Future: The Lifestyle Loop

The Lifestyle Loop builds on the frameworks of the Purchase Funnel and Buyer's Journey — which, by the way, is by no means obsolete. The Lifestyle Loop adds definitive dimension beyond the traditional sales funnel when connecting people with your product. Your communications reach beyond the basic steps in a continuous loop designed to attract and reattract; to engage and reengage. Essentially, this is relationship marketing that connects with your future and current customers well beyond the times they are actively walking down any given purchase path. New considerations from the Lifestyle Loop include:

✔ **Consumers are dynamic individuals:** Humans are fickle, with changing needs, moods, and motivations. Regularly connecting with them with on-point messaging at the right time creates ongoing interactivity between the consumer and your brand, and not just at the point of sale.

✔ **The marketplace is more dynamic and interactive:** People have instant access to massive amounts of information and may just as easily shut your message out with the click of their mouse. The Internet lowers the barriers to entry for competitors, allowing nimble companies to outmaneuver your efforts.

✔ **Marketing actions cause consumer actions and reactions:** Your valuable content, when organized and disseminated correctly, directly causes consumer action. With the ease of social sharing, one consumer action may influence other consumer actions, eventually causing a chain reaction among many people. Messaging that goes viral is the ultimate consumer chain reaction.

✔ **The purchase path or Buyer's Journey is not rational and, therefore, not linear:** Lewis' Purchase Funnel is simplistic and inaccurately portrays the purchase path of today's consumer. With instant access to multiple websites, customer reviews, and price-shopping, the purchase path looks more like a maze than a straight line.

✔ **The buying cycle does not end with a single action or purchase so the first purchase is not the ultimate goal, it's merely a point in the Customer Conversion Chain:** With the Lifestyle Loop, the goal isn't to create a mere customer; it's to create a Lifestyler who lives your brand, influencing others to do the same.

✔ **Space and time affect consumer behavior:** Where and when you connect with prospective and repeat customers matters. Having presence at that exact moment and point when a consumer is ready to purchase increases conversions.

✔ **A customer can be valued beyond dollars spent with you. Value may also be derived by influence:** Influence matters today. Whether it's an individual blogger or an aggregate of customer reviews, customers wield influence way beyond mere dollar transactions with your company.

These concepts behind the Lifestyle Loop are important for inbound marketers because we can now consider:

✔ Marketing to the individual rather than the masses.

✔ Greeting consumers on *their* terms and *their* needs rather than yours.

✔ Creating multiple conversions and multiple consumer reengagement opportunities.

✔ Customers can become loyal customers and loyal customers can become *Lifestylers*. (See the nearby sidebar, "Who is a Lifestyler?")

✔ Recency and frequency of marketing messages can now be timed based on consumer behavior and real-time actions.

✔ Return-on-investment (ROI) potential is higher after the first action (purchase).

Figure 6-3 shows the Lifestyle Loop's multiple points of contact along the consumer purchase path.

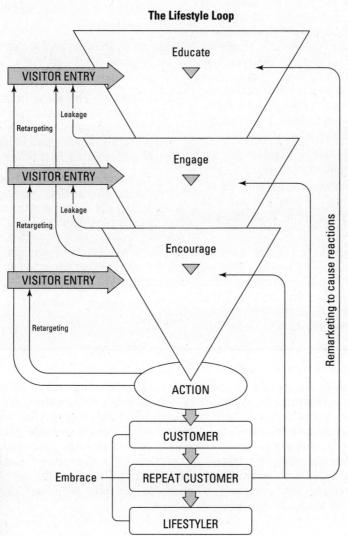

**The Lifestyle Loop**

Educate

VISITOR ENTRY

Leakage

Retargeting

Engage

VISITOR ENTRY

Leakage

Retargeting

Encourage

VISITOR ENTRY

Retargeting

Remarketing to cause reactions

ACTION

CUSTOMER

Embrace — REPEAT CUSTOMER

LIFESTYLER

**Figure 6-3:**
The Lifestyle Loop.

# Who is a Lifestyler?

Some call them brand evangelists or brand advocates. I call them Lifestylers. Lifestylers are those individuals who associate so strongly with a brand that they actually make the brand a part of their identity. The Lifestyler's value can transcend dollars and cents. Through their online reviews, their conspicuous consumption of your product, and their influence among their peers, Lifestylers serve as an example to others. Lifestylers may be public figures or they may be average Joes or Janes. Some companies that have achieved deep relationships with Lifestylers are Apple, Rolex, Starbucks, Red Bull, REI, Disney, and the National Football League.

Loyal Lifestylers aren't created only by multinational giants. By offering a unique, satisfying experience online and offline, smaller companies and start-ups can also cultivate Lifestylers. Consider the example of Trunk Club.

Trunk Club, a men's clothing service, disrupted the men's fashion-buying process, creating Lifestylers and $100 million in revenue in just four short years. They did it by creating a platform that delivered custom-fitted clothing ensembles designed around individual customers' tastes. Trunk Club was built to solve the customer "pain point" — it was created for men who hate to shop. Here's how they made it simple for men to buy:

1. Customers are assigned a personal stylist who helps customers discover their style, sizes, and tastes.

2. The stylist hand picks several clothing items, posting them in the customer's "trunk" for him to preview before shipping.

3. Customers pay only for the clothes they keep. They're permitted ten days to try outfits on, and they only have to purchase the items they like. Any unwanted items can be easily returned; shipping is included.

Trunk Club's reviews are enthusiastic and highly personalized. They have customer *relationships*, not customer relations. Trunk Club created Lifestylers because they know their ideal customer and they satisfy the need for stylish, individualized convenience and the ability to shop on their terms. Sounds a bit like inbound marketing, doesn't it?

Nordstrom bought Trunk Club in 2014 for $350 million.

---

The Lifestyle Loop model assumes a multi-dimensional relationship between a person and product. With this model, customer relationships are defined by consumer interaction with your brand over time and by your subsequent brand responses based on those interactions. Creating meaningful interactions at multiple points on the purchase path elevates your customer relationships above the merely transactional. For a few, these relationships evolve into the ultimate customer relationship. These are the people who connect with your company and products on such a deep level, they actually *live* your brand. These are the *Lifestylers*.

Characteristics of a Lifestyler include:

✔ Brand loyalists

✔ Often early adopters of your new products

✔ Experience your brand as a part of their identity — a Lifestyler "lives" your brand

✔ Influences others through Facebook, Twitter, and Pinterest

✔ Is sometimes a public figure or someone who actively participates in public forums

✔ Are important because they may cause customer chain reactions of product awareness, acceptance, and purchases for your company

Lifestylers' value is more about their influence than on the dollars they spend. Figure 6-4 shows how a Lifestyler's influence can cause a brand movement through a chain reaction by encouraging others to live your brand. This may be the most powerful form of marketing because the messaging is articulated by fellow Lifestylers rather than the brand, resulting in unmatched credibility.

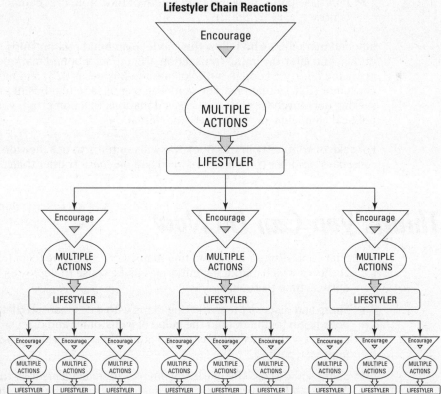

**Figure 6-4:** Lifestyler chain reactions.

The Lifestyle Loop describes your dynamic consumer and their non-linear interactions with your website, your content, and your brand. Connecting and reconnecting with these consumers at key conversion points encourages positive interaction, and results in positive outcomes. For the Lifestyler, these outcomes may mean special offers, perks, or experiences. For you as a marketer, it's a matter of cultivating customer relationships (not relations) that contribute to achieving your business goals.

Understanding the Lifestyle Loop and practicing marketing under its tenets implies:

- ✔ There are multiple points of entry for a consumer's first connection with your company.
- ✔ Consumer movement along the purchase path from first connection to purchase and repurchase is vertical.
- ✔ Consumer movement along the purchase path between different product Purchase Funnels is horizontal.
- ✔ Persona profiles connect with brands based on different sets of criteria. (That is, buyers, say, connect with a brand differently than end-users.)
- ✔ Purchase paths, as well as the length of time from first contact to first contract, vary by profile.

Inbound marketers who follow this model plan build relationships before, during, and after the initial transaction. Of course, inbound marketers can apply the Lifestyle Loop in both business-to-business (B2B) and business-to-consumer (B2C) situations. The model also applies to non-business entities seeking non-purchase actions such as donations to a non-profit, votes in a political campaign, or numerous other situations.

For sake of continuity in this book, we will continue to use the words *consumer/customer* (rather than *donor*) and *purchase* (rather than *action*).

# Things You Can Do Now

- ✔ Share and discuss the marketing maps with marketing team to provide clarity of which marketing initiatives make sense to deploy as well as the optimal time to deploy.
- ✔ Share and discuss the marketing maps with sales team so that you can both begin to understand the value of a customer and discuss how to connect with leads and customers at multiple points along the customer purchase path.
- ✔ Share and discuss the marketing maps with management so they can understand that you have a solid customer-centric approach to attracting and converting leads to customers.

# Chapter 7

# Discovering Customer Needs with Keywords

. . . . . . . . . . . . . . . . . . . . . . . . . . . . . . . . . . . . . . . . . . . .

*In This Chapter*

▶ Understanding keywords as consumers' stated needs

▶ Performing keyword research

▶ Assigning keywords to buyer's place in the purchase path

▶ Segmenting keywords for maximum effect

. . . . . . . . . . . . . . . . . . . . . . . . . . . . . . . . . . . . . . . . . . . .

*T*his chapter is about researching and applying keywords to your inbound marketing efforts. I share some keyword research tools; some of these tools are free to use and some require a paid subscription. Don't worry if you can't afford the software or the subscription right now. Instead, you can use the free keyword research tools to formulate a list of target keywords and keyword phrases. Due to the dominance of Google in the United States (it's two-thirds of all search volume), I use Google as the search engine barometer for this book. Still, you can usually apply your findings to Bing and other search engines to achieve similar results.

After you perform your keyword research, you can apply your findings to improve your content, your onsite SEO, and your paid search campaigns. By applying your keyword rank estimates to your Customer Conversion Chain (see Chapter 15), you can also use your keyword research to begin predicting website traffic volume based on search volume and clickthrough-rates (CTRs). Eventually you can use a large keyword list to estimate market potential; however, at this point, you're better served by learning what search terms mean from the prospect's perspective, and understanding how that applies to your inbound marketing. This chapter helps you learn these things.

Happy researching!

# Finding a Need and Fulfilling It

Marketing 101 states: Marketing exists to find a consumer need and fulfill it. Before the Internet era, before Big Data, before hyper-connectivity, and before Google, marketers had limited consumer data. To discover consumer needs, marketers made assumptions, often rife with incomplete data, inadequate consumer studies/surveys, and personal bias. The most valued skill for the marketer of yesteryear was his or her ability to correctly guess consumer outcomes based on this incomplete information. Sometimes this was just dumb luck.

As a marketer, you must still find needs and fulfill them, but today your most valued skill is your ability to collect, analyze, and parse big datasets from a variety of sources in order to spot opportunities and trends. Keyword research and the application of those keywords in inbound marketing is an important part of this process. Effective keyword research is your starting point for making data-driven decisions, providing value to your prospective customers by addressing their needs, and therefore providing value to your company.

## Discovering customer needs: The early years

In the past, discovering consumers' true needs was much more difficult. Common business sense said, "Build it, and they will come." Accordingly, marketers made assumptions, many of which were wrong. The process was even fuzzier because of the ad agencies who created the "Big Idea," — a mythical silver-bullet solution suggesting that a single creative campaign would solve an organization's marketing problems. This Big Idea was creative but its success was no more measurable than throwing stuff up against the wall and seeing what stuck. In other words, its success was random.

When the Big Idea missed its mark, traditional marketers created surveys and focus groups. At best, this led to limited data, and the assumptions made from that data were questionable, but this was the best information available at the time. The limitations of this approach stemmed from these flaws:

✔ Traditional marketers started by trying to push a product rather than by providing attractive solutions to customer needs.

✔ Traditional marketers started with marketing problems and metrics rather than a financial business solutions. So, instead of focusing on increasing sales volume, marketers focused on metrics like audience gross impressions.

✔ Traditional marketers provided marketing solutions that often were disconnected from business solutions and business results.

✔ Marketing didn't communicate well with sales. With the two departments isolated from each other, there were few shared goals and objectives and frequent misunderstandings defining lead quality.

✔ Marketers didn't have a good understanding of consumer needs. Limited research data resulted in speculative assumptions, sometimes with marketer bias, about consumer needs.

All this has changed.

## Discovering customer needs today

Many companies and organizations today still operate on this antiquated model — and not just the marketing department. These fallacies infect many companies' accountants, product engineers, sales departments, research and development departments, even CEOs and board members.

As your inbound marketing evolves and your organization's understanding of customer needs grows, you customers win. And when the customer wins, so does your organization, provided you're operating responsibly and with a certain degree of transparency and credibility.

Inbound marketing and its associated thought processes is changing the way organizations conduct business today. For example, I've personally seen dramatic results when traditional barriers that exist between the marketing and sales departments are broken down. Keywords serve as a key to unlock the door between these two departments. Why? Because keywords come from customers searching online, and allow us to literally define customer needs.

Inbound marketing is customer-centric. Practicing inbound marketing narrows the focus onto your best prospective customers. Prospective customers signal their intentions and needs every time they type words and phrases into their browser search bar. The value of the terms customers use to search and the number of times that search is made is indisputable. Different marketers may infer different meanings from the same keyword as to where that keyword search term places a consumer in the purchase path; however, the keyword is itself a stated need from the consumer's point of view.

People perform 3.3 billion searches every day on Google alone. Knowing which keyword search terms are important for customers to find and visit your website is an important step in the customer conversion process. Categorizing those keywords by associating word or phrase with a consumer's place in the purchase path, helps you serve optimal content that answers the searcher's query. In other words, you are better meeting customer needs. To understand keywords is to understand your customers. This is the power of keywords and this is why it's imperative to begin or expand your keyword research today.

Performing keyword research and segmenting those keywords into meaningful buckets results in better connective communications with customers. It also allows you to realize better internal connectivity within your organization because you now have a shared understanding of your target customer needs. It's now easier to connect people with your products. With shared goals and accountability between the sales and marketing departments, companies can now reward and financially incentivize sales and marketing personnel based on metrics that contribute to a shared end outcome of generating a measurable number of new customers and sales. That outcome metric should be based on prospect and customer activity.

# Understanding Keyword Research for the Inbound Marketer

*Keywords,* those words you target to attract website visitors based on consumer search terms, are the literal words typed into your browser's search bar or the literal words typed into your *website's* search bar (although it's less common— unfortunately — for marketers to research their onsite search terms). *Keyword phrases,* or *long-tail keywords,* are search terms that are several words in length, and are usually more descriptive search terms.

For example, a keyword might be: *restaurants Nashville.* Long-tail keywords based on this root keyword might be any of the following:

- *vegan restaurants Nashville TN*
- *fine dining restaurants Nashville*
- *romantic restaurants with patio, Nashville*

Because they're more specific, long-tail keyword phrases have a lower search volume. The value of long-tail words is their specificity. Choosing the optimal long-tail keywords results in a more relevant search-engine results page (SERP) and more qualified leads to your website. So although the number of visits and the number of leads generated may be lower with long-tail keywords, the quality of those leads may be higher, resulting in higher lead conversion rates and more customers.

To evaluate keywords, you first prioritize keywords based on their total search volume, ordering them from highest to lowest. High search volume signals high demand. By cross-tabulating keyword search volume with *difficulty* of ranking on the SERP for each keyword, you can formulate a simple equation to discover which keywords you should target. Ideally, you're looking for keywords with high search volume and low difficulty to rank.

Keyword search volume is usually expressed as total monthly searches. You can access this information by creating a Google AdWords account. Keyword ranking difficulty is usually expressed on a scale of 1-99. You can access this information with marketing automation software or by accessing a free keyword tool like the one on the SEM Rush website (`www.semrush.com/info/kdt`) where you can compare ten words at a time with their free version. The higher the number, the harder it is for you to rank for that term. Terms displaying higher than 60 or 70 may be difficult for your company to achieve and maintain a page one rank and the SERPs, unless you're an SEO expert or you've hired one.

## Interpreting keywords as stated needs

Every time you type a search term in Google's search bar, you're stating some type of need. Ditto for your customers searching online. No longer do you have to guess what your customers' needs are. They're telling you every time they perform an Internet search or, better yet, a search on your website. Google's reporting changes make it much more difficult to obtain the keywords consumers used in organic search to find and visit your website. So if you want the most comprehensive, accurate keyword sourcing for your website visits, investing in marketing automation software may make sense.

Look for search terms that a prospective customer would use by researching keywords in Google AdWords and/or marketing automation software tools. Look for phrases from the customer viewpoint. Type those phrases into the Google search bar to see what other suggested terms appear and add those terms to your list. Also check the bottom of the first page SERP for additional suggested search terms. You'll learn a lot about customer problems and the pain points they're experiencing by analyzing these search terms. If geography is a consideration for your business add in those geographic terms to search terms and phrases as additional keywords (such as, for example, *plumber Indianapolis*). Examine additional keyword variations by adding in long-tail keyword phrases and substituting synonyms a person is likely to use. Steer clear of industry jargon or proprietary terms unless your target persona is so specific that they know and use industry terminology.

# Understanding implied keyword meanings

Let's say my car needs new brakes. What do my search terms imply about my place in the purchase path or about the type of content you should serve me in order to create the most meaningful connection? (See Table 7-1.)

| Table 7-1 | Implied keyword meanings | |
| --- | --- | --- |
| *Search Term* | *Place in Funnel* | *Deliverable Content* |
| signs my car needs new brakes | ToFu | "3 Signs You Need New Brakes" |
| best brake shop Honda Accord | MoFu | "ABC Auto: the Best Option for Foreign Brakes" |
| brake coupon St. Louis | BoFu | A brake coupon |

This pattern works for businesses as well as individual customers. Let's say I am the owner of ABC Auto. What if I type in the following search term: *cheapest brake distributor Midwest?*

Because this is not a search term that a typical end consumer would use, this term implies that:

✔ It's a business-to-business search.

✔ Price is important.

✔ The searcher has an interest in wholesale brake products.

✔ Midwest distribution is important.

As a marketer, you may be able to infer additional meanings based on the type of device used to access the Internet, the geographic region from which the search occurred, and so on.

You can gather important information for the data gleaned from inferred keywords. The searcher's location, the method of search, the search engine used, and the device used to access the search — these all suggest things you can use in your inbound marketing.

If, for example, you're generating a large search volume outside your trade area, consider making your SEO keywords location-specific while at the same time limiting your pay-per-click campaigns to your geographic area of service (hopefully, you were doing this anyway). Additionally, the demographic of a Bing searcher is different than that of a Google searcher: If more people are coming to your site from Bing, what does that say about your customers? Further, your clickthrough-rates may vary based on the device your customers used to access the search (mobile phone vs. desktop).

Beyond these, you can make contextual inferences based on search terms. One of the most important uses of interpreting your contextual inferences derived from both short- and long-tail keywords is your ability to use those inferences to begin categorizing keywords into meaningful buckets like the examples above. There is no set rule for this; let your data interpretation be your guide.

# Using Keyword Tools

When performing keyword research, you have several keyword tools at your disposal, some that are free and some that require paid subscriptions. Regardless, your methodology in targeting and segmenting keywords remains the same. Because keywords are literally your customers' stated needs, using keyword tools helps you gain insight into the minds of your prospective customers when they're in a buying state of mind.

## Determining which keywords to target

Your ideal list of keywords and keyword phrases to target should consist of keywords with a high search volume and a low difficulty for ranking on SERPs. (I know. A pet unicorn would be nice, too.) To begin discovering your target keywords, follow this basic process:

1. **Choose a product on which to focus.**

   Sometimes your focus may be dictated by the company. Other times, you may be able to use keyword search volume to determine online demand.

2. **Start with some root keywords that describe your business or the products you offer.**

   Try to use the words a customer would use, not industry jargon.

3. **Load your list into Google AdWords Keyword Planner, or any other paid software you've purchased to perform keyword research.**

4. **Enhance your list by adding in suggested keyword phrases from an analysis tool and from suggestions in the search bar and on the SERP.**

5. **Create a ratio of search volume to ranking difficulty.**

6. **Segment keywords to determine relevancy and to consider conversion rates based on their association with a place in the customer purchase path.**

   *Segment* means to classify. Specifically assign keywords to individual personas that may use any given search term, then associate words with the buyer persona's place in the Purchase Funnel. For instance, someone who searches for *brake coupon St. Louis* should have a higher conversion rate and a greater propensity to buy than someone who searched *signs I need new brakes*. (See Table 7-1.) This is because the former word is associated with a BoFu term and is closer to a sale whereas the latter is associated with a ToFu term and is further away from a sale.

7. **Test your keywords by typing them into Google and Bing to see what the first-page search-engine results are.**

   If the results are relevant, then you're probably okay. If they're not, you may need to dig deeper. This may be because a like term is consuming the top results — for instance, I may never rank on the coveted page one SERP for my term *CTA Map* because I can't compete with the Chicago Transit Authority's "L" trains.

## Researching and choosing target keywords

Your keyword research influences your digital campaigns, your content marketing, the titles of your onsite pages, your SEO, and your pay-per-click campaigns. The actual words and phrases you choose to target affect your ability to attract visitors and your conversion percentages.

As an example, let's say you're a pet food company whose objective is to sell healthy dog and cat food online to U.S. consumers. To begin your keyword research, your first step should be at Google AdWords.

By entering in some basic information and following the prompts, you can create a Google AdWords account (at `https://adwords.google.com/um/Welcome/Home googleadwords.com`) in minutes. (See Figure 7-1.) At this point, don't worry about filling in the budget field with accurate information, because you're just in the planning phase.

Now, you can start your keyword research in Google AdWords Keyword Planner (at `https://adwords.google.com/KeywordPlanner`). You should do this even if you have no intention of initiating a pay-per-click campaign at this point. The Keyword Planner is Google's free tool designed for paid search campaigns, but you can use it in your keyword research for building inbound marketing campaigns and for all your inbound efforts.

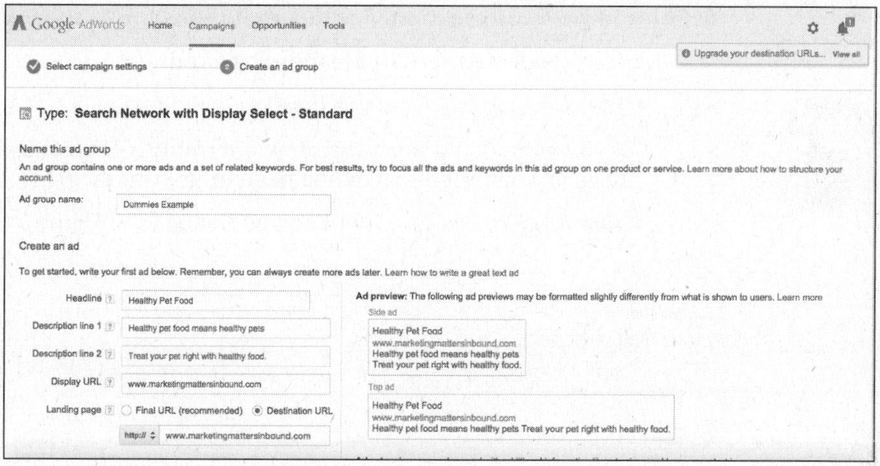

**Figure 7-1:**
Signing up
with Google
AdWords.

In Keyword Planner, you'll search for keyword ideas, research your keywords' historical performance, and enhance your original list of keywords by expanding root keywords into long-tail keyword phrases. If you choose to use paid search as part of your inbound marketing plan, the campaign you create now will also serve as the basis for your pay-per-click campaign.

You can access Keyword Planner by logging into your Google AdWords account. To do so, follow these steps:

1. **Click Tools, then choose Keyword Planner.**

2. **Choose the first of the four options by clicking Search for New Keyword and Ad Group Ideas. (See Figure 7-2.)**

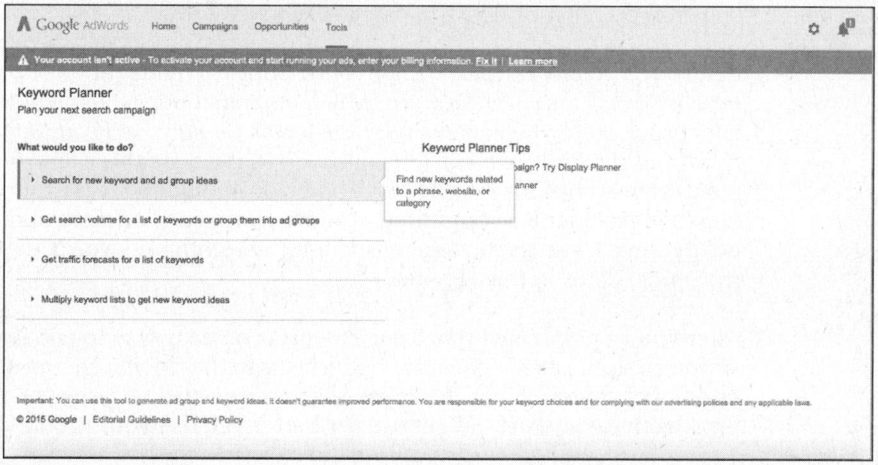

**Figure 7-2:**
Google
AdWords
Keyword
Planner.

**3. Enter in your information. For this example, type in the following:**

- *Your Product or Service:* Healthy Pet Food.

- *Your Landing Page:* Enter a fictitious landing page.

  If you were doing this for real, you'd want to enter the URL of a real page at your site — a landing page or your home page.

- *Your Product Category:* Pet Food & Treats. (See Figure 7-3.)

Keyword Planner
Plan your next search campaign

**What would you like to do?**

▾ Search for new keyword and ad group ideas

 Enter one or more of the following:
 Your product or service

 Healthy Pet Food

 Your landing page

 www.TestLandingPage

 Your product category

 Pet Food & Treats

| Targeting ? | Customize your search ? |
|---|---|
| All locations | **Keyword filters** |
| All languages | **Keyword options** |
| Google | Show broadly related ideas |

**Figure 7-3:**
Filling in the
Keyword
Planner.

**4. Click Get Ideas.**

You get a list of keyword categories to explore.

Before you go any further, head over to Google Trends (at `www.google.com/trends`) and click Explore, which appears under the menu in the upper-left corner. Here you can evaluate the terms *Healthy Pet Food, Healthy Dog Food,* and *Healthy Cat Food.* (See Figure 7-4.) Because there are clearly more monthly searches for *Healthy Dog Food,* you should focus on your healthy dog food product for your initial product pyramid. (For more about product pyramids, see the upcoming section, "Assigning keywords to product pyramids," later in this chapter.)

After you've performed this basic research, an easy way to enhance your keyword research is to begin entering terms into the Google search engine. Type into Google's search bar the keywords and keyword phrases you think your prospective customers might use (or better yet, use your Profile/Persona

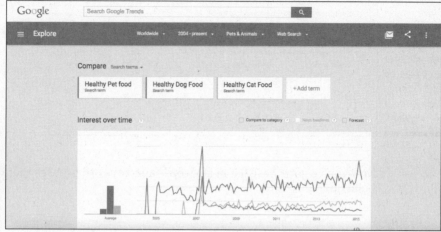

**Figure 7-4:**
Researching
keywords
at Google
Trends.

study from your IMA to predict search terms). Google's auto-suggest feature
populates additional keywords for you to consider. In Figure 7-5, Google's
auto-suggest feature offers up four additional choices related to Healthy Dog
Food that you can now enter into your master keyword list. (Strangely, the
auto-suggest function often provides keywords other than those in Google's
Keyword Planner tool so use both for keyword research.)

**Figure 7-5:**
Using
Google's
auto-
suggest
feature
to find
additional
keywords.

Another simple way to add to your keyword list is to locate Google's list of
related search terms. Enter a target keyword into Google's search bar and
then scroll to the bottom of the results page. In the lower-left Google displays
search terms it sees as related to your target search term. (The related
terms for *Healthy Dog Food* appear in Figure 7-6.) Add these words into your
keyword list for grading and segmenting along with your other terms.

**Figure 7-6:**
Google's list
of search
terms
related your
keyword.

Now you've got a base list of keywords and keyword phrases that you can build upon.

## Using other tools to research keywords

After setting up your AdWords campaign and identifying keywords using Google's Keyword Planner as well as Google itself, you can use other keyword research tools to expand your list.

The free research tool at Keyword.io (`www.keyword.io`) is a good next stop. Typing the keyword *healthy pet food* into this tool generates 407 related keyword terms. (See Figure 7-7.) Purging the list by eliminating geographical terms, retail outlet terms, and homemade dog food recipe terms results in 278 terms related to healthy dog food. You can use this tool to build robust campaigns. In this case, you can download the refined list of 278 terms and upload it to Google Keyword Planner (see Figure 7-8) to get additional suggestions.

**Figure 7-7:**
Researching
keywords at
Keyword.io.

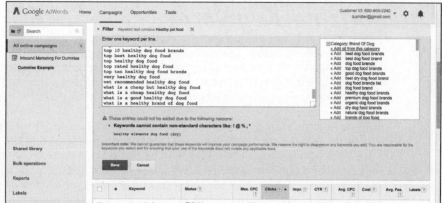

**Figure 7-8:**
Uploading
terms from
Keyword.io
to Google
Keyword
Planner.

This adds a great many more terms to your list. Of course, your ability to build a large keyword base is limited only by your time, budget, and expertise. The following list gives you some other tools, some of which are very sophisticated and require a paid subscription:

- ✔ **KeywordTool.io (`www.keywordtool.io`):** This tool does not offer search volume, but its cut-and-paste function enables you to plan in Google.

- ✔ **SEMRush (`www.semrush.com/info/kdt`):** Free and paid keyword research tool.

- ✔ **Ubersuggest (`www.ubersuggest.org`):** Free keyword research tool that makes it easy to add and download additional long-tail keywords.

- ✔ **Raventools (`www.raventools.com`):** Paid set of robust research tools.

- ✔ **Moz Rank Tracker (`http://moz.com/tools/rank-tracker`):** Free tool with robust set of paid SEO and keyword tools available.

- ✔ **Seed Keywords (`www.seedkeywords.com`):** Scenario-based keyword user testing.

- ✔ **SpyFu (`www.spyfu.com`):** Free limited competitor keyword research which is much more in-depth with the paid version.

- ✔ **Wordstream (`www.wordstream.com`):** Keyword research primarily for paid search campaigns.

- ✔ **Hubspot (`www.hubspot.com`):** Paid marketing automation software with user-friendly keyword research tool.

You can also use these tools to examine your competitors' websites and backlinks. There may be a good reason they've targeted the words you discover.

# Categorizing Keywords

Many marketers perform keyword research but few segment keywords in a meaningful way. By *categorizing* keywords — that is, grouping them by product, persona profiles, location in the purchase path, and other factors — you can create a more sophisticated inbound marketing plan.

By associating your keyword list with these categories you form highly targeted, highly functional sub-groups of keywords. Measuring the performance of a sub-group determines which groups contribute most to facilitating customer conversions, including purchases. Over time, your keyword segmentation makes clear which terms and groups contribute and which don't. As a result, you can increase your marketing investments for the contributing keyword groups and cut the investments for the non-contributing keyword groups.

## All these keywords. What now?

Now that you've performed your initial keyword research, it's time to categorize. You can segment your keywords by any combination of these factors:

- **Geographical relevance:** If you sell spas in San Diego, you probably don't need search terms that include *New York*.

- **Location in the purchase path:** You can sometimes infer a searching customer's position on the purchase path based on the language she uses. If she types in *coupon,* for example, she's most likely at the bottom of the purchase path.

- **Persona profiles:** Procurement buyers often use different search terms than end users. Take this into consideration

- **Inferences:** From my own research results, someone who searches for the term *website grader* is a less knowledgeable prospect than someone who searches for *inbound marketing assessment*. Among the people searching for *website grader* are marketers looking to grade their website and also elementary school teachers looking for an online method of grading papers. The more specific term *inbound marketing assessment,* however, suggests a familiarity with the terms *inbound, marketing,* and *assessment,* and is therefore a more qualified search prospect.

Categorize your keywords. Form them into keyword groups. Match the groups to persona purchase paths.

# Branded search vs. non-branded search

People who arrive at your website from a search with a branded search term tend to behave differently than those who enter via other, non-branded terms. Branded terms may include your company's name as well as the name of your products. For example, someone who enters Apple's website after searching the term *Apple MacBook Pro*, will behave differently than a person who searched for the non-branded term *computers*, say, and will have different conversion rates. Be aware that branded and non-branded terms will have different customer conversion rates. Most SEM professionals track these groups separately and I recommend you do the same. It's easy to set this up in Google Analytics. Just follow these steps:

1. **Sign into your Google Analytics account.**
2. **Click Admin in Google Analytics navigation menu at the top of the page.**
3. **In the View column, click Channel Settings.**
4. **Click Manage Brand Terms.**

   *Brand terms* are keywords and keyword phrases associated with your brand names and products.
5. **Add in the appropriate suggested brand terms by clicking Add.**
6. **Type in additional appropriate brand terms and click Add your company brand terms.**
7. **Click Save.**

   Now your Google Analytics reporting includes the percentages of your visitors arriving from a branded search and non-branded search and tracks the onsite behavior and conversion differences of each.

If 100 percent of your visits are from branded search terms, you're probably not attracting very many new customers. This may be good for a mass-market company like Amazon, but it's probably not good for your company. New visitors mean new opportunities for conversion, and new customers mean new business and new opportunities to create Lifestylers for your brand.

What is a good ratio of branded to non-branded search? There's no set rule. It depends on your company, your company website, your industry, and the desired results you're working toward. The higher percentage of branded search means fewer *new* customers are discovering your website. On the other hand, it may also signal an attractive brand with a large base of loyal Lifestyler customers.

# Assigning keywords to product pyramids

Perhaps the most obvious keyword segmentation is the breakdown of keywords by product. Treat each product as if it had its own conversion funnel. I call each of these product purchase paths *product pyramids*. Each product pyramid is a consumer conversion path to which you should assign keywords.

Let's say you were performing digital marketing for an automotive service company with three key product areas: brakes, tires, and oil changes. Any keywords or search phrases that contain the word *brakes,* then, gets assigned to the brake product pyramid. Likewise, search terms containing the words *tires* or *oil changes* get assigned to their respective product categories. This is pretty simple stuff, but by starting simple, you get a handle on the multitude of keywords on your initial list, allowing you to organize your digital campaigns.

After you've assigned your keywords, you can use them to assess your market opportunity for each product category. Here's how:

1. **Add up the total search volume for all product terms.**

2. **Estimate potential traffic to your site.**

   Because you haven't yet decided on your tactics (such as, for example, prioritizing SEO or PPC initiatives) for now you should use a baseline clickthrough-rate (CTR) of one percent to estimate potential traffic to your site. Of course, CTR varies by your organic rank, and CTRs from your SEO may be higher than paid search.

3. **Calculate market opportunity for each of your products by looking at total search volume for each, volume of search terms for each place in the Purchase Funnel (ToFu, MoFu, BoFu), and your ability to rank for each of these respective terms.**

4. **Apply basic math to calculate market opportunity.**

   For instance, you can use CTRs from the Moz rankings shown later in this chapter to estimate your opportunity. You can refine this calculation later — right now, you're just looking for a ballpark figure. Here's an example:

|  | *Product A* | *Product B* |
|---|---|---|
| Search volume | 100,000 | 50,000 |
| Estimated average keyword rank (SEO) | 11 | 6 |
| Estimated CTR | 1.5% | 2.5% |
| Average sale | $100 | $200 |
| Market potential | Product A has an estimated market potential of $(100,000 \times 1.5\%) \times \$100 = \$150,000$ | Product B has an estimated market potential of $(50,000 \times 2.5\%) \times \$200 = \$250,000$ |

Now you have better intelligence to choose which products to focus on. So, in our simplistic example, shown in Figure 7-9, you should expect 640 visits/month for brakes, 2,000 visits for tires and 2,400 visits for oil changes.

**Figure 7-9:**
Assessing
your
keyword
opportunity.

| | Brakes | Tires | Oil Changes |
|---|---|---|---|
| Targeted Search Terms | 200 | 200 | 400 |
| Total Search Volume | 64,000 | 200,000 | 240,000 |
| Click-thru-Rate (CTR) | 1% | 1% | 1% |
| | 640 | 2000 | 2400 |

## Segmenting keywords in the Lifestyle Loop/Buyer's Journey

Next, further segment keywords by your target profile's place of entry onto the purchase path. Let's continue with our auto-service example, breaking down each product's keywords, classifying each as a research term (top-of-funnel), shopping term (middle-of-funnel), or a buying term (bottom-of-funnel). Table 7-2 shows some search-term examples:

**Table 7-2     Segmenting keywords by their implied location on the purchase path**

| Keyword or Search Term | Position on the Purchase Path |
|---|---|
| signs my brakes are going bad | Research |
| best all-weather tires | Research |
| oil change frequency | Research |
| best brake shop Chicagoland | Shopping |
| Goodyear tire store Kansas City | Shopping |
| premium oil change store | Shopping |
| September brake discounts | Buying |
| current tire promotions | Buying |
| oil change coupons | Buying |

Take your list for each product and assign the keywords to each point in the purchase path. Express this in terms of the number of keywords and the sub-total search volume for each segment. You can record your research in an Excel spreadsheet or you can use marketing automation software. Later, when you're projecting revenues and ROI, you can customize your CTR percentages by purchase path segmentation.

Figure 7-10 shows a hypothetical breakdown for our auto-service company. In this table, you can see that the number of search terms does not necessarily directly rate to the search volume.

| Brakes | Research | Shopping | Buying |
|---|---|---|---|
| Targeted Search Terms | 100 | 60 | 40 |
| Total Search Volume | 30,000 | 20,000 | 14,000 |
| Click-thru-Rate (CTR) | 1% | 1% | 1% |
| | 300 | 200 | 140 |

| Tires | Research | Shopping | Buying |
|---|---|---|---|
| Targeted Search Terms | 90 | 80 | 30 |
| Total Search Volume | 90,000 | 50,000 | 60,000 |
| Click-thru-Rate (CTR) | 1% | 1% | 1% |
| | 900 | 500 | 600 |

| Oil Changes | Research | Shopping | Buying |
|---|---|---|---|
| Targeted Search Terms | 100 | 200 | 100 |
| Total Search Volume | 40,000 | 120,000 | 80,000 |
| Click-thru-Rate (CTR) | 1% | 1% | 1% |
| | 400 | 1200 | 800 |

**Figure 7-10:** A keyword breakdown by purchase path.

Research words used by searchers earlier in the purchase process generally result in end consumer conversion actions less frequently than those close to a purchase action. In other words, the searcher who types in *oil change coupon St. Louis* is much more likely to get an oil change than the one who types in *how often does a Honda Accord need an oil change*.

If a relatively high volume of keywords for your oil-change product pyramid get assigned to the "Buying" stage of the process, you may elect to focus only on the bottom of the funnel, serving up coupons and oil change offers so prospects are more likely to purchase from you.

## *Matching persona action paths with keywords*

Your target customer profiles may also dictate your allocation of resources. To see how, let's continue with our auto-service example. Let's assume we have formed two basic profiles for auto-service customers: foreign vehicle owners and domestic vehicle owners. Even though owners of each make of vehicle may have the same needs (say, new brakes), persona motivation, purchase path, and timeline for each will be different. They may use different keywords to find you. Your inbound attraction and engagement tactics must take this into consideration.

For business-to-business companies, association to target profile personas becomes extremely important, especially when you consider the sometimes vast differences in buying triggers, buying paths, and buying incentives among end users and procurement buyers. An end user of your product, for instance, may be more interested in the product's functionality, benefits, and ease of use, whereas the procurement buyer may be most interested in price. End users commonly buy products one at a time whereas procurement buyers buy in volume. It depends on your business and the products you offer, but segmenting keywords by target profile inference may have significant impact on the success of your attraction campaigns.

## Categorizing keywords for search engine optimization (SEO)

One of the reasons you segment your keyword research is to determine which keywords you may be able to rank for in organic search results. The more detailed your keyword research, the more precise your predictions for online traffic based on your organic rank.

Remember the hypothetical online pet food retailer, the one who is targeting people interested in healthy dog food? For this example, as you may recall, we performed keyword research with the Google Keyword Planner and with the Keyword.io research tool. I uploaded that list into Google Keyword Planner to determine search volume and to see if any of my current website pages rank for the target keywords. For simplicity, I whittled down the list of keywords to 25 by eliminating terms that are competitors' brands, recipes for homemade healthy dog food, and irrelevant terms, then exported my refined list into Excel.

Here are the next steps in the process:

1. **In Excel, rank the terms on your list by difficulty to rank on SERPs (in this case, on a scale of 1 to 100 with 100 being the hardest). Cut any words from your SEO initiative that have a rank difficulty higher than 75.**

2. **Now sort your targeted keywords by search volume, highest to lowest (see Figure 7-11).**

3. **Perform a simple ratio by dividing rank volume by rank difficulty. Add in a formula cell and divide your search volume by rank difficulty.**

| | A | B | C | D | E | F |
|---|---|---|---|---|---|---|
| 1 | Keyword | Difficulty | Monthly Searches | Cost Per Click | Campaigns | |
| 2 | healthy dog food | 68 | 1,900 | 6.97 | Pet Food Test | |
| 3 | healthy dog food brands | 66 | 720 | 6.84 | Pet Food Test | |
| 4 | healthy weight dog food | 61 | 170 | 2.6 | Pet Food Test | |
| 5 | best healthy dog food | 65 | 170 | 7.47 | Pet Food Test | |
| 6 | cheap healthy dog food | 57 | 110 | 3.78 | Pet Food Test | |
| 7 | healthy dog food reviews | 55 | 110 | 6.94 | Pet Food Test | |
| 8 | most healthy dog food | 68 | 90 | 7.03 | Pet Food Test | |
| 9 | best healthy dog food brands | 72 | 70 | 2.45 | Pet Food Test | |
| 10 | healthy wet dog food | 58 | 70 | 2.99 | Pet Food Test | |
| 11 | healthy dry dog food | 76 | 70 | 7.16 | Pet Food Test | |
| 12 | healthy dry dog food brands | 74 | 50 | 5.47 | Pet Food Test | |
| 13 | affordable healthy dog food | 34 | 50 | 5.04 | Pet Food Test | |
| 14 | heart healthy dog food | 43 | 50 | 4.29 | Pet Food Test | |
| 15 | top 10 healthy dog food brands | 17 | 50 | 5.32 | Pet Food Test | |
| 16 | what is a healthy dog food | 76 | 30 | 5.42 | Pet Food Test | |
| 17 | is vegan dog food healthy for dogs | 63 | 30 | 6.25 | Pet Food Test | |
| 18 | good healthy dog food | 64 | 30 | 8.34 | Pet Food Test | |
| 19 | healthy dog food ingredients | 65 | 30 | 8.05 | Pet Food Test | |
| 20 | best healthy dry dog food | 58 | 20 | 5.73 | Pet Food Test | |
| 21 | natural healthy dog food | 71 | 20 | 7.63 | Pet Food Test | |
| 22 | healthy dog food for puppies | 58 | 20 | 1.25 | Pet Food Test | |
| 23 | most healthy dog food brands | 64 | 20 | 1.8 | Pet Food Test | |
| 24 | top healthy dog food | 62 | 20 | 5.62 | Pet Food Test | |
| 25 | healthy hips dog food | 48 | 20 | 4.46 | Pet Food Test | |
| 26 | | | | | | |
| 27 | | | | | | |
| 28 | | | | | | |

**Figure 7-11:**
Keyword volume.

4. **Rerank your keywords based on this ratio, highest to lowest. (See Figure 7-12.)**

Because the ranked numbers are only relevant to each other and are considered a very basic starting point, they shouldn't be viewed as anything other than a simple way to determine which words may be best for you.

| | A | B | C | D | E |
|---|---|---|---|---|---|
| 1 | Keyword | Difficulty | Monthly Searches | Search/Difficulty | Priority List |
| 2 | healthy dog food | 68 | 1,900 | 27.94 | Pet Food Test |
| 3 | healthy dog food brands | 66 | 720 | 10.91 | Pet Food Test |
| 4 | top 10 healthy dog food brands | 17 | 50 | 2.94 | Pet Food Test |
| 5 | healthy weight dog food | 61 | 170 | 2.79 | Pet Food Test |
| 6 | best healthy dog food | 65 | 170 | 2.62 | Pet Food Test |
| 7 | healthy dog food reviews | 55 | 110 | 2.00 | Pet Food Test |
| 8 | cheap healthy dog food | 57 | 110 | 1.93 | Pet Food Test |
| 9 | affordable healthy dog food | 34 | 50 | 1.47 | Pet Food Test |
| 10 | most healthy dog food | 68 | 90 | 1.32 | Pet Food Test |
| 11 | healthy wet dog food | 58 | 70 | 1.21 | Pet Food Test |
| 12 | heart healthy dog food | 43 | 50 | 1.16 | Pet Food Test |
| 13 | best healthy dog food brands | 72 | 70 | 0.97 | Pet Food Test |
| 14 | healthy dry dog food | 76 | 70 | 0.92 | Pet Food Test |
| 15 | healthy dry dog food brands | 74 | 50 | 0.68 | Pet Food Test |
| 16 | is vegan dog food healthy for dogs | 63 | 30 | 0.48 | Pet Food Test |
| 17 | good healthy dog food | 64 | 30 | 0.47 | Pet Food Test |
| 18 | healthy dog food ingredients | 65 | 30 | 0.46 | Pet Food Test |
| 19 | healthy hips dog food | 48 | 20 | 0.42 | Pet Food Test |
| 20 | what is a healthy dog food | 76 | 30 | 0.39 | Pet Food Test |
| 21 | best healthy dry dog food | 58 | 20 | 0.34 | Pet Food Test |
| 22 | healthy dog food for puppies | 58 | 20 | 0.34 | Pet Food Test |
| 23 | top healthy dog food | 62 | 20 | 0.32 | Pet Food Test |
| 24 | most healthy dog food brands | 64 | 20 | 0.31 | Pet Food Test |
| 25 | natural healthy dog food | 71 | 20 | 0.28 | Pet Food Test |
| 26 | | | 3,920 | | |
| 27 | | | | | |
| 28 | | | | | |
| 29 | | | | | |
| 30 | | | | | |

**Figure 7-12:**
Keyword ratio.

**5. Apply CTRs based on your projected rank (be conservative!) for CTRs. (See Figure 7-13)**

Remember, only about one in ten searchers will search beyond the first page of the search-engine results page (SERP). To estimate your traffic volume from SEO rankings, simply estimate your average page rank for all terms and multiply by the total search volume for those terms. Be aware, however, that estimating rank has become more difficult since Google has changed how it displays actual search results. Sometimes the SERP displays a rank list, sometimes it's a visual "carousel" of images. Different queries may bring up different forms of a SERP so exact rank is harder to determine. Use the table in Figure 7-13, compiled by Moz, as a rough guide.

| Position | AOL 2006 | Enquiro 2007 | Chitika 2010 | Optify 2010 | Slingshot 2011 | Chitika 2013 | Catalyst 2013 | Caphyon 2014 |
|---|---|---|---|---|---|---|---|---|
| 1 | 42.3 | 27.1 | 34.35 | 36.4 | 18.20 | 32.5 | 17.16 | 31.24 |
| 2 | 11.92 | 11.7 | 16.96 | 12.5 | 10.05 | 17.6 | 9.94 | 14.04 |
| 3 | 8.44 | 8.7 | 11.42 | 9.5 | 7.22 | 11.4 | 7.64 | 9.85 |
| 4 | 6.03 | 5.1 | 7.73 | 7.9 | 4.81 | 8.1 | 5.31 | 6.97 |
| 5 | 4.86 | 4.0 | 6.19 | 6.1 | 3.09 | 6.1 | 3.5 | 5.5 |
| 1 to 5 | 73.55 | 56.6 | 76.65 | 72.4 | 43.37 | 75.7 | 43.55 | 67.6 |
| 6 | 3.99 | 4.1 | 5.05 | 4.1 | 2.76 | 4.4 | 1.63 | 3.73 (6 to 10) |
| 7 | 3.37 | 4.1 | 4.02 | 3.8 | 1.88 | 3.5 | 1.09 | N/A |
| 8 | 2.98 | 3.2 | 3.47 | 3.5 | 1.75 | 3.1 | 1.04 | N/A |
| 9 | 2.83 | 2.8 | 2.85 | 3.0 | 1.52 | 2.6 | 0.44 | N/A |
| 10 | 2.97 | 3.6 | 2.71 | 2.2 | 1.04 | 2.4 | 0.51 | N/A |
| Top 10 | 89.69 | 73 | 95 | 89 | 52 | 92 | 48 | 71.33 |

**Figure 7-13:** Moz ranking chart

It is important to note that some studies show a higher CTR for position 11 (the first spot on the second page of search results) than some rank positions on page one. Do note, however that only about one in ten searchers will search beyond page one of the search results and that percentage is shrinking.

## Categorizing keywords by device

How someone connects to the Internet matters. Conversion rates from mobile devices, especially phones, are harder to track. Frequently CTR rates from mobile devices are higher, but so is the bounce rate. This usually means the user accidentally clicks (my business partner calls it "fat thumb click syndrome") into your site instead of clicking the "x" to close out.

Because the numbers vary so greatly from one website to another, I do not provide a rule of thumb to account for the CTR difference here. Instead, be aware of these differences and look at your own website statistics to adjust accordingly. Review user flows on your website, comparing desktop/laptop users to mobile users.

# Things You Can Do Now

- ✔ Set up a Google AdWords account to enable your keyword research.

- ✔ Perform your keyword research with Google AdWords Keyword Planner so you can begin discovering customer needs.

- ✔ Segment your keywords based on persona and place in purchase path so you can whittle down to the most relevant, targeted keywords.

# Chapter 8

# Connecting People with Your Products

*Y*ours is a *relationship* business. Nearly every business is. If you're a non-profit, you need relationships with the people whom you serve and the donors who support your cause. If you provide professional services, your "product" may be measured in time and results rather than in physical goods; however, it's still a product, and it's what connects you with your customers. If you're a sole proprietor or consultant, *you* may actually be the product as defined by your reputation. So relationships matter when connecting people with your products.

In this chapter, I cover how inbound marketing creates deeper relationships by connecting your product with people via online content and communications. I introduce the new "4 P's" of marketing and discuss how connecting earlier in the purchase path generates more opportunities to create conversions and customers. Let's begin connecting your products with people.

## Creating Meaningful Connections

Creating connections is at the heart of inbound marketing. When your inbound marketing plan is hitting on all cylinders, you create meaningful connections the following ways:

✔ Connections between people (especially your target personas) and your product

✔ Connections between your marketing and sales departments

✔ Connections between marketing initiatives and business results

Your company offers something people want or need — something prospective customers are searching for online. Your marketing communications should speak directly to those needs, attracting visitors so you can connect with them.

Practicing inbound marketing means connecting with strangers, visitors, prospects, and customers on *their* terms. In practicing your inbound marketing, *how* and *when* you communicate is as important as what you have to say. New digital media consumption habits and new methods of conducting online business necessitates a change in how marketers think and act. That's why I created the *new* "4 P's of Inbound Marketing".

# Remembering the original 4 P's of Marketing

Remember the 4 P's of Marketing from your Marketing 101 class? They are:

✔ **Product:** What you're selling

✔ **Place:** Your distribution channel to get your product to people

✔ **Price:** Your product cost

✔ **Promotion:** Pushing your product to the masses

These 4 P's are fine; however, note how product-centric they are. Their focus is on pushing a product rather than on connecting with likely customers by engaging in a meaningful dialogue. Inbound marketing, on the other hand, is about connecting through attraction. Your aim as an inbound marketer is to *pull* in prospective customers rather than *push* products.

A business-to-business study conducted over the course of five years, (published in *Harvard Business Review* in February, 2013) and involving more than 500 managers and customers, discovered the original 4 P's model undercuts business-to-business marketers in three important ways:

✔ It leads business-to-business marketing and sales teams to stress product technology and quality over consumer wants and needs. Consumers now expect your products to be technologically advanced and well-constructed. So, these are no longer product differentiators but are simply the cost of entry for consumer acceptance.

✔ It underemphasizes the need to build a robust case for the superior value of their solutions. Value is created in the mind of the consumer when the perceived benefit outweighs its cost. When a company's primary focus is product features over consumers needs, the consumer is less likely to see value in the product and the product is commoditized.

✔ It distracts companies from leveraging any advantage to communicate as a trusted source, acting as a thought leader, industry innovator, and customer advocate by solving a customer problem and communicating that solution based on consumer needs rather than product features.

Still, understanding the original 4 P's of Marketing is useful as a basis for evolving your marketing from traditional "push" marketing to inbound "pull" methodologies.

# *Product*

Your product is still important, but it's secondary to consumers' expressed needs. In other words, your products only matter if they're fulfilling customer needs. Marketing by pushing your product doesn't work anymore. In fact, it's often seen as offensive. From the standpoint of inbound marketing, the best approach is actually to build new products and services based on customer needs rather than products pushed promotionally. In this new scenario, products are purpose-built to satisfy needs.

Consider Uber, the fantastically successful driver service. Uber is quickly outmaneuvering the standard taxi business by offering a formerly commoditized product — transportation — in a new, meaningful way. Both Uber and taxi services offer rides from point A to point B. The difference is when you use a service like Uber, you know you'll be riding in a nicer unmarked car with a preapproved driver. By accessing Uber's mobile app (see Figure 8-1), you know approximately how long you'll have to wait before your ride arrives, the approximate time it will take for your ride, and a how much the ride will cost (within a certain range). Plus, because your credit card is on file with Uber from your initial sign-up, you don't have to keep cash handy. Your credit card is automatically billed at the end of your ride, including the prefigured tip. To top it off, you may save time by choosing to have your receipt auto-emailed. Overall, the Uber ride experience is better than hailing a taxi.

Uber isn't necessarily cheaper than taking a taxi, but it's a more predictable experience. In my experience with Uber, I haven't worried about riding in a vehicle with bad brakes and no shocks. There's no fumbling around to pay at the end of the ride and no surprises from a driver demanding cash even though there are credit card emblems on the vehicle. That's not to say that all taxi drivers are bad; it's just that the taxi experience is unpredictable and inconsistent. Uber's product is better because it was built on needs that have been long unmet by an archaic business model. And the free bottled water is a nice touch, too.

Figure 8-1:
An Uber
pick-up
map.

# Place

In the original 4 P's, *place* referred to either your product-distribution method or to your physical, brick-and-mortar stores. Product distribution is as important today as it was then — maybe even *more* important — but a brick-and-mortar store is a product-focused concept which, in most cases, is based on physical product interaction. Visiting the place of a store's physical location requires effort. People no longer need to drive to the mall to make purchases between some predetermined store hours that may or may not be convenient for you. You can shop online when and where you want, at your convenience or whim, on your desktop or your mobile device. Internet access has eliminated the shopping constraints of the past. (This is why travel agents have become a rare species. You can shop Travelocity, Expedia, Hotels.com, AMEX, Priceline, and two airlines all at one time.)

So if your understanding of *place* doesn't evolve, you're not in the game. In the 4 P's, *place* now refers to your customer's location on the purchase path and how you should greet them appropriately based on that location. If your website doesn't excel at creating the right "place" for your customers . . . or if you're not serving up meaningful, relevant, contextual content that also creates engagement opportunities . . . well, you're no place at all as an inbound marketer. Your visitor just bounced!

# Price

*Price* is still relevant in connecting your product with people; it will probably always be a factor. But price isn't the sole determining factor in a product-purchase decision, nor is it necessarily even the primary consideration.

Manufacturing companies often allow average unit price to determine market opportunity and to design their products and features rather than innovating based on consumer's needs. This is a bad idea. Consider the example of Nest, the thermostat company. Nest was co-founded by former Apple engineers Tony Fadell and Matt Rogers in 2010, at a time when basic programmable thermostats sold for $25–$80. In 2011, they introduced their first "learning thermostat," based on consumer research identifying a need for a simple, less confusing programmable thermostat.

The Nest thermostat is a simple, sleekly-designed circular dial with a large digital readout (see Figure 8-2). You turn it up, you turn it down. Oh, did I mention it's Wi-Fi enabled? Nest begins to learn your habits and starts automatically adjusting based on your settings. Simple. Upon product launch, Nest retailed for the premium price of $249, and you could only purchase it online. So instead of relying on product engineers to design more confusing programmable buttons, Nest streamlined the product based on consumers' stated needs and, in the process, redefined that marketplace opportunity, disrupting the industry. Price is, indeed, especially important when conveying value relative to satisfying consumer needs and not merely responding to alternative competitive products. In this case, Nest used premium pricing to connote value rather than a typical discounting strategy that confuses low price with value. Nest matched consumers stated values with a product that satisfied those values, and justified a premium price point.

Google bought Nest in 2014 for $3.2 billion.

# Promotion

Let's run a promotion! Shout a little louder, bang a little harder, discount a little more. Blast out your message and just wait for the hordes of people to show up. That's what *promotion* means.

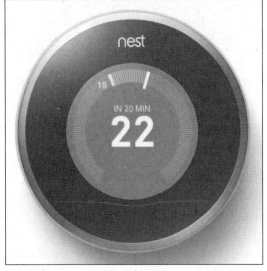

*Courtesy of Nest*

**Figure 8-2:**
A Nest
learning
thermostat.

There is a place for discounts, sales, and sweepstakes within inbound marketing, but there's even more room for engaging with customers by listening to and interacting with them. Inbound marketers prefer to present meaningful content, relevant to the purchase path journey of the customer, over running promotions. Ideally, this creates a connection beyond mere product transactions. Certainly, some purchases are more transaction-driven than relationship-driven, but as an inbound marketer, you can engage with customers after the sale, even if your business model is considered a commoditized transaction. By encouraging reviews and by following up with customer-service information or surveys, you create a two-way conversation. Old-school promotions don't do that. They shout *at* you rather than listen *to* you.

# Introducing the New 4 P's of Inbound Marketing

Now that we know that the original "4 P's of Marketing" do still serve a purpose, let's talk about evolving your marketing into the inbound realm. Here are the new "4 P's of Inbound Marketing" (see Figure 8-3):

- ✔ Profile/persona
- ✔ Product

- ✔ Place in purchase cycle
- ✔ Purchase path to conversion

**4 P's of Inbound Marketing**

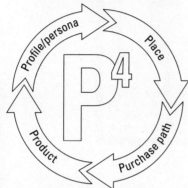

**Figure 8-3:**
The new
4 P's of
Inbound
Marketing.

## *Profile/persona*

Knowing the profiles of your key target customer groups is essential to communicating with those prospective customers. The more you know about who your buyers, shoppers, and non-buyers are, the better you can communicate to their individual needs. This is where profile development of personas plays a big part in developing your inbound plan.

A *profile* is an overview of your target customer group. A *persona* is an individual portrait of a buyer that you develop over time. Figure 8-4 shows an example portion of a director-of-marketing persona. By creating a persona description that zeroes in on the persona's stated needs, your marketing communication becomes impactful and individualized. Using language that "speaks" to an individual persona increases listener acceptance, especially if we create an engagement opportunity — if, that is, we allow our customers to be heard, and if we listen and we respond appropriately.

For instance, for a business-to-business relationship it's quite common to see two distinct buying groups: the end user and the procurement department. If you ran an e-commerce site that sells scientific lab equipment, the wants, needs, desires, and buying parameters of the scientist in the lab will be much different than those of the university accounting department. Talk about different needs and motivations!

**Figure 8-4:**
An example
section of a
director-of -
marketing
persona.

# Product

Of course, your product is still important; it's how you satisfy customers and make money. If you view each product as an inverted pyramid you can see the product as a purchase process, and not simply as an object. Product pyramids are representative of the purchase process in that they're three-dimensional. Each of your products has its own pyramid, which means each path to purchase is unique to that product. Consumers can migrate from one product pyramid to another; in fact you can encourage cross-pollination sales from one product pyramid to another by remarketing and retargeting after a sale conversion. You've probably already seen this on e-commerce sites: When you buy, say, a computer, and you suddenly see ads targeting products such as a charger or carrying case for your brand of computer, or for ancillary products that buyers like you also purchased.

# Place in purchase cycle

Connecting with people is easiest when you greet them on *their* terms. That means your inbound marketing provides entry points other than the home page for visitors to enter your site. These could be onsite pages or landing pages providing entry at each of the four stages of the buying cycle.

Want to see how you're doing in attracting visitors at multiple points on their purchase path? Check your Google Analytics. On the left, under Audience, click User Flow. (Figure 8-5 shows an example from my own website.) Your Users Flow page appears, and among the information here is the starting page where people enter your website. You can see that for my website, the page "/website-review" outperforms my home page "/" as a starting entry point. This means people who are either researching or shopping for a website review are entering directly into one of my product pyramid purchase paths (the one titled IMA) instead of having to navigate through the home page to seek and find the relevant information.

**Figure 8-5:**
The Google
Analytics
Users Flow
page.

It's usually a sign of good inbound marketing if pages other than your home page outrank your home page as the starting point. In this example, forcing a visitor to navigate through my home page to find the website review they're seeking would cause unnecessary friction, taking more time and more clicks for a visitor to get where he's going. In terms of user navigation, providing user shortcuts is usually preferable because it facilitates a positive UX by allowing customers to access their desired content quickly and increasing conversions as a result.

## Purchase path

As you learned in Chapter 6, every one of your customers takes a unique path to purchase. Mapping your customers' well-trodden paths to conversion is therefore of paramount importance to the inbound marketer who wishes to create connections at multiple times and at multiple points in the Lifestyle Loop.

Your call-to-action site map is designed with the Lifestyle Loop in mind. That is, by organizing pages that create a clear, simple path toward conversion, you make it easier for people to convert. Ideally, for any given product pyramid, your website's user interface (UI) navigation path will direct people either horizontally across to like content or downward, closer to an action.

Your first onsite conversion will be the exchange of data during the research (top of funnel) and shopping stage (middle of funnel). To support an e-book, for example, you might provide eight-to-ten engaging blog posts. Each of those posts provides links to another blog in this content group, creating horizontal movement through the Lifestyle Loop. Additionally, each of these posts engages with your visitor with a call-to-action to download your e-book, encouraging downward migration in the Loop and your first conversion. Likewise, your follow-up messaging after the initial download may offer another horizontal CTA, stimulating additional downloading of research/shopping information as well as a vertically downward CTA to encourage, say, a product demo.

Too often, websites provide encouragement only at the bottom of the loop, in a "Contact Us" form, when in reality the majority of your visitors aren't ready to contact you because they're not yet buying; they're only researching or shopping. Of course, you want to provide encouragement to buy or to engage closer to an ultimate action, but this shouldn't be the only CTA on your website.

# Closing Communication Gaps

Two-way communication is difficult at best. This means your inbound marketing efforts must close gaps in your customer communication. Addressing these communication gaps early helps you prioritize your content needs and determine which inbound product campaigns you'll focus on first in order to close these gaps. Continually monitoring your communication gaps simply makes you and your organization better at communicating with visitors, leads, and customers.

Here are some gaps to look for:

- ✔ Content for each of your product pyramids
- ✔ Content that addresses each stage of the Lifestyle Loop purchase path, for each of your product pyramids
- ✔ Engaging content that is non-gated, meaning a lost opportunity for data collection because there is no form required to access the content.
- ✔ Ineffective onsite CTA flow
- ✔ Little to no onsite CTA buttons and forms

✔ Lack of social-media engagement or one-way broadcasting

✔ A preference for traditional media interruptive communication over inbound marketing two-way engagement

✔ Lack of fresh, timely blog content

✔ Overreliance on one content form instead of using multiple formats including video, written, info-graphics, and so on.

✔ Using identical content for different buyer personas with different needs and different buying criteria

Assessing your current content library, analyzing your gaps, and prioritizing your connections begins your process of closing your consumer communication gaps.

# Knowing Your Attraction Factors

To connect, you must attract. Positive attraction is your catalyst to begin a positive conversion process. As an inbound marketer, you need to know which of your marketing inputs are creating attraction, and you need to measure this attraction factor over time. Study each digital media source's attraction to understand each individual medium's input contribution to attracting new visitors, leads, and customers. I cover attraction in more depth in Chapter 10, but this section gives you an overview of your attraction factors.

## Search engine marketing (SEM)

Search engine marketing (SEM) used to be the broad term for digital marketing efforts designed to attract people to your website. Most often, SEM referred to paid search efforts *and* search engine optimization (SEO). Nowadays, search professionals often use the terms *SEM* and *paid search* (not just PPC) synonymously. To avoid confusion, in this book I refer to search engine optimization as SEO and to paid search as either SEM or PPC.

## Search engine optimization (SEO)

The most authentic inbound method of attraction under SEM is SEO. *Search engine optimization* is the practice of assessing and applying an ever-changing set of criteria (mostly dictated by Google) to boost your organic rankings on the search engine results page. SEO consists of:

- ✔ **Onsite optimization:** By this I mean organizing, titling, and publishing in a manner that is easy for the search engines to crawl and evaluate. This includes optimizing the speed at which your website loads, your content, and the titles of your pages and images.

- ✔ **Links:** Is your website fully connected and has no dead-end 404-Errors? How many links do you have from credible websites whose authority Google trusts? Where do your internal website links connect?

- ✔ **Mobile access:** Is your website mobile friendly? I list this as its own SEO factor (separate from onsite optimization) because its importance increases as Internet access from mobile devices increases. Google announced algorithm changes in April 2015, specifically identifying mobile as an increased ranking factor, so it's now a key contributing factor to SEO.

In Chapter 7 I discuss the correlation between a higher organic ranking and CTRs, especially for the top three SERP positions. More searchers click on organic results than paid search ads. So ranking for your brand terms and for your targeted keywords adds greatly to your inbound attraction factor. As the competition increases and opportunities to rank on page one grow scarcer, it becomes even more important to attract based on satisfying a searcher, rather than on satisfying Google. That's not to say you shouldn't organize your website and publish your content to Google's standards; you should. Elevating your content to first serve your target customers is of primary importance to your inbound marketing because people buy products; search engines don't.

## Paid search

Paid search is paid digital advertising (as opposed to earned or owned digital media) and includes pay-per-click ads on search engines, display banner ads on websites and social media platforms, and sponsorships on social media sites. Some inbound purists don't include paid search as an attraction factor because you have to pay for it and because some forms of paid search (banner ads, pop-ups) can be considered interruptive ads. Although it's somewhat true that some of these ads are interruptive, paid search continues to attract. I believe that serving up relevant ads that speak directly to the search term — whether they're paid search or not — qualifies as a good inbound marketing practice. Many websites drive more traffic from paid search than from organic or from social media, so to ignore paid search's importance to attracting visitors would be setting yourself up to fail. Here are some paid search avenues:

- ✔ Pay-per-click (PPC): The three largest PPC providers are:
    - Google (`https://www.google.com/adwords`)
    - Bing (`http://advertise.bingads.microsoft.com/en-us/home`)
    - Yahoo! (`https://advertising.yahoo.com`)
- ✔ Banner ads
- ✔ Facebook ads (`https://www.facebook.com/advertising`)
- ✔ Retargeting ads: Popular retargeting ad providers include:
    - AdRoll (`www.adroll.com/retargeting`)
    - ReTargeter (`www.retargeter.com`)
    - Chango (`www.chango.com`)
- ✔ LinkedIn ads (`www.linkedin.com/ads/`)
- ✔ Twitter sponsorship (`www.ads.twitter.com`)
- ✔ Pinterest "Promoted Pins" (`https://ads.pinterest.com`)

## Content marketing

Great content attracts. For more about content, see Part IV.

## Email remarketing

Implementing email remarketing is a fundamental part of your inbound marketing. Your email remarketing campaigns create the "loop" of the Lifestyle Loop by reattracting and reengaging those visitors and prospects who have fallen off the purchase path. Understanding your profile customers' purchase paths helps you follow up with automated email campaigns. So, knowing where your visitors enter and exit your website helps define their location in the purchase path. With that information you can craft emails that encourage revisits to relevant website pages. Following up with relevant and timely emails based on that persona's place in the product pyramid helps you catch prospects that slip through the cracks. (I cover more on email remarketing in Chapter 18.)

## Social media

Social media makes it easier than ever to connect with your tribe. Your attractive interactions on Facebook, Twitter, Pinterest, LinkedIn, and other social media channels are inbound inputs whose impact can be measured and monetized.

## Traditional media

Traditional media attracts, but unless it's integrated into your inbound plan — that is, unless it specifically directs traffic to your website — it has less impact on your online attraction factor. So a traditional newspaper ad, even one featuring your website URL address, is less impactful than a traditional terrestrial radio ad that advertises an ecommerce site. A digital radio ad on Pandora, say, has more impact than either the newspaper ad or the terrestrial radio ad because listeners to Pandora can actually click through to your website. Although traditional media can be part of your attraction factor, it's more common for it to be separated from your inbound marketing and its desired outcomes.

# Things You Can Do Now

- ✔ Document the sources of your website visitors, discovering how and where the largest volume of high-quality visitors find you.

- ✔ Check your Google Analytics user flow, ranking your starting-point pages versus your home page and checking that you have multiple high-volume points of entry other than just a home page.

- ✔ Study the "4 P's of Inbound Marketing," analyzing whether or not your website provides appropriate "welcome mats" to visitors based on who they are, where they enter, and their anticipated path to purchase.

# Part III
# Building a Customer Conversion Machine

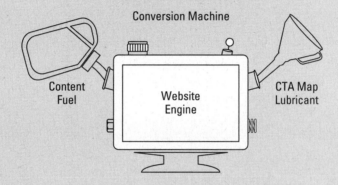

Conversion Machine

Content Fuel

Website Engine

CTA Map Lubricant

For more about the components of a Customer Conversion Machine, visit www.dummies.com/extras/inboundmarketing.

# In this part . . .

- ✔ Building a Customer Conversion Machine.

- ✔ Finding out why your website isn't working as hard as it could be.

- ✔ Creating multiple entry points into your website.

- ✔ Understanding why conversion architecture is as important as design.

- ✔ Getting acquainted with the benefits of an open-source content management system (CMS).

# Chapter 9

# Building Your Conversion Machine

*I*nbound marketers are attraction and conversion architects. As you build and refine your inbound attraction inputs and purchase path flow, you'll be building a system that establishes a series of conversions that culminate in an action (purchase). I call this system a *Conversion Machine* (see Figure 9-1), and it consists of the following parts:

✔ **Website engine:** Building your website based on a conversion-centric architectural blueprint powers your online marketing efforts.

✔ **Content fuel:** Your website engine needs fuel to run. Premium, high-octane content powers your engine to run faster and more efficiently.

✔ **Frictionless user experience:** A Call-to-Action Map lubricates the user experience. Organizing your site based on an intuitive, natural customer path helps to increase engagement and conversions.

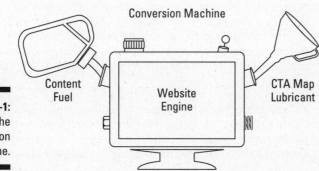

**Figure 9-1:**
The
Conversion
Machine.

Your Conversion Machine runs on a well-tuned website, fueled by great user content that's easy for visitors to access, discover, and engage with.

# Understanding the Importance of a Conversion Machine

Inbound marketers tend to focus on the marketing parts rather than the whole. Envisioning the inbound process as a Conversion Machine with three simple components helps you connect the inbound marketing parts. Your website is the hub of your inbound-marketing activity. As such, it's the key connection point between you and your lead-generation and conversion teams (usually your marketing and sales teams). It's important to build a Conversion Machine that creates meaningful dialogue through publishing dynamic content. Automating marketing and sales functions helps integrate these objectives into your Conversion Machine.

Viewing your inbound marketing as a Conversion Machine working towards an efficient, frictionless conversion process, helps you avoid the pitfall of inbound disconnection. A website with no content is useless because it attracts no visitors. Content with no website hub is a mess. Websites built on traditional architecture aren't consumer-centric and may actually hinder conversions. Remember that inbound marketing is a holistic process with inter-connected, interdependent parts. You'll achieve a higher success rate by connecting these inbound components.

# What's a Conversion Machine?

Building a Conversion Machine means building a hub of attraction and conversion. Your website is probably broken in the sense that it's probably not built on inbound conversion architecture. Most websites are not fully optimized, which causes user friction, stalling or thwarting conversion opportunities. In fact, if yours is like most websites, it's not optimized for conversions at all. A Conversion Machine features a website designed to satisfy your visitors and the search engines by optimizing for both UX and SEO. The result is a frictionless purchase path for your customers and higher SERP rankings, respectively.

Furthermore, a Conversion Machine consistently offers high-quality, engaging content. Organizing your content to encourage a natural, systematic migration toward a purchase increases your conversion rates at many points in the Customer Conversion Chain, helping to achieve your sales objectives more easily.

Begin by designing and building your website as a powerful customer engagement hub. Dedicate resources to developing meaningful content to populate your website and then provide an easy path for customers to convert. That is a Conversion Machine and it's what drives your inbound marketing.

## Connecting with customers

In the last chapter, you learned of the importance of connecting with your customers at multiple levels based on their needs. Building a Conversion Machine facilitates this connection by attracting visitors to your website, serving them relevant content, and facilitating their journey down the conversion path toward a purchase.

You can't really connect on a meaningful level without building this system of content publishing, organization, and distribution. Therefore, it's important for you to build your Conversion Machine with a combination of personalized and automated communications. Backed with marketing automation software, your Conversion Machine enables you to concentrate on the most qualified prospects by connecting deeper and connecting sooner. Automating your attraction and conversion process frees up time for you to focus on strategy and personalized communications with those most likely to convert while automatically following up with those that may not be as qualified or are further away from a conversion action.

## Connecting your internal parts

Building a Conversion Machine results in better internal communications. This is especially true between the two key departments that drive your business: marketing and sales. Practicing inbound marketing means blurring the boundaries between these two departments. This is a positive outcome if your company is adaptable because a Conversion Machine measures lead quality based on shared input from both your marketing and sales departments.

When your marketing and sales efforts are connected — truly connected — wins and losses are shared. So, the intent of building a Conversion Machine is to bring these two departments together to mutually define the characteristics of a quality lead and then to begin attracting and converting those leads. When you connect your website with analytics and measure those statistics versus your known sales and marketing objectives on a regular basis, you'll have the information to refine your definition of a marketing qualified lead

(MQL) and sales qualified lead (SQL). Once you have trend data from your Conversion Machine analytics you can now perform several worthwhile exercises including:

- ✔ Define and improve your cost-per-lead (CPL).
- ✔ Define and improve your cost-per-acquisition (CPA).
- ✔ Measure which conversion links are broken and fix those problems more quickly.
- ✔ Begin predictive marketing based on your known collected conversion data.
- ✔ Budget more efficiently based on the sources that are best at attracting and converting.
- ✔ Integrate marketing automation software and sales CRM for bi-directional internal communication.
- ✔ Reverse-engineer proven purchase paths by replicating the purchase paths taken by your most valuable customers.
- ✔ Follow up earlier in the purchase process and more quickly based on real-time alerts.

Connecting your internal process through your Conversion Machine is almost as important as connecting with your customers.

## Building your conversion chain links

In Chapter 22, I go into detail about building your Customer Conversion Chain, which consists of a series of conversion links from first contact through first contract and beyond. For purposes of building your Conversion Machine, it's important to understand the basics of the links that make up your key conversion points. They are as follows:

- ✔ Impressions
- ✔ Visitors
- ✔ Leads
- ✔ Opportunities
- ✔ Customers
- ✔ Repeat customers
- ✔ Lifestylers

Combining these important conversion points with your average ticket CPL and CPA elevate your marketing higher than your competitors who are not implementing inbound marketing best practices while creating connections between your marketing efforts and measurable results.

# Building a Super-Powered Website Engine

Inbound marketing, by definition, requires a website. So what? You have a website just like everyone else. But is your website powering attraction and conversion? Ask yourself:

- Does my website act as a lead generation mechanism rather than a static brochure?
- Is my website customer-centric?
- Does my website provide engaging content?
- Do my website pages download quickly?
- Does my website allow visitors easy entry and quick navigation?
- Can I easily track onsite visitor behavior?
- Are there different visitor experiences for new visitors, returning prospects, leads, and customers?

Answering "no" to any of these questions should give you pause because you're going against for inbound marketing best practices.

# Fueling Consumer Connections with Content

Your website engine needs fuel to run. Content is that fuel. This topic is covered more in-depth in Part IV, but for now you should just understand the role of content as a part of your Conversion Machine.

Just like your car's engine, your website engine needs to be refueled on a regular basis. Filling up with premium content and refueling often creates onsite engagement, and having more engagement opportunities helps your inbound efforts.

Premium content includes:

- ✔ Informative blog posts
- ✔ White papers
- ✔ E-books
- ✔ Online tools
- ✔ Videos
- ✔ Webinars

Publishing premium content means distributing meaningful, interactive content that encourages attraction and engagement.

# Creating a Frictionless Buying Experience

If your website is the engine of your Conversion Machine and your content is your fuel, then the lubrication in creating a well-oiled machine is your Call-to-Action (CTA) Map (covered more fully in Chapter 11). Applying CTA Maps to your website navigation links and to your inbound campaigns increases fluid user flow. By allowing prospects to easily and intuitively navigate your site through your onsite structure, you pave the way for customers. CTA buttons, forms, and internal page links are the components you'll use to build this streamlined path. Execute these tactics inside your marketing campaigns and don't forget to measure and report!

# Achieving Unusually High Performance (Success)!

When you're building a Conversion Machine, you're essentially optimizing the buying experience. After building your website, populating it with content, and organizing that content based on conversion, there are several things you can do as an inbound marketer to achieve a higher level of performance.

Figure 9-2 shows the conversion rates for digital marketers.

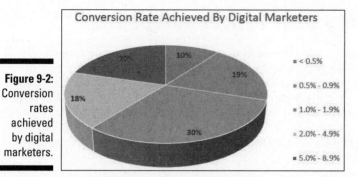

**Figure 9-2:**
Conversion
rates
achieved
by digital
marketers.

Where do you fit in? What's your conversion rate? Whatever your current conversion rate, building a holistic Conversion Machine, complete with conversion-based campaigns, helps you increase your conversion rates.

Building your Conversion Machine may seem like a daunting process. Quite frankly, it can be. First, get your website in order and begin generating quality content. Next, build out campaigns for your product pyramids, populating each product purchase path with appropriate content and CTAs to lead your visitor down the purchase path.

# Testing Your Attraction and Conversion Points

The last thing you do after changing a simple task like changing a light bulb is to flip the switch to test the light and make sure it illuminates. Yet, according to Adobe's 2014 Digital Marketing Optimization Study, 54 percent of companies do not test their digital marketing efforts. Traditional marketers have not been conditioned to perform testing. I believe this is primarily due to a historical lack of available data and the accompanying lack of accountability. Your inbound marketing must include testing because:

✔ Testing ensures that the website/campaign you built works.

✔ Testing helps you discover which CTAs work best.

✔ You can't optimize your website, your campaigns, nor your processes without testing.

✔ Testing helps you determine your main conversion for each product pyramid and the resulting ROI.

That same Adobe study found that 73 percent of the top quintile of performers implement testing on a regular basis.

## Measuring your conversion points

I highly recommend you invest in measurement tools beyond Google Analytics. You set your milestones and metrics in your SSB (refer to Chapter 5) and now that you've built your Conversion Machine, it's time to monitor your success. It may seem counterintuitive at first, but it's important to measure more than just the end sales result. At the very least, you'll want to measure each point of conversion, each link in your Customer Conversion Chain. Successful companies go further in their measurements as seen in Figure 9-3.

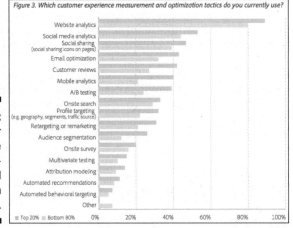

Figure 3. Which customer experience measurement and optimization tactics do you currently use?

- Website analytics
- Social media analytics
- Social sharing (social sharing icons on pages)
- Email optimization
- Customer reviews
- Mobile analytics
- A/B testing
- Onsite search
- Profile targeting (e.g. geography, segments, traffic source)
- Retargeting or remarketing
- Audience segmentation
- Onsite survey
- Multivariate testing
- Attribution modeling
- Automated recommendations
- Automated behavioral targeting
- Other

Top 20%   Bottom 80%   0%   20%   40%   60%   80%   100%

**Figure 9-3:** Customer experience measurement and optimization tactics.

Measuring each conversion point, rather than just the end conversion point, acknowledges that each link in your conversion chain influences the other conversion links. So, although your end goal may be a number in dollars, the method of achieving that number may vary. You may need to attract more visitors or you may need to convert more leads, but you won't know which will help you achieve your desired sales outcome unless you measure each conversion point.

## Tweaking your conversion points

As my business partner, Nate Davidson, says, "Do more of what works. Do less of what doesn't work." Now that you've set milestones and you're monitoring the success of each link in the Customer Conversion Chain, begin tweaking your traffic numbers, conversion numbers, or quality numbers to improve your end results. Examine your attraction and conversion data over time (at least over the last three months initially) and begin to assess which conversion points are excelling, which content engages, which social media channels attract better quality leads, and so on.

Start with your base conversion metrics and look for your top-performing conversion points. Drill deeper to assess why a particular link in your Customer Conversion Chain is overperforming. Take the overperforming component and insert that component into another campaign. Is a particular landing page converting at a high level? Determine why, and then apply a similar landing page to another product pyramid in a different inbound campaign. Is a certain e-book getting more downloads? Discover why, and then create similar content for your other campaigns.

Start slowly, but A/B test the new component against the existing component to see which performs better. Don't make wholesale changes — it's preferable to change only one component at a time when replicating success.

Likewise, look for your most underperforming conversion point and drill deeper to find the cause. Are you underperforming? Do you need more traffic? Do you need to improve the quality of your leads? Form your hypothesis about why this is happening and then continually make changes to improve.

# *Things You Can Do Now*

✔ Begin building your Conversion Machine website engine, taking into account your website/IMA assessments.

✔ Form a hypothesis as to which of your conversion links are weak and which are strong. Test your hypothesis.

✔ Attempt to populate all the links in the Customer Conversion Chain (if you need help, see Chapter 11).

# Chapter 10

# Organizing Your Website for Attraction and Conversion

*W*hy do you have a website? It's a deceptively simple question with as many answers as there are websites. Yet, when I ask this question to prospective clients and marketers I'm frequently met with blank stares and silence. From an inbound-marketing standpoint, the reason your organization has a website is to attract and convert. That's it.

Organizing your website for SEO helps you attract visitors because you'll rank higher in the SERPs. Organizing your website to please your visitors causes conversions because you're delivering what a customer (or prospective customer) wants. Both contribute to attraction and conversion.

## Making Your Website Attractive

Your website is probably broken. Most websites are. That's because most websites aren't built on conversion architecture. In fact, if your website is like most websites, it's not optimized for conversions at all.

Optimizing your website makes your website more attractive everywhere it could be. You create a more attractive website when you:

✔ Create a user experience that fulfills shoppers' needs and facilitates a natural series of conversions along the path to purchase

✔ Organize and optimize your website for SEO

✔ Design a pleasing look that matches your overall brand and encourages visitor action.

Unfortunately, most websites are given the green light solely on graphic design. Although graphic design is an important factor, it should contribute to attraction and conversion, not be the end-all deciding factor for building and launching your new website.

## Creating a great user experience (UX)

According to Don Norman, the cognitive scientist who coined the term, *user experience* refers to "all aspects of the end user's interaction with the company, its services, and its products." Customers search for your product offerings. After they find you and enter your website, it's your job to make their path to purchase simple. This means paving your website navigation path with a better user experience (UX) structure and designing a more pleasant, intuitive user interface (UI) for your visitors.

The term *user interface (UI)* refers to:

✔ The look, feel, and graphic design of your website

✔ The placement of images, buttons, and copy to facilitate website navigation and conversion

✔ The physical onscreen branded look of your website

The term *user experience (UX)* refers to:

✔ Improving the interactions between your users and your website in order to increase customer satisfaction and loyalty.

✔ The structure upon which your UI is placed. So, your UX consists of you website page wireframes and logical page links upon which your cool, intuitive clickable UI graphics can delight customers.

✔ Seamless integration between your customers' onsite and offsite experience.

✔ A designed customer process that goes beyond the computer screen. For example, building a real-time interactive website customer service connection featuring options for website visitors to either chat live onsite or directly call on the phone. This creates comprehensive UX design that facilitates positive UI online and off.

## Positioning your website to be found by people and Google

One part of good UX is creating entryways that make sense to visitors, whether they're first-time visitors or repeat visitors. For instance, constantly directing return visitors through your home page forces them to undergo unnecessary navigation and many extra clicks, and this doesn't contribute to a positive UX.

By using relevant keywords in the titles of your pages and by connecting those pages with search terms that make sense, your website is more attractive to the search engines. More importantly, it provides an easier, quicker path for your visitors to consume the content they desire. It's like giving users a short cut to avoid a traffic jam. Make it as easy as possible for the search engines and your target profile personas to find you.

## Designing a pleasant onsite brand presence

Your website is a reflection of your brand. Sometimes it's even the first impression a prospective customer has of your company. As a friend of mine says, you never get a second chance at a first impression.

Good website design goes beyond graphic design. Though your graphic presentation is important, it is trumped by good UI. In other words, aesthetically inferior sites that present obvious conversion opportunities tend to perform better than pretty sites with no opportunities to convert. Superior website design focuses on simplicity, making it apparent which action a visitor should choose next.

Consider Google's home page (see Figure 10-1). It's pretty clear which action a Google visitor should take next. Although your website doesn't have to be this stripped down, simplifying your page design down to a few key user choices improves visitor navigation and ultimately your conversion rate.

**Figure 10-1:**
Google's
home page.

# Defining a Content Management System (CMS)

A CMS, also known as a web content management system, is a system used to manage your website's editorial content. Your CMS allows you to create, publish, manage, and store your content on web pages. Web content includes page text, embedded graphics, photos, video, audio, and code (for, say, apps or tools). A CMS basically helps you manage anything that your website visitors see or interact with. There are hundreds of CMS platforms.

Your CMS enables the management of your website information from content creation through distribution. A CMS helps you do this with content management application (CMA) which simplifies content management by allowing you to add, edit, and remove content from your website without IT's involvement. A CMS's content display application (CDA) compiles that information, updating your website.

CMS functionality is important to managing your website page content, your blogs, articles, and product pages. You need CMS technology to capture data, manage your content, access stored information, and deliver your content onsite and through campaign workflows. As an inbound marketer, it's more important to understand the need for an easily accessible, user-friendly CMS than to know the technology behind it.

# Choosing Your CMS

Choosing a content management system (CMS) for your website is no easy task for the inbound marketer. Your website platform choices are broad and deep. The needs of (say) an enterprise e-commerce site are vastly different than those of your typical mid-sized business-to-business company. You may need tons of customization, and then again, you may not. Only you, or your trusted advisors, can answer the question of which CMS is best for your inbound marketing needs.

Open-source means there are a lot of developers with access to the code which usually results in a large choice of enhancements, plug-ins, and apps to help automate your back-end information and display cool visual enhancements/tools. These features make your job easier while improving your UI. An open source CMS enables you to easily use third-party application plug-ins to:

- ✔ Post content quickly
- ✔ Easily A/B test forms, buttons, and landing pages
- ✔ Change visitor navigation paths when analytics data says it's appropriate to do so
- ✔ Quickly add website pages according to best practices and your company rules

To research your CMS options, check out the in-depth reviews at www.cmscritic.com.

# Involving Your Developer with Your Marketing Efforts

Developers know code — it's what they do for a living — but they don't tend to know or understand inbound marketing. They may know information architecture, but they're usually not familiar with *conversion* architecture. If your developer has been trained on conversion architecture, congratulations, you're way ahead in the game.

It's important to involve your developer or IT department in your onsite business goals and conversion objectives. Focusing on conversion metrics encourages internal inter-departmental conversations about which factors contribute most to online success. This includes the attraction inputs (like content, SEO, and PPC) affecting those conversion metrics (positively or negatively) which, in turn, influence the end onsite business outcomes. Ultimately, these business objectives determine success.

Using your website developers to code your website based on user attraction and conversion factors build the framework for success. Developers and IT personnel often get a bad rap for developing cryptic code. In my experience, IT people are brilliant, however, they're trained to look for problems. The language they use may seem to marketers as if they're constantly creating roadblocks for the functionality of your website. They're probably not; they may just want you to understand the importance of planning outcomes in advance rather than in building a new site on the fly, resulting in extra work and additional coding. Involve your developer early in the planning process and be sure to include business outcomes as your common reference point for measuring success.

Sometimes, when your IT department is unwilling or incapable (due to corporate structure or time) of making content changes on a short timeline you may need to create a specific area on your website for consumer and promotional messaging, controlled by marketing. In some cases, you may even need to build conversion-based microsites, possibly geared toward a specific digital product inbound campaign. These microsites consist of only a few website pages, usually separate from your main website, that are geared primarily for conversion of a specific product or promotion. Although building microsites is not ideal for long-term traction, it is an option if:

- ✔ Your site is extremely cumbersome.

- ✔ Marketing has limited access/influence to the main website.

- ✔ You want to test a one-time conversion campaign separate from your main website.

- ✔ There's an unusually quick turnaround time to launch for market.

# Gaining Access to Your Website

Your website is your online kingdom. Inbound marketing demands frequent updating of content, forms, buttons, blogs, pages, and landing pages. In order for you to operate nimbly and address the dynamic needs of your customer, you need the keys to access your company's website kingdom. Certainly there are those organizations who must restrict access by law (healthcare, financial, and so on) for security and privacy purposes. In this case, it's imperative to work hand-in-hand with your IT and compliance departments.

Inbound marketers can't afford to be locked out of website access. An enterprise organization's IT department can (intentionally or unintentionally) put a chokehold on inbound marketing campaigns. If you're a smaller organization, relying on a sole developer as the only access point is dangerous and downright irresponsible. Any business that relies on inbound marketing for leads and customers can't afford for its website to be down.

Be sure your developer is customer-centric (with *you* being the customer). Your development team must understand why you need access. Discuss and come to an agreement about the limitations of website access: Who in your organization is allowed access and to which parts of the site? What parts of the site are off-limits to everyone but the developer?

In a larger company, this means that certain responsible individuals have access to onsite information and can post new content on a regular basis. Consider using different levels of accessibility — such as one level for your blog and another for the rest of your site — making it easier for you to access and update your blog content. Sometimes this means creating your blog in a blog-friendly CMS like WordPress and then connecting it to the rest of your website, even if it's built on a different CMS.

# Building Your Website on Conversion Architecture

*Information architecture (IA)* is the backbone of your website and is tied into user experience (UX). Good IA organizes and connects your website information in a manner that appears natural and logical to your viewer. My Call-to-Action Map (see Chapter 11) is an example of information architecture designed to encourage a customer purchase through a series of systematic, progressive purchase path conversions.

IA influences both your user experience (UX), which is the technical connective tissues, and your user interface (UI), which is the graphic "skin" displayed to your visitors. Your website may have great skin, but no one will care about it unless it also has the skeleton and connective tissue to support it. User experience (UX) is the sum total of all the factors influencing your users' onsite visit. Great UX is supported by information architecture created with:

- Structured hierarchy
- Intuitive navigation
- Meaningful content
- Consistent onsite experience
- Visitor interactivity
- Design simplicity
- User empowerment

Inbound marketing works best with conversion-based websites built on conversion-based architecture.

## Building with search engine optimization (SEO) in mind

You want your website to be found. Search engines "read" your web pages differently than humans do. Building your website based on SEO best practices makes your website more attractive to search engines, helping you to rank higher. To establish page authority, make sure you:

- Create your pages in HTML so your site is indexable.
- Title your page URLs to include keywords people use.
- Build your pages for quick load speeds.
- Ensure your website is mobile-friendly.
- Use keywords in headlines and within the copy at least two-to-three times (but don't "stuff" keywords).
- Use alt-tags for images.
- Create text to supplement any video and Flash components.
- Make sure your developer builds your links so they're crawlable by the search engines.
- Have your developer submit a sitemap to the search engines.

For more about attractive SEO, see Chapter 17.

## Blueprinting with your Call-to-Action Map

A Call-to-Action (CTA) Map is an IA blueprint designed for onsite visitor conversions. In other words, it's formatted primarily to facilitate onsite conversions. Creating your CTA Map before you begin building your website encourages good inbound marketing practices because you're designing with an end conversion action (purchase, donation, subscription) in mind.

CTA Maps include:

- Conversion paths for cornerstone content pages
- Conversion paths for product campaigns
- Conversion and reconversion paths through email remarketing and paid retargeting

Because it's a component of your UI, your CTA Map is your conversion backbone. I cover CTA Maps in more detail in Chapter 11.

# Identifying Wireframes That Work

If your CTA Map is your conversion-based site blueprint, your *wireframes* are your page templates, populating your CTA Map with pages designed to inform, navigate, and convert. Effective wireframes, those that reduce bounce rate and encourage further exploration deeper into your site, have traits in common with the research, shopping, and purchase decision.

Remember, there are three types of website pages:

- ✔ Navigational
- ✔ Educational
- ✔ Conversional

When building a new website, or when retooling your current website, try to create two-to-five wireframe templates for each type of page (beginning, then, with a total of 6 to 15 templates). Of course, you should design your pages so they're graphically pleasing, but it's even more important to design pages based on function.

## Understanding navigation pages

Navigation pages help direct website visitor flow. Good navigational pages consider the user's intent to improve ease of movement throughout your site.

The keys to building good navigation pages on your website are:

- ✔ Have clear, simple directions explaining what users should do next.
- ✔ Make it obvious to visitors where they can click next.
- ✔ Limit options so your page isn't confusing.

Because your website menu is present on most of your pages, design it purposefully. Use only the most meaningful headers for drop-down menus, titling them with commonly understood, user-friendly terms.

## Understanding information pages

Informational pages have more copy than other pages. Design yours so that a visitor can consume the information based on their persona and reading style. An engineer persona researching a lens purchase for a giant observatory telescope will probably seek educational data, product specs, and perhaps scientific white papers. Conversely, a teenager looking to purchase the most recent *Call of Duty* game probably requires interactive video content for maximum effect.

Even if the product category is the same, design your information pages based on the buyer. For instance, you'd expect an e-commerce shoe store to display women's dress shoes much differently than men's athletic shoes.

The keys to building good informational pages on your website are:

- ✔ Include meaningful text for deep readers.
- ✔ Use headlines, bullet points, and text callouts for people who are skimmers.
- ✔ Add video content for tutorials and storytelling.
- ✔ Make onsite tools available for problem solving.
- ✔ Try using webinars for a deeper dive into education.
- ✔ Use infographics to make complex information simple to digest.

## Understanding conversion pages

Conversion pages have one goal: cause a conversion. As such, effective conversion pages have few navigational opportunities. Provided you've communicated the right offer with the right value, limiting on-page navigation increases your conversion rate. If they get stuck, visitors can always click the Back button on their browser tool bar.

According to a 2014 study performed by WordStream, the median website conversion rate is 2.35 percent, which means half of all websites convert at a rate below that number and half convert higher than that number. The same study shows that about one in four websites convert at a rate less than one percent. Clearly you want to build your conversion pages to achieve as high a rate of conversion as possible.

The keys to building high-performing conversion pages on your website are:

- ✔ Using simple CTA buttons for easy clickthrough.
- ✔ Using forms with a reasonable amount of fields.
- ✔ Offering little to no navigational opportunities (that is, no menu bar).

✔ Including action words with clear communication as to the next step.

✔ Listing the bullet-pointed benefits of completing the conversion.

One method of limiting your website bounces and exits is to create a conversion page that opens up in a separate window. Instead of linking to a page that navigates the user totally off the site, your original website page remains open. So instead of being directed offsite in a manner that requires the user to either reenter your website URL or click the Back button on his browser, your original page remains accessible for your visitor to delve deeper, which, in turn, helps with UI and SEO.

## Affirming the visitor's entry

Nobody wants a visitor to bounce. To avoid bounces, populate your website with pages that affirm that your visitors have arrived at the right place. If you're attracting visitors whose needs are aligned with your product offerings, you're off to a good start. That means your attraction factors like social media, paid search, and SEO are working.

After you've attracted your visitors, they decide in seconds whether they'll stay on your site or leave (bounce). Sometimes visitors bounce because the content on their entry page makes them think they're in the wrong place. This is why affirming that your visitor is in the right place is of paramount importance.

When you're developing your wireframes, always ask yourself (or your developer) this question: "Based on my visitors probable search term and source of entry, will my visitors believe they're in the right place?" Sometimes addressing this is as simple as matching your page headline with the search term.

## Validating the visitor's position

After you've attracted a visitor and affirmed your page as the correct place to be, it's now time to validate your visitor's position.

Visitor validation means your website demonstrates that you understand where your visitor is coming from by serving up content acknowledging your visitors' needs. Understanding your target personas and creating content that "speaks" to their needs helps you connect with content and cause conversions.

## Confirming your position as solution provider

After you've attracted visitors, affirmed their presence on your website as being in the right place, and validated their needs, you may now confirm your position as a solution provider.

## Converting visitors to the next action

You've learned that an end action sale is the result of multiple conversions. Your desired visitor conversion depends on which page the visitor is on and where that page exists in the buyer's purchase path. The CTA you use also depends on an understanding of your buyer profile path for your industry. If the customer purchase path is quick and the visitor has an imminent need, your CTA will be an encouragement to act now, whereas a longer purchase path for a complicated purchase requires an engagement CTA so you're able to secure lead data and reconnect through lead nurturing. The home page CTA for an individual seeking an emergency room for a broken bone will be different than the home page CTA for a procurement department of a country's defense department purchasing fighter jets.

# Creating Your Website Content

Now that you've wireframed your navigational, informational, and conversion-based pages, it's time to create content! Matching your content with the intent of each page-type is important. So is using language that makes sense to your target personas.

Creating content is one of the most difficult inbound marketing initiatives because good content is subjective, takes time, and is so hard to get right. Make sure your website content creation process provides enough time for several edits, reedits, and even reformatting. Focus your messaging on user benefits rather than on product features. Create content that is both concise enough to be easily scannable and offers in-depth information when required. You don't want your website to be an electronic version of your company brochure.

Lastly, vary your content-type to appeal to different visitors. I may be partial to viewing videos and you may prefer to read technical data. Most importantly, remember to create content that is timely, relevant, and contextual.

# Populating your website pages

Create content for your visitors first and for search engines second. To make sure you're hitting all the targets you aim for, it's best to write a content strategy (see Chapter 4) based on your target buyer profiles. Here are some recommended steps for developing your page content:

1. **Determine the page type. Is it informational, navigational, or conversion?**

2. **Identify which target persona is most likely to visit this page and the search term most desirable for you to attract that persona.**

3. **Determine the next desired action for your visitor to take upon completion of this page's content consumption.**

4. **Choose your content form (text, video, graphic).**

5. **Choose a wireframe, including any appropriate CTAs for that page.**

6. **Populate your wireframe with relevant content, using keywords appropriately.**

7. **User-test the page.**

# Building your blog

I dislike the word "blog" because it suggests an individual with nothing better to do than sit at home and write about the mundane details of life. For a well-written blog, nothing could be further from the truth.

A great blog:

✔ Features attractive content, creating interest with thoughtful, clever, and sometime humorous editorial content

✔ Generates a following of customers and non-customers alike

✔ Creates opportunities for thought leadership in an industry or around a certain expertise

✔ Provides an opportunity to convert

✔ Organizes a collection of categorized content

You can have your developer custom build your blog as part of your website or choose a free option that integrates with your website content management system (CMS). The top free blogging platforms are WordPress, Tumblr, and Blogger, with WordPress being the most popular. Choosing a platform like WordPress enables you to easily and quickly make changes without a developer's involvement. Because creating timely blogging content often requires instant access coupled with easy content posting, I tend to lean towards this option. (I cover blogging in more detail in Chapter 15.)

Create blog categories based on the keyword research you performed in Chapter 7. Matching blog categories with products and their respective inbound campaigns makes sense in a couple ways. It helps you focus on the areas of attraction early in the Lifestyle Loop, where people are seeking educational content. Aligning blog categories with product campaigns makes it easier for you to connect the links in your Customer Conversion Chain.

# Applying Website Metrics

The only way to know if your website is working as a Conversion Machine is to measure outcomes. Here's how:

1. **Start with your inbound marketing Customer Conversion Chain goals.**

2. **Use Google Analytics and tracking codes.**

3. **Employ marketing automation software.**

4. **Begin with your desired business result in mind.**

5. **Hypothesize conversion metrics based on what you know today.**

6. **Reverse-engineer each link metric in your custom Customer Conversion Chain.**

7. **Measure your data against your hypothesis.**

8. **Analyze by asking "Why?"**

9. **Recalibrate your hypothesis.**

10. **Retool the Customer Conversion Chain links that data tells you can be improved.**

11. **Repeat.**

# Hooking up Google Analytics

If you're currently using Google Analytics, skip this. If you're not using Google Analytics, see Chapter 24 to learn how to quickly set up Google Analytics for your website. If you don't have Google Analytics attached to your website, make this a priority. Even if you're not yet ready for a website redesign and relaunch, it's helpful to measure and document a baseline of visitor traffic and page visits for future comparison. Plus, Google Analytics is a common language for marketers discussing website analytics.

## Using marketing automation software

If you're serious about inbound marketing, you're going to want to automate your processes at some point. Marketing automation software creates tremendous efficiencies in the application phase of inbound marketing.

Marketing automation software helps you do the following:

- ✔ Conduct keyword research
- ✔ Report visitor attraction sources for your Customer Conversion Chain
- ✔ Create CTA buttons and forms
- ✔ Perform conversion analytics
- ✔ Create inbound campaigns for your products
- ✔ Send automated emails
- ✔ Score and qualify your leads
- ✔ Create seamless lead hand-off from marketing to your sales team
- ✔ Connect marketing initiatives with results

Not all marketing automation software features all of these benefits, however. Ultimately, you'll need to evaluate your software options according to your company's individual needs. I cover marketing automation software in more detail in Chapter 22.

## Connecting your sales CRM

One of the benefits of instituting inbound marketing is connecting your sales and marketing efforts. Many marketing automation software (MAS) platforms connect to sales CRMs like Salesforce.com so you can synchronize the marketing data you collect with your sales team. Some MAS platforms, like Hubspot, feature an integrated CRM. Either way your sales department now has customer intelligence, providing each salesperson with individual visitors' onsite behavior and email clickthroughs so they may follow up with meaningful dialogue. This is just one more way of addressing each individual's specific demonstrated needs.

## Customer service add-ons

In order to complete the Lifestyle Loop, consider adding customer feature plug-ins and add-ons into your website CMS. For instance, consider installing a real-time, onsite customer assistance plug-in, easing communications and encouraging conversions. Following up with customers afterwards, along with collecting data from customer purchase patterns and website navigation, encourages reconversion. This may include data that helps you identify people most likely to become Lifestylers for your product or company.

Customer service add-ons may also include intranet options for current relationships to gather your company information, take product training tests, post on private message boards, or create forums for preferred customers.

## Billing/payment connections

If you're currently responsible for an e-commerce website, you've connected or embedded customer payment options into your website with a shopping cart feature or with, say, PayPal. If you're *planning* to build an e-commerce site consider a payment connections such as one of the following:

- ✔ Google Wallet
- ✔ PayPal
- ✔ Amazon Payments
- ✔ Dwolla
- ✔ Authorize.Net

One of the benefits of connecting online payments is the ability it gives you to segment customers based on the following:

- ✔ Size of purchase
- ✔ Average frequency of purchase
- ✔ Annual dollar value per customer

Modeling your most valuable customers and then embracing them through special incentives or rewards is a particularly powerful method of creating Lifestylers for your company.

## Things You Can Do Now

- ✔ List your website pages and associate each with a page-type.
- ✔ Research and choose a content management system for your website.
- ✔ Decide whether your website needs to be retooled or rebuilt.

# Chapter 11

# Creating a Call-to-Action Map

*T*here's a path to every purchase. Each consumer must find you and your products and establish a perceived value for those products before they act. Your website is the engine of your Conversion Machine so building your site map to accommodate your visitors' needs will increase your conversions. This chapter introduces a new information architecture concept called a Call-to-Action (CTA) Map. The CTA Map provides a website blueprint. In other words, a CTA Map is simply a site map designed with a series of conversions in mind, each one bringing your visitor one step closer to a desired action: a sale, donation, or free trial.

## Building a Call-to-Action Map

Your website CTA Map is not going to tell you whether to take the blue line or the red line on Chicago's "L." (We'll leave that to the Chicago Transit Authority.) But *your* CTA Map, the one you're using for your website blueprint, will outline a path to help direct your website visitors closer to a conversion.

A Call-to-Action Map charts the interaction of individual wireframes inside your site map, linking them based on creating the quickest paths to purchase. A CTA Map is designed as a blueprint to create a streamlined UX. A wireframe is a blueprint of your website page templates. Your *site map* technically reports to the search engines the organization of these pages based on how they're linked. Hence, connecting conversion page wireframes by using a CTA Map to improve website user flow and conversions helps with

SEO. Reduced visitor bounces and exits because of your improved design is viewed by the search engines positively when automatically reported via your site map submission. So designing your website with a proper CTA Map sends positive signals to Google and Bing.

Figure 11-1 demonstrates the different types of content that facilitate a frictionless path toward conversion. Creating content based on the Lifestyle Loop naturally navigates prospects closer to a purchase.

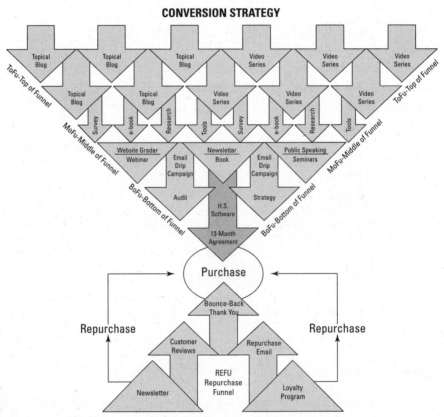

**Figure 11-1:**
Navigating the conversion path.

A CTA Map:

- ✔ Creates a frictionless experience for the user, resulting in higher conversions.

- ✔ Allows for customer self-selection and self-segmentation. In other words, your visitors choose the most suitable navigation path based on the clickable choices you display. Upon clicking, a visitor may automatically be segmented into like groups enabling you to send more and more relevant messaging based on those collective onsite actions.

    ✔ Is designed for purposeful conversions at multiple points of website
      engagement.

    ✔ Appears natural and intuitive to your website visitors.

    ✔ Nurtures a visitor horizontally or downward in the Purchase Funnel.

# Creating Wireframe Templates as Part of Your CTA Map

Remember, the three types of website pages are navigation, information, and conversion. Populate your Call-to-Action Map with page wireframes before you worry about the actual copy on the pages. Doing so helps you think about creating conversion paths. As you expand from your home page, branching out based on your product offerings, use the keywords from your keyword research to formulate titles for the logical, customer-centric entry point pages into your website.

After populating your CTA Map with keyword-titled pages, think about the possibilities for your first conversion point for each of your products. Is your first prepurchase conversion an e-book? Is it a webinar? You'll possibly have multiple points of engagement for first conversion. Start with the conversion point you hypothesize will create the highest numbers of leads, then work backwards, connecting each point in this path of engagement with the entry point wireframe pages you originally created. Try to create the shortest possible path to conversion as possible. You've now begun creating a CTA Map that will elevate your website conversions.

## Building navigation pages

Design your navigation pages to quickly direct visitors to where they want to go. There may be many options or there may be few, but your wireframe should be designed so that the navigation helps users find the path to conversion on their own, based on where they click and their flow from that page.

Create navigation pages so that it is clear to visitors which options are meant to be taken next while setting a clear expectation as to what they'll find upon clicking to the next page.

Figure 11-2 shows a simple example of a navigation page wireframe with two options to convert. Notice there are plenty of navigation opportunities in the top menu and the bottom footer. The two featured images, however, make it clear that there are two main options for your visitor to choose the next click, allowing the user to self-select which path to follow. This wireframe facilitates a click by making the main headline clickable, the image clickable, and the sub-headline clickable. If either of these two choices isn't what your visitor was seeking, she is still able to navigate elsewhere through the navigation menu or the multiple links in the footer. Although there is a conversion form option, it's subservient to the two navigation points. So, there is an opportunity to convert, but it's not the main focus of this navigation page wireframe.

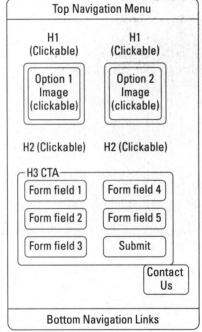

**Figure 11-2:**
A navigation page wireframe.

Freshbooks (see Figure 11-3) features a home page that presents clear actions for the first-time visitor to its home page. Although it offers conversion opportunities quickly with a simple form for a free trial and a "Free Trial" button among the main navigation options, it's also easy to scroll down or click to learn more about Freshbooks. Three benefit statements encourage the visitor to learn more or the visitor can click on the top menu navigation to learn about Freshbooks' features (though I would have made these clickable), get pricing, or a variety of other actions. For those more comfortable connecting by phone, the number is conveniently displayed on the top banner. Current customers may log in from the home page.

You can scroll down to learn more about the product features and their customer support and, at the bottom footer (see Figure 11-4) you can dive much deeper into their company, their product, their partners, and, of course, there's another CTA to encourage a free trial.

**Figure 11-3:**
The
Freshbooks
home page.

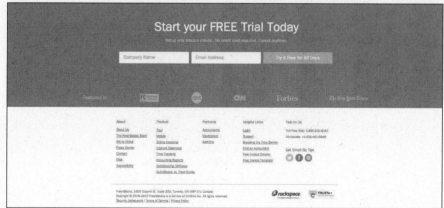

**Figure 11-4:**
The
Freshbooks
footer.

# Building information pages

Information pages are an important way for you to tell your company story, feature your product benefits, and educate visitors during their research and shopping steps in their individual customer purchase path. Because they are designed to inform and educate, information pages can be more copy-heavy and will naturally have more detail. As such, it's important to provide obvious visual clues so visitors clearly understand their next expected steps.

Write copy for your information pages with clear headlines, callouts, and graphics so a reader may choose to either skim the information or read all the details. Use images to help your visitors see their choices.

Figure 11-5 shows an example wireframe for an informational page suited for a business-to-business website. Note this wireframe includes:

✔ Top and bottom navigation

✔ A headline with keyword

✔ A scannable checklist of benefits

✔ Detailed product information with links

✔ A product image

✔ A CTA button

✔ Bulleted links to similar products

✔ An educational product video

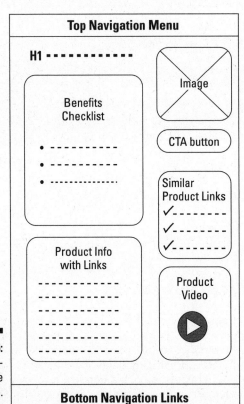

**Figure 11-5:**
An informa-
tion page
wireframe.

This wireframe could be simplified even more if the product is well-known, requiring no explanation, or if there weren't similar product lines featured on the page.

## Building conversion pages

Many times, creating a landing page specific to your offering makes more sense than creating an onsite cornerstone conversion page. Even so, nearly every page on your website should offer an opportunity to convert. Figure 11-6 shows an example of a conversion page wireframe.

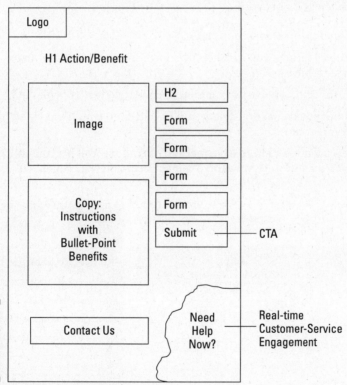

**Figure 11-6:** A conversion page wireframe.

Notice the top and bottom navigation options have been removed so the only way to navigate further into the site is to click the Back button in your browser (or, for most websites, to click on the logo which will direct the visitor back to the home page). Conversion pages are designed with one goal in mind: to convert. That's why the wireframe doesn't offer navigational direction.

This wireframe features:

- A simple, action-oriented headline
- A relevant image
- Brief, bullet-pointed copy displaying the benefits of completing the form
- A form to be completed by the visitor
- Opportunities to convert further down the purchase path with a "Contact Us" CTA and a real-time customer-service live chat feature

Salesforce.com features an exemplary conversion page (see Figure 11-7).

This page excels because:

- Benefits are clearly outlined.
- The UI directs you to fill out the form (notice the subtle arrow directing you to the form).
- Form fields are easily completed, collecting just enough data.
- It includes an action-oriented CTA button to watch the video upon form completion.
- It provides an alternative method of contact (toll-free number) for those who may wish to speak to a human being on the phone.

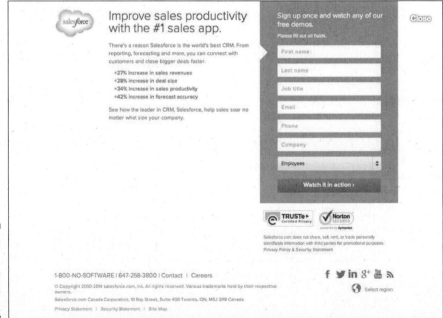

**Figure 11-7:**
Salesforce.
com's
conversion
page.

## *Creating CTA forms*

Forms are your method for collecting consumer data. The amount of information you ask for (the number of form fields the visitor is required to fill out) should correlate directly with the following three parameters:

- ✔ Visitors' perceived value of benefit in exchange for their personal data
- ✔ Degree of upfront prospect screening you wish to use to filter the quality of your leads
- ✔ Immediate demand for your deliverable

When a visitor perceives something as more valuable they're willing to release more of their personal information. Conversely, the lower the perceived value, the less information a visitor will be willing to part with. A customer may hand over their credit card information to purchase a product, but that same customer isn't going to give you credit card information for your free e-book. Still, they'll probably give you their name and email address. Likewise, visitors will only fill out a certain number of fields before they get "form fatigue" and give up to move on somewhere else. I usually recommend a form with no more than five fields for the initial conversion. It's become quite common to ask for:

- ✔ First name
- ✔ Last name
- ✔ Email address
- ✔ Phone number

If you have an anchor engagement piece (tool, e-book, webinar, etc.) for a given product pyramid, consider adding a consistent standard form, anchoring your conversion efforts on each of your information pages (your conversion pages by definition will have a form or CTA button included). Designate the important information as a "required" field while classifying the information that would be nice to know as "optional."

Some marketing automation software allows you to progressively profile a customer, which means you collect additional pieces of information important to the buying process with each subsequent conversion. For business-to-business companies, these form fields may include:

- ✔ Title
- ✔ Company revenue
- ✔ Number of employees

✔ Budget

✔ Timeframe for purchase

✔ Any problems currently facing the prospect

### Designing CTA buttons

Call-to-action buttons are the clickable icons that direct you to a conversion page or landing page with the sole intent of navigating your visitor to conversion. CTA buttons range in size, color, and copy, but there are some common traits that make some CTA buttons convert at a higher rate than others including:

✔ Designed to clearly communicate the deliverables

✔ Short, simply-worded buttons outperform long, cluttered descriptions on buttons

✔ Clear, literal instructional button copy (such as "Click here for download") performs better

As an inbound marketer responsible for lead conversions, you'll want an easily accessible button design so you can build and test effectiveness quickly. Ideally, you'll find a program or marketing automation software that helps you easily create CTA buttons so you can A/B test different buttons to learn which convert better on your website. As outlined in my discussion of user testing (see Chapter 23), ensure your sample size is big enough; otherwise you may detect changes in conversion that are not long-lasting. Some studies have shown that A/B test on CTA buttons conversion differentials tend to diminish over time, so changing your button's color, size, or shape may not have as big an impact as you first think.

# Using Your CTA Map as Part of Your Site Map

A sitemap is a list of all pages accessible to users or to search engine crawlers. A CTA Map is a visualization of these pages based on conversion architecture. The goal of your CTA Map is to provide a clear, natural, frictionless path for users to engage on their terms and at their speed of engagement.

Using your CTA Map as art of your sitemap results in a conversion-based website. Your website's CTA Map:

✔ Provides relevant points of entry

✔ Creates a streamlined conversion path

> ✔ Helps others in your organization understand why your website content is organized in the manner it is organized
>
> ✔ Provides a common internal conversion touchstone to which you can refer back when building out new pages, campaigns, and workflows
>
> ✔ Creates a future reference point from which you can observe and analyze conversion path roadblocks
>
> ✔ Increases conversion rates on your website, when implemented properly

Figure 11-8 shows an example of a simple CTA Map. Each page in the CTA Map would have a keyword in its URL, as determined by your keyword research. In this case, the website conversion map is incorporating the blog for attraction, writing to keywords at different points on the purchase path, and directing visitors to appropriate content based on their proximity to making a purchase.

On this CTA Map, Product #1 is a primary product because it's linked to the home page, whereas Product #2 is not. (So Product #1 might be a John Deere lawn tractor and Product #2 might be an optional mower bagging system.) There is an informational product information page that connects to points lower in the purchase loop, including another informational page about pricing, a conversion page with a downloadable, and a link straight to purchase the tractor. Both of these information pages are to be populated with educational content with opportunities to move further down the purchase path (CTA buttons and links).

The second information page on pricing also connects lower in the purchase loop, with two opportunities to engage (the downloadable and the pricing tool). These two middle-of-the-funnel engagement pages cross-pollinate by offering up mutual links to create multiple engagements. Each of these two pages also share a CTA to "purchase now" by vising the Purchase page (conversion page).

This CTA Map features a Purchase page with an enticement for a quick reconversion for an additional sale. This was designed with the objective of creating a higher average ticket in mind. Because of this, the Purchase page offers a reconversion opportunity to price out Product #2 (the bagger) or just learn more about Product #2 on an informational page, which starts the conversion process all over again.

This is just a simple example of a CTA Map to help you begin creating your own CTA Map.

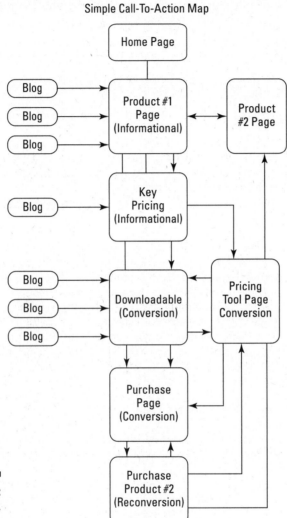

Simple Call-To-Action Map

**Figure 11-8:** A CTA Map.

# Things You Can Do Now

- Populate the example CTA Map with content from your digital marketing creative assets.
- Take a page count of the number of pages that have a CTA button or form. Express this as a percentage of your total pages using 75 percent as your minimum metric.
- Examine from what source or page a conversion occurs and what occurs after a form is filled out or a button is clicked.

# Part IV
# Fueling Visitor Needs with Content Marketing

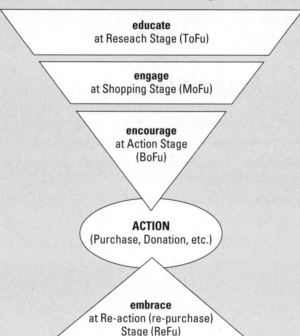

**4 E's of Content Marketing**

**educate**
at Reseach Stage (ToFu)

**engage**
at Shopping Stage (MoFu)

**encourage**
at Action Stage
(BoFu)

**ACTION**
(Purchase, Donation, etc.)

**embrace**
at Re-action (re-purchase)
Stage (ReFu)

For more about creating engaging, three-dimensional content, visit
www.dummies.com/extras/inboundmarketing.

# In this part . . .

- ✔ Creating a content strategy.
- ✔ Learning the different forms of inbound-marketing content.
- ✔ Understanding the way content connects with customers based on the 4 E's of Content Marketing.
- ✔ Creating a content calendar.
- ✔ Assigning content ownership.

# Chapter 12

# Creating Valuable Content: The 4 E's of Content Marketing

*W*ithout content, inbound marketing is nothing. Content connects you with your customers. Creating, publishing, and distributing meaningful content fuels engagement and interaction. Making sure your content is relevant to your individual target personas during each step of the purchase path opens opportunities for a customer dialogue, which in turn empowers your customers to trust your brand — simply because you're listening.

## Why Content Is King, Queen, Jack, and Your Ace in the Hole

You've heard the cliché: *Content is king!* When it comes to inbound marketing, content goes beyond fueling your website engine; it is the connective tissue between you and your customer for every step of the Buyer's Journey. Your goal as an inbound marketer is to create content that facilitates meaningful connections.

# Creating Content Strategy

As an inbound marketer, you make meaningful connections by creating a systematic publishing calendar, producing content designed to attract and engage. This is your *content strategy,* and it includes the following:

- A formal documented content process
- The profile personas you'll target
- Product pyramids for which you'll create content
- A CTA Map populated with content designed for SEO and conversion
- Content campaigns
- Content asset gaps and recommended list of content to be produced for each step of the purchase path
- Purposeful blog page structure encouraging interactivity
- Publishing calendar

Improving your content strategy starts with creating purposeful content that is measurable. Figure 12-1 displays the top objectives for business-to-business content marketers, providing insight into some objectives for your own content strategy. Great inbound marketing content:

- Resonates with each of your target persona customers because it "speaks" to them in their language
- Displays over multiple formats
- Provides value to an individual
- Is shareable
- Builds meaningful relationships beyond a mere transaction
- Encourages a natural progression from a stranger who is having first contact with your company through a trusted product advocate (or Lifestyler) who lives for your brand.
- Offers opportunity for further connections

Pardot published a helpful white paper about content creation. Use it as a guide when creating your content strategy. You can download it here: http://www.pardot.com/whitepapers/content-creation-guide/.

## Knowing your content

Content is anything your target market finds engaging, relevant, entertaining, or informative. Delivered as text, video, audio, or imagery, content addresses the particular needs, pain points, or interests of your visitor. It should be engaging, useful, relevant, easily consumed, and contextually accessible across multiple device platforms.

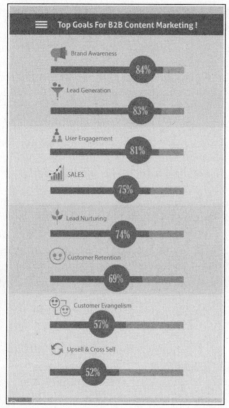

**Figure 12-1:** Top goals for business-to-business content marketing.

# *Making Purposeful Content Connections*

You now know that content is a powerful agent in fueling prospect and customer relations. There are three content attributes that create value to the consumer of that content. Making purposeful connections with inbound content requires content with three key attributes. Those attributes are:

✔ **Timely:** Timely content creates urgency, and encourages action. Timely content also connotes a certain positive company progressiveness, whether that's being viewed as "hip" or as a trusted cutting-edge thought leader. Creating timely content increases your attraction and conversion at least a couple ways:

- It allows your external attractive content to be published and distributed in coordination with current events and trends.

- It allows your internal conversion content to be published and distributed at meaningful points in the purchase path.

*An example of external timely content:* An automotive repair shop that recommends oil changes every three months sends out an automated oil change reminder email two-and-a-half months after a customer completes an oil change. This stimulates reengagement and produces a positive customer reaction (multiple customer purchases).

*An example of internal timely content:* SciQuest is a provider of automated cloud-based business-process-automation solutions, including procurement management software. Their home page (see Figure 12-2) features, among other CTAs, an unobtrusive "Contact SciQuest to Learn More" chat box that slides up when you click the header, providing an engagement opportunity. The chat box provides an opportunity for visitors to move more quickly down the purchase path, right now.

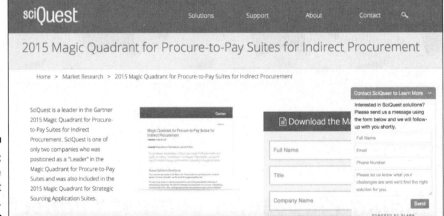

**Figure 12-2:**
The
SciQuest
homepage.

Although chat boxes aren't revolutionary and certainly may also provide "live chat" (a good idea when you have a dedicated person/team monitoring and communicating), simply having an alternative engagement tool provides timely content; in this case it's when a customer has decided she's ready to communicate.

✔ **Relevant:** Creating relevant content causes user engagement, which is the fundamental conversion component for inbound marketing. The mindset of the consumer is, "I want to read about me." Content that speaks to this mindset creates relevance to the visitor's needs at your website, increasing engagement between consumer and content:

- The more sharply relevant your external content, the more you'll be viewed as possessing expertise.

- Increasing content relevancy by distributing a logical set of content pieces, each associated with a step in the purchase path, also increases conversions.

*An example of external relevant content:* This book you're reading, *Inbound Marketing For Dummies,* is an example of external relevant content. You're interested in inbound marketing. You identify yourself as an inbound marketer. This book provides relevant inbound marketing information, serving as learning tool for you and as external relevant content for me.

*An example of internal relevant content:* Creating an immediate, automated "Thank You" email is a simple way to create content that's both relevant and timely. Figure 12-3 shows an example "Thank You" email I send out directly after my prospect completes an inbound marketing assessment survey on my website.

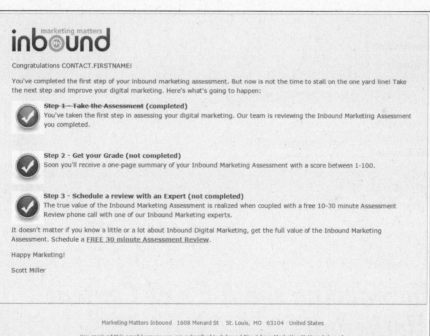

**Figure 12-3:** An automated thank you email.

✔ **Contextual:** Creating relevant content and delivering that content contextually adds a familiarity factor, increasing attraction and engagement. Designing inbound marketing campaigns (see Chapter 13) creates context for your buyers, providing consistency and a clear path. Figure 12-4 is a simplified example of the most basic inbound marketing campaign. Contextual content may be classified by:

- Medium (video, ebook, blog)
- Form (desktop, video game)
- Depth (white paper vs. ebook)
- Solution-centric (that is, serves a need)
- Persona comfortability with form (think young male inside a video game)
- Place in the purchase path

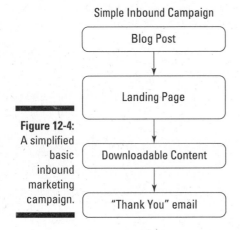

Simple Inbound Campaign

**Figure 12-4:**
A simplified
basic
inbound
marketing
campaign.

Deciding on your content's context becomes much easier when you break down the purchase path into the Lifestyle Loop and assign content accordingly. That's where the 4 E's of Content Marketing become so helpful.

# Introducing the 4 E's of Content Marketing

As discussed in Chapter 7, keywords signal customer intent and indicate the customer's place in the purchase path. Keywords represent your customer needs as they were expressed by the customers themselves. Every time a search is performed (and there are over 100 *billion* every month on Google alone) a person signals a need.

Before you begin creating content for your inbound marketing campaign, you perform an assessment, and part of that assessment is keyword research. You identify keyword roots and long-tail versions of those keyword roots; you segment those keywords and keyword phrases into places in the old Purchase Funnel. Now it's time to overlay your words onto the Buyer's Journey and the Lifestyle Loop.

By overlaying your segmented keywords onto the Lifestyle Loop, you create a template for the type of content you can use to greet the prospect, customer, or Lifestyler on their terms.

The four types of content are best expressed as The 4 E's of Content Marketing (see also Figure 12-5):

- ✔ **Educate:** Top of funnel (Researching)
- ✔ **Engage:** Middle of funnel (Shopping)
- ✔ **Encourage:** Bottom of funnel (Buying)
- ✔ **Embrace:** Repurchase funnel (Reconnecting/reacting)

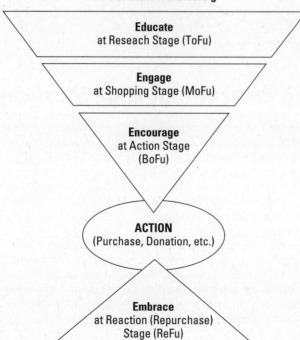

**4 E's of Content Marketing**

Educate
at Reseach Stage (ToFu)

Engage
at Shopping Stage (MoFu)

Encourage
at Action Stage
(BoFu)

ACTION
(Purchase, Donation, etc.)

Embrace
at Reaction (Repurchase)
Stage (ReFu)

**Figure 12-5:**
The 4 E's
of Content
Marketing.

## Creating content that educates researchers

Think of your educational content as a visitor's introduction to your company and the products and services you deliver. When you direct researchers to that educational content, you've begun the inbound-content marketing process.

A person who begins research into a product purchase needs a reliable, trustworthy source from which he or she can form an opinion. This is the stage in which you serve up educational content. Educational content may be any of the following:

✔ Blog posts

✔ FAQs

✔ "How To" Tips sheets

✔ Product Spec sheets

✔ Infographics

✔ Informational videos

✔ Resources

✔ Social media posts

✔ Industry overview reports

## Creating content that engages shoppers

A stranger becomes a visitor upon being attracted to and landing at your website. Initially you won't know much about these visitors except what you can learn from Google Analytics. Reviewing your Google Analytics uncovers aggregate visitor trend information but displays nothing about your visitors as individuals. So, you're limited to some basic demographics as well as to some limited geographic and lifestyle information and an ISP address (which you may use to retarget and reengage).

Your engagement content is usually the point of first conversion. The customer lead information you request should be proportionate to your target persona's perceived value. You wouldn't ask someone for their credit card number for downloading a basic e-book. Engagement content is designed for lead interaction for your visitors and data collection for you, the marketer. Engagement content may include any of the following:

✔ E-books

✔ White papers

- ✔ Interactive tools
- ✔ Research
- ✔ Buying guides
- ✔ Webinars
- ✔ Podcasts
- ✔ Newsletters
- ✔ Workflow emails

Creating landing pages (for more on this, see Chapter 22) specifically for each of your engagement content pieces provides a gateway through which visitors interact and you collect customer information relevant to your chosen persona's buying qualifications.

After you've collected lead data, you can begin to communicate with your leads, offering reengagement opportunities and directing the prospect toward the encouragement stage. Communicating on a personal level with your prospects requires data collection through engagement. Ideally, your engagement content:

- ✔ Provides user value
- ✔ Captures lead data
- ✔ Creates interaction with your visitors
- ✔ Nurtures a prospect closer to the next desired set of conversions

## Creating content that encourages an action

After visitors exchange data for your content, they are now a *contact* or a *lead*. By knowing your ideal target customer personas, you can segment leads, allowing you to direct relevant content their way, paving the path towards further action. Encouragement content includes assets that help persuade your leads to take action. Serve encouragement content to those leads who have expressed a demonstrated interest. Encouragement content may include any of the following:

- ✔ Onsite incentives
- ✔ Product demos
- ✔ Free trials
- ✔ Custom presentations

- ✔ Coupons
- ✔ Pricing estimates
- ✔ Customer reviews
- ✔ Onsite live chat
- ✔ Workflow emails
- ✔ Prewritten emails from the sales department

Your bottom-of-the-funnel encouragement content facilitates sales and therefore often requires involvement from your sales team. Ideally, your encouragement content achieves the following objectives:

- ✔ Positions your brand/products above competitors
- ✔ Shortens the purchase cycle
- ✔ Causes an action like a sale or donation

Often encouragement content features a Contact Us form as the CTA, but this doesn't always have to be the case. Allowing purchases online makes it easy for people to take action on their terms. Creating a customer sign-up process with little to no human interaction is sometime preferred by your customers and often makes things easier for you. Just be sure to provide human engagement when it's needed, particularly if there is a long sale cycle, a complex buying process, or the need for product demonstration or training.

## Creating content that embraces repeat customers

It's probably clear to you by now how challenging it is to generate relationships that attract strangers to your website, and to nurture them into customers. Reengaging customers with content is a great way to maintain customer communication, and it lowers your cost-per-acquisition of additional sales. After a lead becomes a customer, inbound marketing uses content like a great big "thank you" hug. This is the embrace stage. Embracing content is delivered to customers directly after a purchase and periodically thereafter, for four reasons:

- ✔ To cement and reinforce the customer relationship
- ✔ To provoke reengagement
- ✔ To provide opportunity for customer feedback
- ✔ To deliver rewards for your best customers, especially your Lifestylers

Here are some forms of embracing content:

- ✔ Automated "Thank You" emails sent immediately after purchase
- ✔ Product shipment notifications
- ✔ Private sales
- ✔ Rewards/loyalty points
- ✔ Customer feedback surveys/reviews
- ✔ Onsite live customer support
- ✔ Workflow emails

# Knowing Your Content Forms

Different consumers consume different types of content. Likewise, the form in which you deliver that content matters. Knowing when to prefer video content over the written word may mean the difference between a prospect consuming your content or leaving your website. An understanding of basic content forms and which forms your personas are more likely to consume helps you build your educational web pages and your downloadable engagement content. For instance, an engineer looking for a supplier of technically sophisticated electronics may prefer a white paper whereas a teenager interested in buying basketball shoes may prefer to view cool videos of the ten best basketball dunks ever. In the following sections, I describe the basic content forms to help you choose the one that works best for your target customers.

## Blogs

Blogs are designed as educational attraction content. Writing relevant blog articles and posting often is a proven inbound attraction factor. Categorizing your blog posts makes it easy for you to assign those posts to product campaigns. Optimizing your blog content increases your ranking on SERPs so your content can be found online. Publishing often (three-to-five times a week) and posting in multiple digital media creates traffic traction. You can read more about blog posting in Chapter 13.

## E-books

Posting e-books as engagement content is an effective conversion tool. Because this is often the first conversion point in an inbound marketing campaign, it's a good idea to start your content production with an e-book.

Take care to structure your e-book to clearly identify the problems you're helping a target persona solve and break those down into manageable, digestible sections. Later, you can use these sections as fodder for your blog posts, essentially republishing parts without giving away all the content inside.

Branding your e-books with a common layout and an unobtrusive logo creates a consistency that's important to your inbound marketing efforts. Just don't overdo it. It's okay to have hyperlinks in your text, and even a CTA; however, be sure to let your content do the work. Don't interrupt the reader with a huge logo or with continual "Contact Us" messages. Remember, this is the engagement phase, so your content is designed to answer questions that help your reader. This works best when you create e-books that:

- Make readers realize they have a business problem or a pain point that you're addressing
- Provide some ideas as to how to address this problem
- Position your company as the expert (not by literally telling the reader you're an expert, but by sharing enlightening information with thoughtful solutions that make sense)
- Do not contain pushy or sales-oriented language
- Talk more (way more) about the reader's needs than about your company
- Provide readers an opportunity to take the next step in the purchase path

Consider listing a highly visible "total reading time" in the introduction so your reader knows what to expect. You can break each section into a reading time so your readers can either skim what's important to them or consume your e-book in chunks.

## *Whitepapers*

Publishing white papers positions your company as an expert in your field. The term "white paper" has been a bit diluted from the times when it referred only to collegiate professor's published papers. Generally, these days, white papers are:

- Written more formally
- Feature a longer format than an e-book
- Appear more scholarly
- Are research-oriented and contain data, facts, and figures
- Dive deeply into the subject matter

So, what's the difference between an e-book and a whitepaper? Check out Table 12-1 to compare these two engagement content pieces.

| Table 12-1 | Components of E-books and Whitepapers | |
|---|---|---|
| *Component* | *E-book* | *Whitepaper* |
| Pages | 5-15 | 10-200 |
| Downloadable | Y | Y |
| Title page | Y | Y |
| Table of contents | Y | Y |
| Intro/Executive Summary | Y | Y |
| Body Copy | Y | Y |
| Conclusion | Y | Y |
| CTA | Y | Y |
| Formal language | N | Y |
| Informal language | Y | N |
| B2B Focus | Y | Y |
| B2C Focus | Y | N |
| More Graphics | Y | N |
| More Copy | N | Y |
| Complex Info | N | Y |
| Overview Info | Y | N |
| Skimmable | Y | N |
| Technical | N | Y |
| Research-oriented | N | Y |

# Videos

Videos are a great way to capture the attention of buyers during the education phase. Lately, many companies specializing in custom video creation have sprung up as an affordable alternative to written content. Business-to-business companies can also use video content during the post-sale embrace stage as training videos or product information videos. Take the following into consideration when including video as part of your content strategy for your inbound marketing campaigns:

- Brand your videos without being interruptive.
- Use your videos to educate, rather than selling product.

✔ Keep educational videos to under two minutes. Often, only one minute is enough time.

✔ If you have complex educational messaging due to a sophisticated product or a systemized procedure, break videos into short, manageable chunks. In other words, using ten one-minute videos is usually better than using one ten-minute video.

✔ For training after a sale, it's fine to have longer format videos

Posting your videos on your website and on YouTube broadens your content's reach. Make sure you optimize your video content for both.

## Webinars

Webinars are a fantastic way to engage prospects, especially for business-to-business companies. Webinars can feature content for each of the 4 E's of Content Marketing. Often, creating a webinar from an e-book makes sense either as a free engagement tool or as a paid means of diving deeper into a topic. You can even create a webinar series for regular customers to subscribe to and to watch. However, it's easy to mess up a webinar, especially a live one, so before creating one consider the following tips:

✔ Start with a small group for your first webinar.

✔ Seek questions from attendees ahead of time so there are no surprises.

✔ Test the webinar software *several times* before you go live.

✔ Start the log-in time for your webinar at least five minutes before the official start time.

✔ Record the webinar so those who don't attend may view it later and so that future visitors to your website can engage by downloading and viewing the webinar.

✔ Keep the material concise. Don't try to cover too much information.

✔ Ideally, keep your webinar to at least 20 minutes but no more than 30. Even if you allot a follow-up period for questions and answers, stick to your total time limit.

✔ Consider prerecording your webinar, allowing questions and comments only at the end.

✔ Use simple graphics and bullet points. Keep one thought per slide. Don't feature every word you say onscreen.

You can create an automated email workflow for each webinar in the following manner:

1. **Send an immediate thank you upon signing up.**
2. **Email a 24-hour webinar time reminder.**
3. **Email again with a one-hour webinar time reminder.**
4. **Send a post-webinar thank you with next CTA for attendees OR**
5. **Also, send a post-webinar "Sorry You Couldn't Attend" email with link to recorded webinar.**

There is a huge selection of webinar-hosting software in the marketplace. Among the hundreds available are the following:

- ✔ Adobe Connect
- ✔ Citrix GoToWebinar
- ✔ ClickWebinar
- ✔ WebEx

The most important features of any webinar-hosting software are dependability (that is, that it doesn't crash during your live webinar) and ease of access for attendees. Test drive a few before you commit to any software choice.

If you plan on regularly hosting webinars with fewer than ten people, several free options are available. You can even host a Google+ hangout. These programs are really more geared toward online meeting facilitation rather than webinar hosting.

# Infographics

Consumers are visual creatures. As such, creating an infographic is one of the most powerful, yet often overlooked, content type. Infographics simplify complex information by visually telling a story. Your infographics will have more impact if you keep the following tips in mind:

- ✔ Keep them as simple as possible.
- ✔ Tell a story.
- ✔ Design compelling (sometimes interactive) graphics aligned with your brand standards.
- ✔ Create a CTA inside your infographic.
- ✔ Make it sharable on social media.

Use infographics to create interest and onsite interactivity. You can hire a professional to design your infographics or check out these free tools:

- ✔ Piktochart
- ✔ Easel.ly
- ✔ Visual.ly
- ✔ Venngage

## Online tools

There may be no more powerful form of educational and engagement content than the well-built, intuitive tool that solves a specific problem for your target persona. Tools encourage interactive problem-solving for dynamic situations — think mortgage calculators for home buyers.

Thoughtfully designed online tools:

- ✔ Are interactive
- ✔ Illuminate problem areas for prospects
- ✔ Help solve problems, even problems with multiple factors
- ✔ May feature engagement opportunities by offering prospects additional information/solutions if they engage with your company consultant or if they try a paid version of your product.

One of the most-used tools in the inbound marketing industry is HubSpot's Marketing Grader (formerly Website Grader) (`www.marketing.grader.com`), which crawls your website, accesses a variety of APIs for your website metrics, and then provides very detailed first-step solutions to fix the problems it identified.

# Fueling Offsite Engagement with Premium Content

Your inbound content strategy extends beyond your website. Premium content — that is, content that's perceived as more valuable — helps your inbound efforts by using external communications to drive website visitors and onsite engagement. According to Wyzowl.com, only one out of five content marketers publishes content *outside* of the website. This means 80 percent of content marketers limit their content exposure to only their website visitors. You should be the exception by publishing content offsite as well as on your website. Here are some opportunities for you to consider for offsite content engagement:

- **Traditional media:** You can still use traditional media to promote your content. For business-to-business companies, consider industry trade publications. For business-to-consumer, consider using a blended medium like Pandora Radio, which mixes radio messaging with clickable ads. Be creative.

- **Events:** Holding seminars offsite or hosting webinars online is an effective means of engaging targeted prospects.

- **News coverage:** Creating newsworthy content and gaining news coverage builds your value as a trusted authority.

- **Thought leadership:** Are you generating fresh, new cutting edge content that attracts followers? If so, you may be a thought leader. Writing a book, speaking at events, and writing guest blog posts for prominent websites will, in turn, attract visitors to you and your website. Not everyone can be a thought leader, but there are some industries, particularly in business-to-business-related manufacturing and in some other segments that haven't fully embraced content marketing, offer tremendous opportunity for thought leadership.

- **Online forums:** Using forums in LinkedIn or Quora and publishing in industry group discussions creates online engagement. When choosing forums, be selective; target forums that provide meaningful opportunities to connect. If forum rules permit publishing of links to articles, do so in a helpful, thoughtful manner. Don't be spammy or use sales language.

- **Social media:** Add content to social media, including YouTube, Facebook, Google+, Twitter, Pinterest, and LinkedIn.

# Improving Your Content

Creating content isn't easy. It seems that you can never generate enough, and the process for creating great content can be an arduous one. You want to ensure that your content

- Displays correctly

- Uses proper spelling and grammar

- Is not plagiarized

- Provides worthwhile information while still being skimmable

- Is clear, concise, and easy-to-read

- Has working links

- Adheres to any legal or industry requirements

Here are some other resources to help you improve your content marketing:

- **MarketingProfs** (`www.marketingprofs.com`) is a popular resource for content marketers and inbound marketers. This website provides a wealth of free educational content geared toward content marketing. Additionally, they offer paid services like Content Marketing Bootcamp, access to premium research content, and events. MarketingProfs is a great resource for your inbound marketing content because they practice what they preach: great content marketing.

- **Copyscape** (`www.copyscape.com`) is a free program that scans the Internet to see if anyone has plagiarized your content. Simply visit the site and input your website address, and it delivers any duplicate content results.

- **Grammarly** (`www.grammarly.com`) has a free program to check your written copy for grammatical errors. Simply import your content into Grammarly and run your scan to check for correct grammar, correct spelling, and vocabulary enhancement by suggesting alternate optimal words for clear messaging. It's a good tool to fine-tune your written communications.

- **Clarity Grader** (`www.claritygrader.com`) is a paid subscription program that grades your website on two things: language clarity and consistency. You can grade your content against competitors and improve your overall website UX by identifying your worst content and then either rewriting it or removing it.

## Things You Can Do Now

- Run a free online content checker program to learn how to improve your current content.
- Perform an inventory of your content assets.
- Assign your content to target personas and their place in the Lifestyle Loop purchase path.

# Chapter 13

# Creating Inbound Campaigns with Content

C reating content is at the heart of inbound marketing. Organizing your content consumption path to match the buyer's purchase path is the fundamental backbone of an effective inbound marketing campaign. In this chapter, you discover key components in building an inbound campaign that attracts and converts. You learn how to map and build an inbound campaign and how to determine which content fits into your inbound campaign.

## Connecting the Dots to Provide Conversion Flow

When building an inbound marketing campaign, connecting the dots means associating content with each link in the Customer Conversion Chain and each step in the buyer's purchase path. You'll begin by choosing conversion content and develop attraction content later, which is the opposite of the way most content marketers think.

A successful inbound marketing campaign:

✔ Limits the campaign to one product/service

✔ Matches the product with persona-based content (matches by form, type, and medium).

---

## The five basic components of a successful inbound-marketing campaign

Creating a successful inbound marketing campaign requires five basic components:

- Attraction inputs
- Conversion inputs
- Conversion mechanisms

- Action inputs
- Systematic flows

There may be additional components, however, you need to include, at a minimum, these five.

---

- Qualifies prospects through a series of onsite actions (also known as lead scoring)
- Measures multiple steps along the buyer purchase path

Although your attraction inputs vary based on your specific marketing tactics (blogs, organic search, and so on) you'll always have at least one attraction component and it usually involves content. Likewise, every campaign has at least one conversion input (although most have more than one). Your conversion input must have a conversion mechanism in order to work. This mechanism may be complex, such as a website built on a CTA Map, or it may be simple, like a landing page with a CTA button or form. More sophisticated campaigns will have additional inputs designed to reengage and reattract. Lastly, by definition, an inbound marketing campaign is a systematic flow with specific starting and ending points. Campaigns may stand alone as a single campaign or these starting and ending points may be connected to other campaigns.

# Creating Connective Campaigns

An inbound marketing campaign is a system of content connection points for any given product or service. Typically, you create campaigns based on product pyramids. By using tactics like offsite publishing, automated emails, online (but offsite) product demos, and webinars, your inbound marketing campaigns may attract and convert beyond your website. Inbound campaigns are different from traditional campaigns in that they are:

- Attractive rather than disruptive.
- Feature multiple interconnected, highly measurable points along the purchase path as opposed to the traditional, highly limited and disconnected points that are measurable only at the starting (impressions) and ending points (sales).

✔ Easily adjusted in real-time as opposed to "set it and forget it" traditional media.

# *Knowing what an inbound campaign looks like*

Inbound marketing campaigns have very specific components that serve to pave the path to frictionless purchasing experiences. Knowing these components and learning how to populate each step with relevant, timely, and contextual content helps you build the framework for achieving online success.

Think of each component in your inbound marketing campaign as an input. Each input is an influential factor in your Customer Conversion Chain. Each input affects the other inputs in the chain. Each input has a different level of influence on the outcome. So, though each input is a factor contributing to your successful outcome, every input should not be treated equally. Consider an attraction campaign that drives thousands of visitors to a broken website page that says "Under Construction." No matter how much traffic you drive to that site, you'll never create a conversion. So, if the sole focus of that campaign was attracting traffic, the initiative will fail. This example may seem extreme, but similar mishaps — in which marketers drive traffic to websites that aren't designed to convert — occur all the time.

Every inbound marketing campaign consists of inputs that affect the successful outcome. Let's take a look at these inputs:

✔ Attraction inputs, which include:

- A website built on conversion architecture (if you don't have this, you can do a workaround by creating a microsite that acts as a robust inbound marketing campaign)

- Organic search from SEO

- Social media sources

- Paid search advertising

- External links

- Referrals

- Traditional media advertising

- Lists cultivated from events (such as, for example, from tradeshows)

- Database marketing via email

- ✔ Engagement inputs, which include:

  - Middle-of-the-funnel engagement piece (an e-book, tutorial, or whitepaper)
  - Further engagement content for the first and subsequent conversions
  - Onsite engagement tools
  - A website chat box
  - Contact Us forms

- ✔ Reengagement inputs, which include:

  - Email workflows
  - Invitations
  - Webinars
  - Online training
  - A website chat box

- ✔ Action inputs, which include:

  - Product trials
  - Product/software demonstration
  - Consultation
  - The purchase of a product
  - A subscription
  - A donation

- ✔ Reaction inputs, which include:

  - Reviews/referrals
  - Customer service connection
  - Product return shipping
  - Private events
  - Suggestive selling at online shopping cart checkout
  - Rewards programs
  - Email campaigns

## Establishing campaign objectives

When designing your inbound campaigns, start with your business objectives. What is your measurement of success? Is it units sold? Dollars generated? Donations made?

Note that I didn't mention Facebook Likes or Twitter retweets. Although those can be important inputs to measure and view, and may actually increase your visibility on social media sites, these metrics alone are not usually used for inbound marketing campaign objectives. In fact, marketing metrics are subservient to the _business_ objective. Using business objectives that tie into your business plan, your marketing plan, and your Shared Strategic Blueprint is the preferred inbound marketing measuring stick. Measuring the degree of influence of your tactical marketing inputs in achieving the desired business outcome or objective is an important part of whether or not your inbound marketing campaign succeeds or fails.

Establish your inbound marketing campaign objectives by stating them in terms that connect to your overall business. And remember, to keep your objectives S.M.A.R.T.

## Designing your inbound-marketing campaigns

Inbound marketing is consumer-centric so you'll begin with your target customers in mind when designing your inbound marketing campaigns. By focusing on one product or service, you can better identify which target profiles are likely to purchase, uncovering their needs and pain points for that specific product. This is how inbound marketing campaigns connect your product with people.

Here's how to design your inbound marketing campaign:

1. **Discover a need.**

2. **Choose a product.**

3. **Articulate a campaign outcome hypothesis.**

4. **Work with your sales department to establish the parameters for defining an MQL.**

5. **Review historical conversion data, including your cost-per-lead (CPL) and cost-per-acquisition (CPA) information.**

6. **Populate your Customer Conversion Chain. (Refer to Chapter 9.)**

7. **Recalibrate your hypothesis based on your initial Customer Conversion Chain inputs.**

8. **Measure and test results; replicate successes and discard underperformers.**

9. **Report and make adjustments.**

## Mapping your inbound-marketing campaigns

If you built a Call-to-Action Map as the basis for your website map, it's much easier to map your campaigns. Because your CTA Map is, by definition, organized based on conversion this is a good starting point. Figure 13-1 shows a campaign map created by Eloqua, the marketing automation software company.

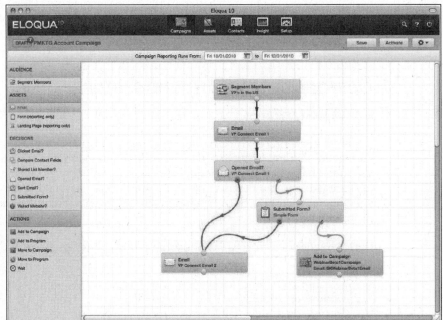

**Figure 13-1:**
An Eloqua campaign map.

You can see how there's a logical flow that connects. Mapping your inbound marketing campaigns with this tool, or something similar, helps you create an organized, logical conversion flow. Keeping it simple makes it easier for your visitors to navigate closer to an action, which is what you want.

## Understanding the campaign build process

Here's a simple process to follow when building inbound marketing campaigns:

1. Use the product your persona is most likely to purchase and create your product pyramid.

2. State your end business objective for the chosen product, defining it in measurable terms.

3. Assign a budget based on this objective.

4. Identify the most likely first conversion point.

5. Assess your current content assets to determine if you have existing content that connects people with your product. Use current relevant content or develop new engagement content that better serves your needs.

6. Build a dedicated landing page for your engagement content at the first conversion point.

7. Identify the attractive content that will act as input feeders to your engagement content.

8. Create your CTA buttons and forms to connect your attraction content with your conversion content.

9. Design email workflows to follow up at each point of engagement, creating a specific CTA with clear action for the prospect to take the next step for reengagement.

10. Connect and track the digital media you'll use as attractive inputs (social media, PPC, SEO, and so on), assign a budget to each and link to the appropriate content for this particular product pyramid.

11. Set up analytics to measure your success as compared to the campaign objective.

To see campaign mapping and building in action, take a look at an example from my own website. Figure 13-2 illustrates an inbound campaign map overlaid with different attraction and conversion content. You can see how this campaign extends beyond my website. Consumer action begins off site, enters into the properly designed CTA Map, continuing with engagement remarketing emails and reengagement opportunities and ultimately through offsite conversion to those people demonstrating interest. When my inbound marketing campaign connects my profile persona with my product, culminating with an offsite sale, the campaign is performing its job. The degree to which this job is being performed well may now be measured and expressed as ROI.

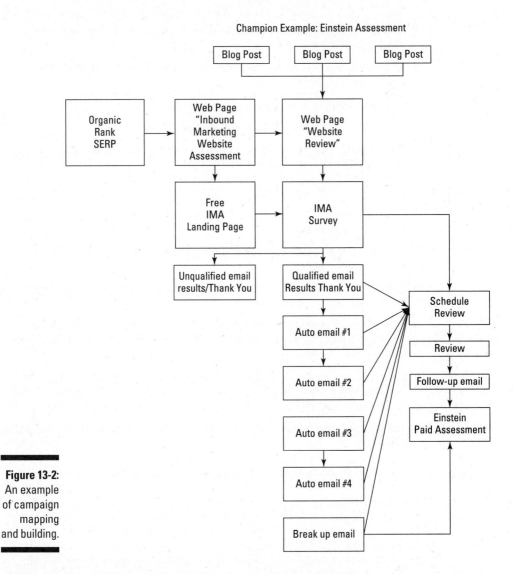

Champion Example: Einstein Assessment

**Figure 13-2:**
An example
of campaign
mapping
and building.

# Building Your First Campaign

After you've assessed the current state of your digital marketing and performed a tune-up on your website, you're ready to build your first inbound marketing campaign. I recommend starting with a very simple campaign, one that consists of:

✔ **Choosing your featured product or service.** Because this is your first inbound marketing campaign, shorter sales cycle and/or higher unit sales volume are preferential.

✔ **Deciding on one existing engagement content piece.** If you don't currently have an engagement content piece, create one.

✔ **Building a product-specific, conversion-based landing page with form fields that collect necessary contact information and information relevant and influential to the purchasing process.**

✔ **Connecting your engagement content by designing on-page CTA buttons or forms, placed prominently on multiple pages on your website.** Note: choose onsite pages that have relatively high page visits.

✔ **Building a simple email workflow of no more than three automated email follow-ups.** Note: you'll need some form of email software, such as MailChimp (`www.mailchimp.com`), or marketing automation software to accomplish this.

✔ **Connect and communicate your lead flow information system with your sales team.**

✔ **Choose which digital media to use for attracting visitors and add different tracking codes to measure individual media performance.**

## Organizing your campaigns for conversion

You've created an inbound map and taken stock of your content assets as well as the additional content you'll need to create an effective campaign. You've seen how to assign content to different steps in the customer purchase path. Now, organize that content as a user would consume it. This means creating new content and organizing it in a way that provides the quickest intuitive path to conversion while still allowing your visitors and leads to explore other information on your website on their terms. Remember, this includes creating reengagement emails that direct people to return to your site to reengage.

## Creating new content for your campaigns

When you perform your content asset census, chances are you'll discover you have content gaps. These may be one of the following, in order of importance to your campaign:

✔ Content gaps for purchase path alignment

✔ Content gaps for target personas

✔ Content gaps by form

✔ Content gaps in relevance

✔ Content gaps in timeliness

✔ Content gaps in contextuality

You'll probably discover that you don't have the optimal *amount*, nor the optimal *type* of content. That's okay. Start by populating your inbound campaign map with existing content, even if it's not optimal. Next, list the "must have" content to populate the campaign. Last, create your optimal list, ranked by overall importance to the success of the campaign based on the priority list above, and then create that content to populate your inbound marketing campaign.

Your first inbound campaign won't be perfect — in fact, there is no such thing as a perfect campaign. All inbound marketing campaigns are imperfect. Likewise, initially you won't have the optimal content. Creating a hierarchy of content needs helps you prioritize content creation.

## *Overlaying content for inbound campaigns*

Effective inbound marketing campaigns are fueled by compelling content. When it comes to content, one size definitely does not fit all. Buyers are unique. Each buyer persona has different needs. Because people are searching for different things at different times, it's important to match your content with your buyer's profile and place on the purchase path. HubSpot provides a handy tool for just this purpose — the blank content map. (See Figure 13-3.) Content mapping can be complex so this tool breaks it down into five simple steps:

1. **Name the persona (from your list of previously created personas created in the diagnostic assessment stage) to whom your content is targeted.**

2. **Identify the problem that persona is attempting to solve.**

3. **Generate educational content ideas for the first step in the purchase path (awareness).**

4. **Generate engagement content ideas for the second step in the purchase path (consideration).**

5. **Generate encouragement content ideas for the third step in the purchase path (decision).**

Of course, I recommend you add a sixth step, which is:

6. **Generate embracing content for the customer reattraction phase in the Lifestyle Loop.**

You can download these templates to map out your own content at `http://cdn2.hubspot.net/hub/137828/file-799282870-pdf/HubSpot_Concepting_worksheet_editable.pdf`.

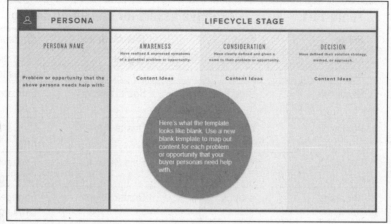

*Courtesy of HubSpot*

**Figure 13-3:**
HubSpot's
blank
content
map.

If you're having trouble generating content ideas, HubSpot has another great content tool — the content map — which breaks down content generation even further. It's a simple one-page content organizer, as shown in Figure 13-4. You can download it for free at `http://blog.hubspot.com/marketing/content-mapping-template-personalize-marketing`.

| PERSONA | LIFECYCLE STAGE | | |
|---|---|---|---|
| PERSONA NAME<br><br>Jimmy Gym Owner | AWARENESS<br>Have realized & expressed symptoms of a potential problem or opportunity. | CONSIDERATION<br>Have clearly defined and given a name to their problem or opportunity. | DECISION<br>Have defined their solution strategy, method, or approach. |
| Problem or opportunity that the above persona needs help with:<br><br>Jimmy is new to gym ownership. He needs to buy some gym equipment, but is unsure where to begin, how much he should spend, etc. | Content Ideas<br><br>• Beginner's Guide to Buying Gym Equipment [Ebook]<br><br>• New or Used: When to Stretch Your Gym Equipment Budget & When to Splurge [Infographic] | Content Ideas<br><br>• Gym Equipment Budget Template [Excel spreadsheet]<br><br>• Purchasing Timeline for Gym Equipment: What Should You Buy First? [PowerPoint worksheet] | Content Ideas<br><br>• Request a quote<br><br>• Phone assessment of equipment needs |

*Courtesy of HubSpot*

**Figure 13-4:**
HubSpot
content
map.

Table 13-1 shows some of the creative content assets I used in setting up this particular inbound marketing campaign. Here's how the content for this campaign is classified when you apply the 4 E's of Content Marketing:

Keywords: *Inbound Marketing Assessment* and *Website Review*

Target Profile: Chief Marketing Office/$20M+ in annual revenues

| Table 13-1 | Creative assets for campaign set-up | | |
|---|---|---|---|
| *Place* | *Form* | *Connection* | *Content* |
| Research | Video/Written | Organic | Educational Website Page |
| Research | Blog Post | Social Media | Educational Blog Page |
| Research | Written | Onsite Page | Conversion Assist Page |
| Research | Video/Written | Paid Search | Engagement Landing Page |
| Shopping | e-book | Onsite Page | Engagement Landing Page |
| Shopping | Written | Email | Reconversion |
| Shopping | IMA Survey | Onsite Page | Conversion Page |
| Buying | Emails | Personal email | Reconversion Engagement |
| Buying | Graphic Table | Onsite Page | Encouragement |
| Buying | Contact Us | Landing Page | Encouragement |

For this campaign, my keywords are *inbound marketing assessment* and *website review* (first *contact*) and my product funnel is an Einstein Assessment with the desired action being a customer acquisition via a paid assessment (first *contract*). My content is written to CMOs. Here's a summary of the content I deliver to connect with different content forms and at different times, based on a prospect who discovers us via organic search by searching the term *inbound marketing assessment:*

1. Stranger's entry point that's linked to the search term is my inbound marketing assessment page (see Figure 13-5), which offers an Einstein informational video and written content (educational).

2. By clicking "Website Grader" in the body copy, my visiting persona may choose to move laterally in the product pyramid to learn the difference between a website grader and an IMA (educational), and they may also download an e-book (engagement). (See Figure 13-6.)

3. Leads who download the e-book receive an email for a free IMA (engagement).

4. The visitor can engage by clicking "Get My Free Assessment" CTA button, which navigates to my IMA survey landing page (engagement). (See Figure 13-7.) My visitor is moving down the purchase path, becoming a marketing qualified lead.

**Figure 13-5:**
Inbound
marketing
assessment
page.

**Figure 13-6:**
A lateral
move in the
product
pyramid.

5. By submitting the form on the landing page, my visitor is now a lead.

6. The lead completes the IMA survey (engagement) and upon submission becomes a sales qualified lead.

7. Alternatively, my lead may wish to click on the Einstein Pricing CTA button, migrating much closer to the desired action (engagement).

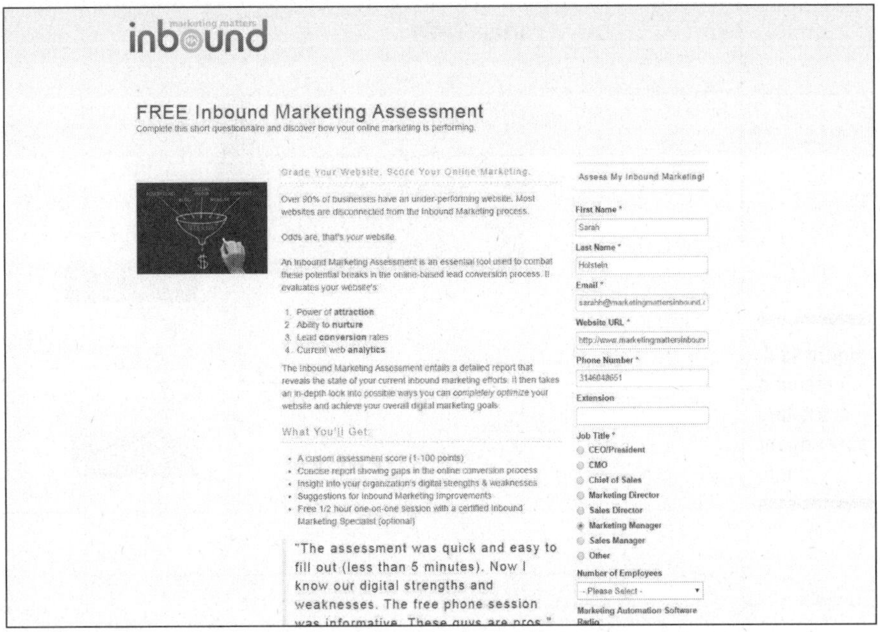

Figure 13-7:
Inbound
Marketing
Assessment
survey land-
ing page.

8. Upon contact — either via the "Contact Us" form or through completion of an IMA survey — leads receive automated and personal emails to schedule a review of the results via phone (encouragement). (See Figure 13-8.)

9. SQLs review IMA results with assessor (encouragement).

10. Timely automated emails are sent as a follow-up reengagement SQL purchases an Einstein Assessment, becoming a customer, receiving the occasional newsletter, topical email (embrace), or encouragement to participate in another product offering like strategic consultation (reengagement).

## Matching content form with function

Deciding between all the options of content form, content function, and content types based on a content map in a content strategy will make your head spin! One of the best tools I've discovered for matching form with function is the simple one-page sheet that HubSpot created, seen in Figure 13-9.

There are other navigational paths a stranger may take, resulting in the same conversion. For instance, visitors may seek my educational content about IMAs by clicking on social media links connecting to educational blog content, then follow the same, or similar, path to purchase.

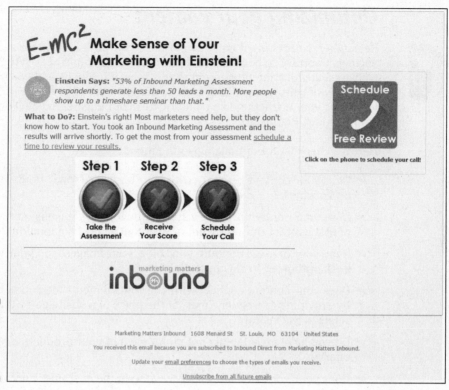

**Figure 13-8:**
An auto-
mated email
offer.

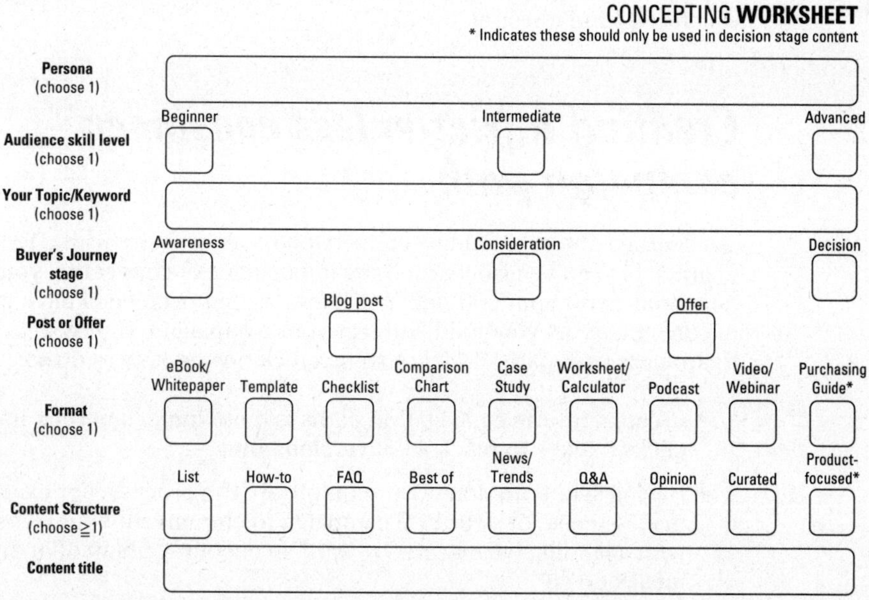

CONCEPTING **WORKSHEET**
* Indicates these should only be used in decision stage content

**Figure 13-9:**
HubSpot
content
sheet/
checklist.

## Optimizing your content

Remember, your content must be optimized for both UX and for search engines. Contrary to common thought, UX should trump SEO. Why? Because truly meaningful content, content that is relevant, timely, and contextual, has a way of being found. That's not to diminish the importance of SEO. SEO facilitates your attraction like oil lubricates your engine. But SEO doesn't buy your product. People do.

Here's a checklist for optimizing your content:

✔ Does your content resonate with your target persona? How do you know?

✔ Does your content provide a systematic logical progression from point of first contact through point of first contract (at a minimum)?

✔ Have your on-page content, your blog, your images, and your videos been optimized to SEO best practices?

✔ Does your content connect with your digital media attraction inputs by providing a "welcome mat" at the place of website entry that makes sense to the visitor?

✔ Do you have meaningful content for each of your product/service offerings?

✔ Does your content align with each step in the customer purchase path?

In essence, you're asking yourself this: "Do I have a content strategy?" — which is a good question to ask.

## Creating a frictionless consumer campaign path

You learned about creating a conversion-based website with CTA Maps in Chapter 11. You've also learned the importance of connecting your attraction inputs with your content. You know the importance of paving the path to conversion. As you build and test your campaigns, your goal is to create a frictionless user path. Here are some quick tips on how to do so:

✔ Creating intuitive navigation paths is more important than how many clicks it takes to reach a conversion point.

✔ Having said that, don't over-complicate the process. For example, if it makes sense for your PPC campaign to circumvent your website entirely with a landing page geared toward an encouragement offer, by all means do so!

✔ Link your pages in a conversion path that directs a visitor either laterally or downward toward an action.

✔ Provide obvious navigation signs so that it's very clear which action a visitor should naturally take next.

✔ Resist the urge to provide too many click options. You may overload your visitors with too many options resulting in a bounce out from your site.

✔ Create and connect side entryways into your home page other than your home page.

✔ Perform user-testing after you think you've got it perfect. You'll discover further opportunities for refinements.

✔ As time passes, look for trends of sources, pages, CTAs, and landing pages, using that analytics data to inspect conversion opportunities and roadblocks.

✔ As you gain customers, model the paths to conversion so you can replicate those paths with other products by building similar campaigns.

Creating a frictionless path to an ultimate action creates a happy customer. Pay attention to how your visitors interact with your site and you'll spot opportunities to obtain more customers and garner more market share.

## Measuring and replicating campaign success

Although Part VII of this book covers analytics more in-depth, it's worth mentioning some ways to track and test your inbound marketing campaigns. This includes:

✔ **Google Analytics:** Creating campaigns in Google Analytics that match your inbound marketing campaigns is usually a smart idea. Depending on your needs, it may not provide the depth that marketing automation software does; however, it's industry standard to track campaigns, especially conversion events, in Google Analytics. You may want to build custom campaigns in Google.

✔ **Tracking codes:** Attaching an Urchin Tracking Module (UTM) to a custom URL in order to track a source, medium, and campaign name. This enables Google Analytics to tell you where searchers came from as well as what campaign directed them to you. Figure 13-10 shows Google's URL builder, which enables the tracking you'll need. If this all seems intimidating, hire a developer!

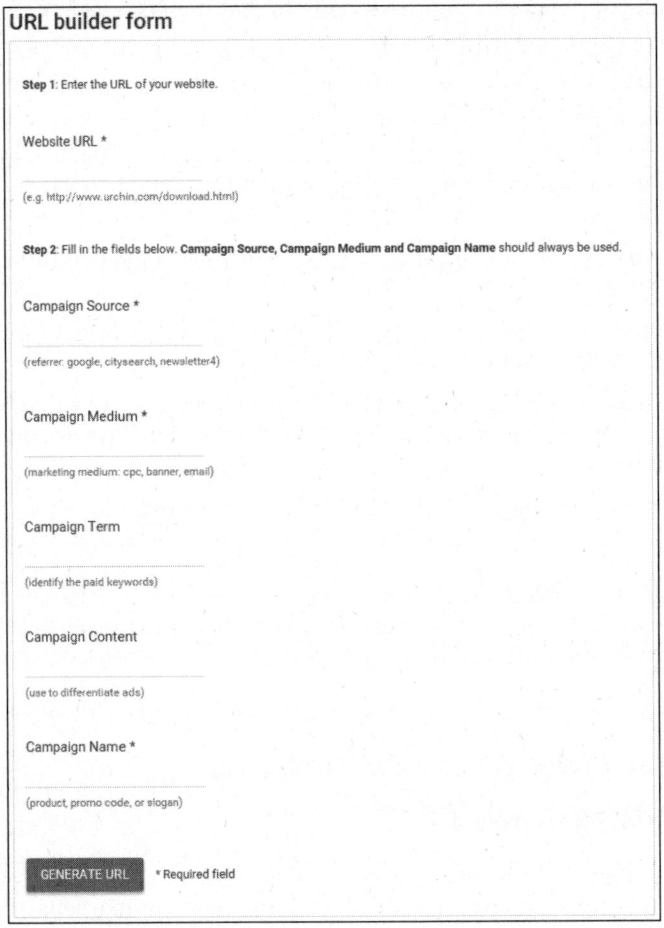

**URL builder form**

**Step 1**: Enter the URL of your website.

Website URL *

_____

(e.g. http://www.urchin.com/download.html)

**Step 2**: Fill in the fields below. **Campaign Source, Campaign Medium and Campaign Name** should always be used.

Campaign Source *

_____

(referrer: google, citysearch, newsletter4)

Campaign Medium *

_____

(marketing medium: cpc, banner, email)

Campaign Term

_____

(identify the paid keywords)

Campaign Content

_____

(use to differentiate ads)

Campaign Name *

_____

(product, promo code, or slogan)

GENERATE URL    * Required field

**Figure 13-10:**
**Google**
**UTM.**

You can see that the URL builder features other tracking fields to add to your code which is helpful in tracking specific keywords or content. You may also track by medium (social media), a source (Twitter), and campaign.

Creating and applying tracking codes to your attraction sources and conversion pages help you understand what's occurring every step of the way down the customer purchase path.

✔ **User testing:** Consider these tools to test your campaign path:

- Clicky

- UserTesting.com

- Morae

- Camtasia

- Ovo Logger

✔ **Customer Conversion Chain ROI analysis:** Measure your attraction and conversion hypothesis as well as your business objectives versus your outcomes to determine your degree of success.

✔ **Marketing automation software:** If you can afford it, buy marketing automation software to help you track your campaign results. If you can't afford it, try to find a way to afford it. If you still can't afford it, measure every point in the conversion chain as best you can.

The unmeasured campaign is like Major League Baseball without statistics. The game can still be played, and the final score can be tallied, but you won't be able to consistently maximize your wins and systematically avoid your losses because you're missing important data. Although that data doesn't guarantee a win every time, it may stack the odds of outfoxing your competition in your favor. Anything worth doing in inbound marketing is worth measuring. So, if it's worth doing it, measure it. If it's not worth measuring, don't do it.

# Things You Can Do Now

✔ Based on fulfilling customer needs, choose a product funnel on which to focus.

✔ Map out your first inbound marketing campaign.

✔ Create content to populate your inbound campaign.

# Chapter 14

# Blogging for Attraction

. . . . . . . . . . . . . . . . . . . . . . . . . . . . . . . . . . . . . . . . . . . . . . . . . . .

## In This Chapter

▶ Learning why you need a blog

▶ Creating your blog

▶ Categorizing your blog posts

▶ Building a blog calendar

. . . . . . . . . . . . . . . . . . . . . . . . . . . . . . . . . . . . . . . . . . . . . . . . . . .

Creating content is paramount for inbound marketers, and blog posts make great educational content. In this chapter, I show you why you need a blog, how to categorize your blog, and how to build a publishing calendar that makes sense for you and your readers. Featuring meaningful content in your blog is a proven, effective way of generating attraction to your website. Your blog is a way to connect people with your products and acts as a means to achieving your inbound marketing objectives.

## Going Beyond the Traditional Blog

Maybe it's just me, but the word *blog* conjures images of a lonely soul typing rambling, stream-of-consciousness posts about the insignificant details of his or her life. Still, the word *blog* has stuck, and I use it here because of its commonality in the business world. Blogging is serious business.

At the very least, you need to blog. It doesn't matter if you're business-to-consumer, business-to-business, or nonprofit: blogs are important, and they get results.

Blogging achieves much in the inbound marketing process, including:

✔ Attracting new visitors

✔ Serving as a stepping stone to engagement content

✔ Positioning you as a reliable source of information

✔ Increasing your visibility with search engines

✔ Creating sharable content, the "word of mouth" in our digital age

✔ Connecting with individual prospects, customers, and Lifestylers

In other words, blogging attracts more visitors, generates more leads, positions your company as a thought leader, positions you higher against your competition, and facilitates customer reengagement. That's why you need to blog.

# Creating Your Blog

Marketers who prioritize blogging are 13 times more likely to enjoy positive ROI. To begin creating one yourself, follow these steps:

1. **Identify the engagement content proven to assist in the next logical step in a buyer's purchase path.**

2. **Review your keyword research in order to formulate blog titles that include those keywords.**

3. **Create a series of blog posts (five to ten), providing a logical link for the reader from blog post to your engagement content.**

4. **Assign these blog posts to a predefined category (usually based on the product or conversion path).**

5. **Write your blog posts for the reader first and for search engines second.**

6. **Publish your blog posts in a consistent manner (usually two-to-five times a week).**

7. **Promote your blog posts via social media and other outlets.**

If you currently have a blog, measure your current state against the steps above, determining if any gaps exist. No matter whether you're creating your first blog or whether your blog has been around for years, you should *activate* your blog rather than maintain it. Blogging only one time a month may be better than nothing, but it's hardly an active blog. In fact, 87 percent of daily bloggers acquire customers via their blog whereas only 54 percent of monthly bloggers do so.

# *Building your blog*

Before you start building your audience, you must build your blog platform. This involves:

- ✔ Creating an onsite blog, preferably on an open-source platform like WordPress
- ✔ Categorizing your content, grouping it around customer needs and product conversion paths
- ✔ Making logical connections between your blog and engagement content
- ✔ Creating an editorial calendar

### *Opening doors with open-source platforms*

Over half of all blogs are written on WordPress (see Figure 14-1) and there are reasons for that. WordPress is a user-friendly, open-source platform so it's easy to access, update, and publish your blog content. (Tumblr is a good platform for blogging and it allows your blog to be imbedded into your website.) Using WordPress means either building your entire website and blog on that platform, or simply building your blog in WordPress and connecting it to whatever platform on which your website was developed.

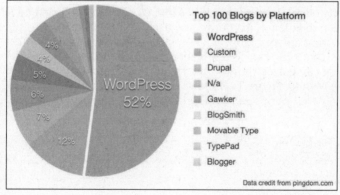

**Figure 14-1:**
The top 100
blogs by
platform.

Building your blog on WordPress makes it easier to concentrate on blogging great content rather than on playing the frustrating role (frustrating for most marketers, anyway) of developer. A multitude of WordPress plug-ins make it easier for you to create graphically pleasing, user-friendly content that's designed for SEO best practices. Building on any open-source platform means you have the freedom to post when you want and how often you want. Rather than relying on your IT person or department, it empowers you to share great content based on your marketing objectives rather than on IT's time-line, and that's usually a good thing.

There are literally thousands of templates available for creating your blog. Most are easy to access and update with fresh content. Be careful to ensure your blog matches your online brand image, even if it requires a custom blog build. Keep the blog form simple and the content clever. People don't want to have to think when navigating, but they don't mind laughing because of something funny you wrote.

## Categorizing your content

When building your blog, it's important to categorize your content. If you built your website with a CTA Map, this categorization should be relatively easy. You'll categorize and tag your blog posts. What's the difference between categories, blog content, and tags? I discovered this little gem on the Internet from John Haydon (@johnhaydon):

> *"Categories are like aisles in a grocery store and tags are like ingredients in the various different foods. Tags (ingredients) link together all of your posts (food items) across your categories (aisles)."*

When assigning categories and tags, think about your content as food. Which aisle (category) would a visitor find it in? And after they found your blog post, what would the interesting details (tag) be?

It's pretty easy to create categories in a WordPress blog. Simply identify your desired end actions onsite and use that information as a category when setting up your blog. In its most simplistic form, product categories serve as your blog categories. There's nothing wrong with this because your blog categories should be very literal descriptions instead of clever creative writing. Figure 14-2 shows where to create categories in WordPress (https://en.support.wordpress.com/posts/categories).

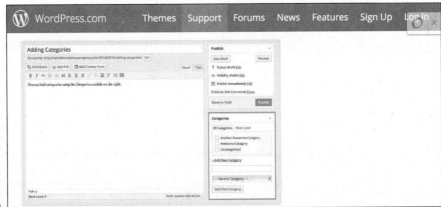

**Figure 14-2:** Creating WordPress categories for your blog.

Looking at Figure 14-2, you'll see how easy it is to create Categories in your blog. The hardest and most important part is creating a hierarchical categorization that makes sense when connecting your product with people.

Tags, as opposed to categories, are optional but recommended. Tags connect a group of related blog posts, making it easier for your readers to discover similar relevant content. The easiest visualization of this is if you were to write a four-part "How To" series with one blog post for each part. Each of the blog posts would tag each other allowing your readers to discover more content and the search engines to know more about your website. WordPress makes it easy to add tags (see Figure 14-3) and you can learn in more detail on their website (`https://en.support.WordPress.com/posts/tags/`).

**Figure 14-3:**
Adding tags to your blog posts.

In the past, blogs simply populated in the chronological order they were published. Categories create blog content segmentation so a visitor may easily access content containing similar subject matter, all under one category, by filtering a search for your blog posts to the categories in which the reader is interested. If you're blogging on WordPress, categories are a mandatory feature when setting up your blog. In fact, you won't be able to publish a blog post without assigning it to a category. It's important to plan your categories in advance so you don't end up with too many for a visitor to wade through. You can create up to three sub-categories in WordPress, so thinking ahead about the hierarchy of your content avoids blog content organizational headaches later on. Categorizing and tagging your blog posts also contributes to your SEO efforts so it's just a good inbound marketing practice.

### Connecting your blog content with engagement content

Blog content is usually educational in nature. Designing attractive blog content is one thing; connecting it with middle-of-the-funnel engagement content in a meaningful manner is another. That's why it's best to begin with your engagement content and let the blog posts flow from there. Formulating blog material from your engagement content creates contextual relevance for your readers. That's why you link your blogs to that downloadable engagement content.

Imagine you marketed for a university, and you created an e-book directed toward high school juniors entitled "Four Secrets to Choosing the Best College for You." For this example, let's say the four decision factors are:

✔ Geographical location

✔ Enrollment size

✔ Areas of study available (majors)

✔ Financial cost

Blog posts derived from this e-book could include titles like:

✔ "6 Benefits for Choosing an Out-of-state Private University"

✔ "Small College or Large University — What's Best For You?"

✔ "How to Choose a College When Your Major is 'Undecided'"

✔ "Securing Scholarships for College: Looking Beyond a University's Published Tuition"

I can think of about a hundred more blog ideas stemming from just these four topics. I'm sure you can, too! Use your engagement content to stimulate your blogging content. Link blog content to the original engagement piece and with the other relevant blogs in the campaign. Gate the engagement content with a form for lead data collection and now your inbound marketing is beginning to work.

### Creating your blog editorial calendar

When you first start blogging, it's a struggle just to keep up. Give yourself enough time, say 30-60 days, to create content ahead of the publish date so you can begin working further out. Not only does this encourage strategic thinking, but it also allows some cushion time for when publishing hiccups occur, which they most certainly will. The best method for keeping track of your blogging efforts is to create a blogging editorial calendar. In its simplest form, your editorial calendar will be a forward-thinking plan that includes:

✔ Blog category

✔ Blog campaign (often this is the same as your category, but it doesn't have to be)

- ✔ Keyword focus
- ✔ Blog title
- ✔ Engagement content CTA
- ✔ First-draft deadline
- ✔ Publish date

For this calendar, a simple Excel spreadsheet will suffice. You can even link it to a calendar format if you wish. Some marketing automation software includes blogging and social media calendars, which is very helpful for your content planning.

## Writing your blog

You've built your blog. Now what? How do you know what to write about? How often should you publish your posts? What's the best content? Here are some things to consider when planning:

- ✔ What problems are your customers attempting to solve.
- ✔ Note seasonality or holidays important to your business.
- ✔ First, focus on one category/campaign and then vary among two or three before branching out even further.
- ✔ Compile a sizable library of written content before you expand into other forms, such as video.
- ✔ Align your frequency of blog publishing with capacity. A one-person marketing "department" can only produce so much. Likewise, relying on inside non-marketing employees to produce blogs may initially seem like a good way for management to save money; however, this usually ends in frustration, unmet deadlines, and eventual dwindling of content publishing to a trickle. Only use internal employees for non-crucial, "guest" posts so your blogging efforts, and hence your content attraction efforts, aren't stymied.
- ✔ Ideally, work toward publishing 60-90 days in advance.

## Knowing what to post

Let's start with the written word because written content represents the vast majority of the content populating today's blogs.

### Knowing your audience

Probably the most important tip when writing your blog is to write for your audience. Yes, you should use keywords. Yes, you should optimize your content. But, if your blog posts are sterile, keyword-stuffed posts with stilted, unemotional language, well, good luck!

You're writing to human beings. The purpose of your blog posts is to connect with people. Effectively connecting and communicating requires knowing your audience. If you've performed an IMA that includes customer profile and/or persona information, congratulations! You're ahead of the game because you've peeked into the minds of your customers to understand their individual needs and buying motives. That's not to say you're going to use pushy sales language. Rather, your blog, using educational information, is one of the first steps in helping a person solve a particular problem. Write to that problem by listening to your customer base, identifying with them, and pointing out how much better the future looks when their particular problem is solved. Help your audience envision their problem is solved and your first onsite conversions will grow higher.

### Choosing your keywords

The smart inbound marketer performed keyword research in Stage 1, which is an inbound marketing assessment. This process includes sorting and categorizing keywords based on the inferred needs of your target customer persona, the product on which you're focusing, and the location of your persona in the purchase path. Knowing this information is powerful when blogging because you now identify with your reader on a three-dimensional plane, speaking directly to their needs based on who they are and where they are in the purchase path at your point of contact.

Use keywords to direct your blogging efforts but use them sparingly and appropriately. In other words, don't try to trick Google by keyword stuffing.

### Identifying authors

You have several options when choosing whom will create your content. Here's a handful of options:

- ✔ You could write the content yourself.
- ✔ You could dedicate a content producer to be responsible for all your blog content.
- ✔ You could outsource your content production.
- ✔ You could share responsibility for the blog among a number of employees.

Previously, I've shared with you the pitfalls of relying on employees to create content. I don't recommend it unless you use those posts as bonus posts, like icing on your blog cake. If you have the time and no other marketing responsibilities, you should create content yourself. This often starts with a bang and then fizzles as the novelty of content creation wears off and the realization of the discipline, strategy, and organization required to effectively produce, post, and distribute your content. But it can be done.

Provided you have the resources, hiring a content producer is a viable option. The internal company and product knowledge is beneficial because there's no learning curve to hinder content production. Allowing this individual to write and produce customer-centric inbound content rather than product-centric interruptive messaging is sometimes a problem but that can be managed.

Outsourcing for help makes sense in three scenarios:

✔ Your dedicated content producer understands the strategic direction, possesses the organizational and delegation skills to work with freelancers, or with a content service or content marketing firm. In this scenario, your internal employee acts as the hub of content production and distribution.

✔ You don't have the internal resources to produce the volume of content you want or need. In this case, your first choice may be a content marketing firm specializing in content strategy and content creation to guide your blogging efforts.

✔ The content you wish to produce requires specialization, technical skills, or specific expertise. In this case, you're outsourcing to someone whose specialization is online tool building or you need a videographer and editor to produce quality video content.

## Creating your blog content

Whether you produce your content in-house, outsource it, or a combination of the two, it's important to follow an editorial calendar, to publish consistently and follow a strategic content plan. Often the importance of blogging content is overshadowed by the need for quick results. Even more often, the discipline required to run a blog results in intermittent posting that span weeks or even months. All content, including blog content, is too important to the inbound process to ignore. Assign ownership of your content with deadlines and begin blogging for attraction.

## Sharing interesting visual information

Not all blog content is the written word. Pictures are worth a thousand words and video must be worth a million. After you've perfected the art of consistently creating, posting, and sharing written content, consider expanding your blog formats into images, videos, and infographics, all designed to attract through educational content. Here are some options to create more interesting blogs:

- ✔ Photographic images
- ✔ Illustrations
- ✔ On-page links to relevant videos
- ✔ Infographics
- ✔ Graphs, charts, and tables
- ✔ Callouts and quotes

Tagging your images also improves your SEO slightly so make sure you're tagging all your blog post images. Lastly, including a video script in an inoffensive location at the bottom of your post enhances your SEO because search engines can't crawl videos for the content you've created within the video.

## Creating offsite visibility

Great content attracts more than just visitors. Great content attracts influential people and publishers who share and/or feature your content. This may be achieved through:

- ✔ Guest blogging on relevant sites
- ✔ Public relations
- ✔ Social-media sharing
- ✔ Turning your blog into an article for traditional and electronic media

There is no magic formula for defining great content, but, just like great art, you know it when you see it. And, then there's timing. I've had prospective clients ask me to create viral content. "Make my video go viral!" That's not how it works, folks. This is a basic misunderstanding in the fundamentals of the ways content strategy, publishing, and dissemination work. A consistently planned, targeted, and customer-centric blogging platform is more likely to achieve success than the random attempts at viral videos that litter YouTube.

# Vlogging with video content

*Vlogs* are simply video blogs, hence the name. With a vlog you create and publish content regularly; it's just in video format rather than in the written word.

For your vlog you can choose to create screencasts or to shoot video featuring "talking heads" (head and shoulder shots) or in the question-and-answer style of an interview. Unless you're adept at videography or you've hired a professional, avoid shooting "on location." When creating your vlog, you don't want to look cheap or create negative UX due to poor audio. To avoid looking like a bad "B" movie, you'll need to invest in some equipment including:

- A good camera that shoots video. (If you can't afford a professional video camera consider a Canon EOS 5D Mark III or EOS 7D Mark II cameras, which both feature video.)

- A green screen if you don't have a suitable shooting environment and want to edit graphics into your vlog.

- A professional microphone for superior audio quality.

- A good lighting kit. Don't skimp on this, because lighting creates a more professional look.

You can edit your video blog in iMovie or Windows Movie Maker or hire a professional.

The alternative to a full video vlog is creating screencasts. If you choose this route, remember to avoid your typical type-based PowerPoint or SlideShare deck. You're not creating a tutorial or product demo with a vlog; you're creating interesting content. Use compelling visuals combining infographics, photos, bold headlines, quotes, charts, and graphs. You can screencast a vlog with screencast software programs, such as

- Camtasia
- Screencast-O-Matic
- Open Broadcaster Software

Keep your individual vlogs short; no longer than two-to-five minutes each. Remember to optimize your vlog title, tags, and description, including backlinks to your site where necessary. If you post your vlogs on YouTube rather than on your website, you'll want to optimize your video there, too.

Vlogs require an investment of time and money so it's usually best to use vlogs as an enhancement to your core content strategy rather than as core content itself.

## Things You Can Do Now

- ✔ Choose a blog category on which to focus.
- ✔ Write a series of blog posts supporting that blog category.
- ✔ Connect blog posts with each other and with one specific piece of engagement content that has conversion potential.

# Part V
# Attracting Visitors to Your Website

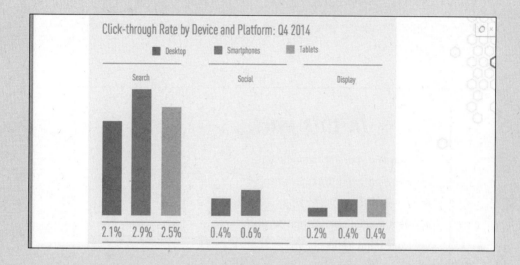

For more about inbound marketing attraction factors, see www.dummies.com/extras/inboundmarketing.

# In this part. . .

✔ Learning your attraction factors

✔ Knowing your attraction types

✔ Generating website traffic

✔ Reattracting visitors with email

✔ Measuring traffic quality

# Chapter 15

# Growing Your Organic Traffic

This chapter is a basic overview of search-engine optimization (SEO), so if you consider yourself an SEO expert, feel free to skip this chapter. This is not a deep-dive into SEO.

Understanding the ways organic search results contribute to your inbound marketing efforts is important. People will find you if you've optimized your website, your content, and your inbound system. Understanding the importance of organic (free) traffic as an input to your Customer Conversion Chain requires a basic understanding of how SEO connects to your inbound marketing system.

## Improving Your Organic Traffic

Depending on which research you study, somewhere between 66 percent and 83 percent of people searching on the Internet click on organic rankings. Roughly two-thirds of these people click on the top five results on the first SERP displayed (page one). So it's no surprise that every online marketer wants to rank as high on that list of results as possible. This makes sense as the primary visitor source to the average website is from organic search.

Ranking higher doesn't happen accidentally. By researching keywords, analyzing click-thru-rates, optimizing your content, and promoting your content through social media channels, you can begin to improve your rank. In the future, it will be harder and harder to rank higher since there are an ever increasing number of competing sites and the search engines display only so many positions on any given page. That's one reason it's important to accelerate your SEO efforts sooner rather than later. Organic traffic is earned traffic. As such, it takes time and effort to begin seeing results from your SEO.

## *Looking at SERPs*

Search engine results pages (SERPs) are the pages a search engine displays after you enter a search term. SERPs include paid advertising from pay-per-click campaigns and organic rankings from your SEO effort. Historically, SERPs displayed ten results per page, but that is changing. Figure 15-1 shows the top results displayed after I typed *steak house San Antonio* into Google's search bar: one paid ad from Bob's Steak & Chop House, some locally reviewed San Antonio steakhouses, followed by typical SERP organic rankings.

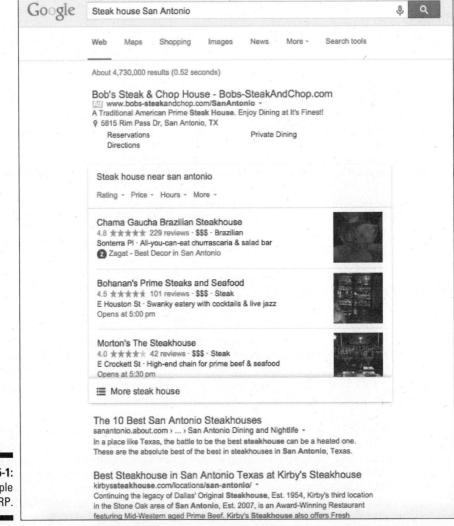

**Figure 15-1:**
An example
SERP.

When I searched *restaurant* from my office in St. Louis, Google's SERP displayed three restaurants within proximity to my search location (all three are fantastic by the way!), followed by a listing for Restaurant.com and other restaurant listings for the St. Louis area (see Figure 15-2).

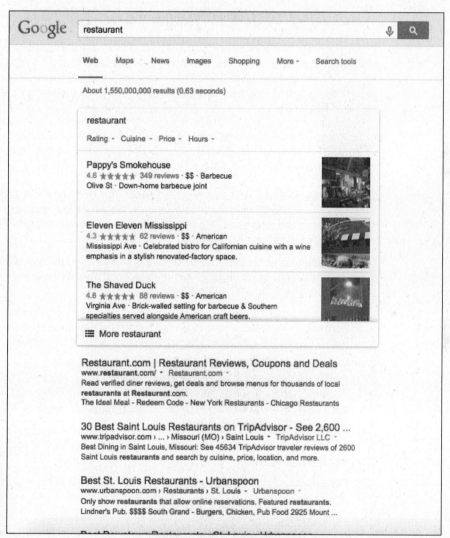

**Figure 15-2:**
A localized, geospecific SERP.

The look of your SERP changes as Google and the other search engines attempt to create more opportunities on the SERPs. So, other dynamic factors, such as your geographic access point to the Internet and your known search habits, affect the SERP displayed by the search engine. In other words, as the search engines become more sophisticated in attempting to serve relevant, individualized results, what displays for you may be different than what displays for me, even if we use the same search term.

## Knowing organic page rank factors

It's impossible to know all the factors that affect how you rank on SERPs. It's equally impossible to understand the weight of each factor in relation to page rank. We can, however, infer relative factor importance through testing and experimentation to make educated guesses, especially when it's performed by SEO industry pros.

In September 2014, David Mihm of Moz compiled a list of ranking factor correlations, compiled from 128 industry experts. Overall ranking factors for local SEO from that survey looked like this:

- ✔ **On-page signals:** A high website domain authority (a score, derived from search engine inferences of search engines' trust and strength of your website); the presence of name, address, and phone number (NAP); keyword in titles; and so on.

- ✔ **Link signals:** Inbound anchor text (keywords used in hyperlinks, signaling importance), including linking domain authority (quality) and the number (quantity) of linking domains.

- ✔ **External local signals:** Internet Yellow Pages (IYP) aggregator, name, address, and phone number consistency displaying across all local platforms (for instance, Yelp, Yahoo!, and Internet yellow pages).

- ✔ **Your business signals:** Blog categories, which make it easier for search engines to classify your content; keyword in business title ("ACME Roofers" when "roofers" is the keyword); proximity of literal keywords in your page copy compared to the actual long-tail term searched.

- ✔ **Review signals:** Online consumer review quantity, velocity (positive or negative trend), and diversity (number of sites on which your business has been reviewed).

- ✔ **Personalization:** Dynamic display of personalized information. In other, words, a website displaying custom content based on who you are or previous actions performed onsite.

- ✔ **Behavioral/mobile signals:** Click-through rate, mobile clicks-to-call (direct dialing from your mobile device), check-ins, offers, and so on.

- ✔ **Social signals:** Google+ authority, Facebook Likes, Twitter activity, and so on.

Figure 15-3 shows a graph from Moz displaying other correlating factors contributing to higher organic page rank.

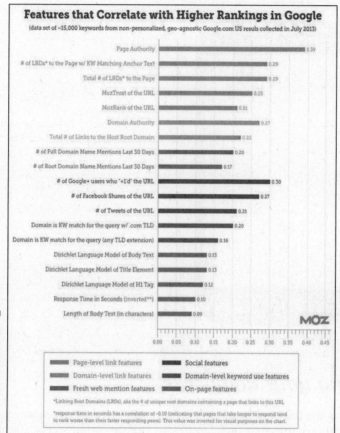

**Features that Correlate with Higher Rankings in Google**

(data set of ~15,000 keywords from non-personalized, geo-agnostic Google.com US results collected in July 2013)

| Feature | Value |
|---|---|
| Page Authority | 0.39 |
| # of LRDs* to the Page w/ KW Matching Anchor Text | 0.29 |
| Total # of LRDs* to the Page | 0.29 |
| MozTrust of the URL | 0.25 |
| MozRank of the URL | 0.21 |
| Domain Authority | 0.27 |
| Total # of Links to the Host Root Domain | 0.22 |
| # of Full Domain Name Mentions Last 30 Days | 0.20 |
| # of Root Domain Name Mentions Last 30 Days | 0.17 |
| # of Google+ users who "+1'd" the URL | 0.30 |
| # of Facebook Shares of the URL | 0.27 |
| # of Tweets of the URL | 0.21 |
| Domain is KW match for the query w/ .com TLD | 0.20 |
| Domain is KW match for the query (any TLD extension) | 0.16 |
| Dirichlet Language Model of Body Text | 0.13 |
| Dirichlet Language Model of Title Element | 0.13 |
| Dirichlet Language Model of H1 Tag | 0.12 |
| Response Time in Seconds (inverted**) | 0.10 |
| Length of Body Text (in characters) | 0.09 |

MOZ

Page-level link features
Domain-level link features
Fresh web mention features
Social features
Domain-level keyword use features
On-page features

*Linking Root Domains (LRDs), aka the # of unique root domains containing a page that links to this URL

**response time in seconds has a correlation of -0.10 (indicating that pages that take longer to respond tend to rank worse than their faster responding peers). This value was inverted for visual purposes on the chart.

**Figure 15-3:** Page-rank correlation factors, according to a Moz survey.

Brian Dean of Backlinko compiled a list of 200 ranking factors that is too long for this book, but is valuable and easily accessible (http://backlinko. com/google-ranking-factors). Remember, however, that these factors are constantly changing in weight of importance so the impact of one factor today may change significantly tomorrow.

Making your website mobile-friendly is increasingly important for Google, but you should be maintaining a mobile-friendly website anyway because of the ways today's consumers access the Internet. Quickly test your website with Google's Mobile-Friendly Test (www.google.com/webmasters/tools/ mobile-friendly). Simply type in your website URL and review your results. Figure 15-4 shows the result for my website.

**Figure 15-4:**
My results
on Google's
Mobile-
Friendly
Test.

## Using your keywords

Knowing the importance of keywords means knowing which words to target.
Keywords are the basis of SEO; after all, they are what you're attempting to
rank for. Search engine algorithms have evolved over time; whereas they
once "crawled" only the technical structure of your website, nowadays they
infer value from your visitors' onsite activities. So, proper structure and
keyword usage are important basics for SEO.

Using keywords for your content, for your on-page website targeting, and for
logical link building enhances your SEO. Eventually, you should rank higher
for the keywords you've targeted.

Make sure you're leading people to an authentic page that matches their
intent so that you're not penalized for "pogo-sticking" — that's when searchers click to a page and bounce right back to the SERP because they didn't
find what they were looking for.

Threading your targeted keywords throughout your inbound campaigns
is important for your SERP rankings. This requires using your keywords

technically for the search engines and naturally for your readers and future customers. (For more on using keywords, refer to Chapter 7.)

## Learning clickthrough rates (CTRs)

A click-through rate is simply the percentage of people who saw your listing, paid ad, social media link, or on-site CTA, and clicked on it. So, if you reached 100 people and 1 person clicked through to your website, your CTR is 1 percent. CTRs vary by source. Typically, I've found CTRs are higher from SEO than PPC (though visitor to lead conversions may be a higher percentage from PPC). Similarly, how high you rank affects the CTR, sometimes quite dramatically.

You can begin predicting your website traffic with a simple multiplication formula: Traffic = Search Volume × CTR by position

Problem is, which CTR do you use? Even the experts don't agree on what a particular page rank position's CTR will be. Keep in mind, also, that the SERPs themselves have changed. With the advent of Google's "carousel" results, it's a bit more difficult to define what exactly constitutes the number one position. The point is, use this data as a broad-based planning tool. Then, as you track progress in Google Webmaster tools and marketing automation software tools, you may formulate a better idea of which ranked keywords are driving visitors to your site.

# Optimizing for Organic Rankings

Google continues to be the search engine of choice in the U.S. Generally speaking, the tactics for ranking higher on Google apply to Bing/Yahoo! and to the other search engines as well. Hence, I don't differentiate among the various search engines in terms of optimization techniques.

## Optimizing technical SEO

Making your website visible is the most basic element of SEO. If the search engines can't find your website pages, or if they can find them but they have broken links, misdirected pages, or duplicate content, you'll be penalized in SERP rankings, or not even show up at all. Structure your website so that it's search-engine friendly — that is, so that it can be easily crawled by search engines in a clear, structured hierarchy. You can then begin on-page content optimization efforts.

Here are the steps you should follow to improve your technical SEO:

1. **Do a site:search to ensure Google has indexed your website.**

   First, make sure Google is indexing your site by performing a *site:search*. Simply type in *site:YourWebDomainHere.com* and press Enter. Figure 15-5 shows a site:search for my own website.

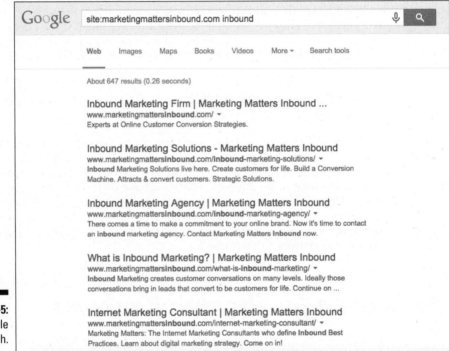

**Figure 15-5:**
An example
site:search.

2. **Check your page title URLs for correct structure.**

3. **Check for duplicate content and fix issues with 302 redirects and canonical tags (see your webmaster).**

   Set up your webmaster accounts for Google and Bing. If your website is new, submit a sitemap to Google to expedite the crawling process.

   If you don't feel comfortable doing this, contact a webmaster for help. Also, have your webmaster make Robots.txt files to tell the search engine spiders what not to crawl. Make sure that you have text-based navigation, and not JavaScript- or Flash-based navigation since the spiders can't crawl those.

4. **Always check your new content for plagiarism in a program like CopyScape (`www.copyscape.com`), especially when that content is created by outside content partners.**

5. **Test your site speed and make adjustments to decrease site load speed.**

   Sites that download quickly reduce visitor bounce rate while positively influencing your search engine ranking. Checking your speed is easy. Visit `https://developers.google.com/speed/pagespeed/insights` and type your URL into the bar then click Analyze. The resulting report displays your site speed score on a 100-point scale. Performing this quick test also displays the results of a User Experience test, also based on a 100-point scale.

   A 60 requires immediate action because you're probably being penalized due to poor site performance.

6. **Examine your server response time in Google Webmaster Tools and make appropriate adjustments to any "404 Not Found" errors. Check for the Crawl Errors Report and eliminate any problems listed there.**

   For other possible technical issues, log in to Google Webmaster Tools and check for any manual penalties that Google may have levied against your website. Lastly, while you're logged in to that tool, navigate to Health and click Crawl Errors to see any server errors. Here you'll find any of your pages that deny access and cause "404-Page Not Found" errors. Again, seek the help of a webmaster if this exceeds your technical capabilities.

## Going mobile

In 2014, mobile-device Internet access surpassed that of connected Internet devices for the first time. More people are connecting to the Internet with smartphones and tablets than with desktops. People are also connecting via alternative means like gaming consoles, smart TVs, and now smart watches and wristbands. Google responded accordingly. As of April 2015, in an algorithm change commonly referred to as "Mobilegeddon," Google elevated the importance of a website being mobile-friendly, including penalizing sites that aren't mobile-friendly.

So how mobile-friendly is your site? The process is simple. Go to the Google mobile-friendly tool (`https://www.google.com/webmasters/tools/mobile-friendly/`), type in your website URL, and click Analyze. Don't forget to make sure your landing pages are mobile-friendly, too. Checking your website's mobile-friendliness across all browsers is as easy as going to BrowserStack (`www.browserstack.com`) and typing in your URL. (You'll need to start a free trial, but it requires no credit card.)

## Ranking locally

Local business listings are an important consideration for small- and medium-sized businesses, especially business-to-consumer businesses.

Listing your business for local search is important because it:

- ✔ Increases your website's visibility
- ✔ Creates links to your website
- ✔ Generates website traffic and, eventually, business

According to a BIA/Kelsey study conducted with Constat, a full 97 percent of all shoppers use the Internet for local searches. Another survey discovered the following:

- ✔ 90 percent of local searchers use search engines
- ✔ 48 percent use online Yellow Pages (which also sometimes show up on SERPs)
- ✔ 42 percent use price-comparison websites
- ✔ 24 percent use vertical (scrolling) sites

So, shoppers are using local search. Factors affecting your local rankings include:

- ✔ Claiming your listings
- ✔ Performing localized SEO
- ✔ Optimizing local landing pages
- ✔ Monitoring and encouraging customer reviews

Claiming your local listings with the search engines is free, and it enhances your visibility on SERPs. You likely have listings on Google+ Local (formerly Google Places) and Yelp. If not, claim them right away. There is a checklist of other local listings to claim later in this chapter.

When considering local listings, the first step is claiming your listings. Here are the steps for local listings:

1. **Claim your listings.**

2. **Clean up data for accuracy.**

3. **Include business name, address, telephone number, and hours, using the information consistently across all local listings.**

4. **Upload photos and descriptions with keywords using alt tags for images and logos.**

5. **Distribute to data aggregators and direct to publisher.**

Because the majority of searches are on Google start claiming your local listing with Google My Business (`www.google.com/mybusiness`) and then Yahoo! (`https://smallbusiness.yahoo.com/localworks`). For about $30/month Yahoo! lists your business information consistently on over forty other local directory services. Then, consider listing locally with the sources listed in the checklist below.

Next, focus on your SEO by localizing title tags, on-page content, and meta-tags. Then create local landing pages for each of your locations, optimizing them for geography. Making your landing pages mobile friendly and including links to customer (like Google Places or Yahoo Local) and review pages helps your local SEO efforts.

Since local search is becoming more important to SEO, it makes sense to claim as many listings as you can for your company, especially if you're business-to-consumer. You can do this by visiting each of the sites below, or use the paid Yahoo! tool or the free Moz tool mentioned in Figure 15-3. Here's a checklist:

- Google+ Local
- Yahoo Local
- Bing
- Yelp
- Facebook
- LinkedIn
- Twitter
- Pinterest
- Foursquare
- Swarm
- Citysearch
- Yellowpages.com
- SuperPages
- Yellowbook
- Whitepages
- SuperMedia
- USYellowPages
- MapQuest
- MerchantCircle
- Etsy
- Biznik
- ThinkLocal
- Local.com

If you operate within a specific industry vertical, consider listing in appropriate directories and review sites. For instance, attorneys may consider FindLaw.com and plumbers may consider Angie's List. If you're a restaurant, gain presence on TripAdvisor and Urban Spoon. Research your own industry to see what's appropriate for your company.

## Optimizing content

You've learned that content is at the heart of inbound marketing. Generally speaking, from a search-engine perspective, your website pages should contain at least 250 words. A page with more than 500 words may signal more meaningful information to the search engines.

By focusing on one target keyword or keyword phrase per page, you provide consistency for your visitors and signal clearly to the search engines why your page exists. There are several factors to consider when optimizing your on-page content, including those listed below and those in the infographic from Moz shown in Figure 15-6.

Optimize your page title because it's the most important on-page SEO element and because it facilitates relevant search engine display and rank. Make sure you have your most important keyword in the title, placed toward the beginning. Use fewer than 70 characters in your title or the search engines will truncate its display. Use a unique title for each of your website pages.

Next optimize your meta-description. This is the information displayed that explains what a searcher will find by clicking on your result. While it may be a less important SEO ranking factor than in the past, writing your tags with clear, engaging, and directive copy will increase your CTR resulting in more visitors. Use fewer than 150 characters in your description.

Use the target keyword in your on-page headings, especially the main heading, known as an H1. If you're unable to use your keyword naturally, you've probably chosen a poor target keyword. Write the headline using the keyword so it appears natural to a reader. Again, make sure the headline is unique to your website. Feel free to include your target keyword in other headings (H2-H6) as well, though the SEO impact may be very little.

When you're writing body copy, incorporate the target keyword in the first paragraph and in the last paragraph. Aim for 500–1,000 words per page, though there are certainly exceptions to this rule, especially for navigation pages. Still, try to maintain at least 250 words on any given page. Write your copy with plenty of breaks, bullet points, and headlines so your reader can skim and easily digest the content, if he or she prefers. Don't go overboard; do not practice "keyword stuffing." There is no magic number for your keyword density percentage; however, pages with more words create opportunities for using the keyword more often at the same percentage of keyword density. A good rule is to create valuable content for the reader first and for search engines second. Using keywords makes sense for both objectives.

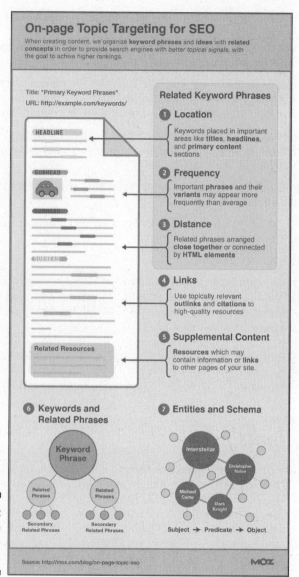

Source: http://moz.com/blog/on-page-topic-seo

**Figure 15-6:**
On-page topic target-ing for SEO.

Using images as content enhances the look, feel, design, and readability of your web pages. Creating visual interest is important to keeping visitors on your site. Because search engines can't interpret images, you have to inform the search engine about the content of the image by including an image tag. Additionally use your keywords in your alt text to populate the pop-up box visitors can read when hovering over an image with their mouse. Be descriptive so your visitor knows what the image is, even if it doesn't display properly.

To optimize your content, make sure you're doing all of the following:

- ✔ Optimize text content including your title tags, meta-descriptions, and page title URLs for each page using your target keyword.

- ✔ Optimize images with alt tags and title tags and file names, using your target keyword for the page on which they display. Make sure your image file size isn't so big that it slows your page download speed.

- ✔ Optimize videos using targeted keywords for title, description, and file name. Embed codes from YouTube and Vimeo so visitors can watch your videos on your website.

- ✔ Optimize your blog posts, using target keywords and linking to relevant content both on- and offsite.

- ✔ Make sure your pages have enough content to signal important, quality content.

- ✔ Include a privacy statement.

- ✔ If your physical address is important to your business, add your full address and contact information on your home page and your regular website pages to enhance your local SEO. Adding a map on your "Contact Us" page contributes, too.

 If you're using WordPress, consider using a plug-in like WordPress SEO by Yoast (www.yoast.com), which makes it easy to check your content to ensure it's SEO-friendly.

## Building links

Building links may be the biggest contributor to enhancing your SEO efforts, but it can also be damaging to your rankings when not performed correctly. Link building is also the most difficult SEO tactic, requiring time and effort. Link building is most valuable when done naturally, by creating and distributing high-quality content. Search engines view links to your website as signs of credibility, trust, and authority, so higher-quality links from trusted domains have more value than the spammy link farms of yesteryear, which now only penalize you.

To start building links, follow these steps:

1. **Check inbound links to your website.**

   Check the number of links to your home page by typing *link:YourDomainName.com* in the Google search bar. (Note that the omission of the "www" provides broader results.)

2. **Check Google Webmaster Tools for a more comprehensive list of links to your site.**

**3. Check competitors' websites, discovering their inbound links.**

Check your competitors to see who is linking to their website. Here are some tools for checking competitor links:

- Ahrefs (www.ahrefs.com)
- Majestic SEO (www.majestic.com/reports/compare-domain-backlink-history)
- Link Diagnosis (www.linkdiagnosis.com)
- Open Site Explorer (www.moz.com/researchtools/ose)

**4. Create valuable, relevant content and distribute it on social media platforms and via influencers.**

Because links are essentially connections to your content, focus on links that make sense based on your inbound content strategy. Create interesting, shareable infographics and distribute that content to influencers more likely to share, creating valid, authentic links to your website.

Distribute valuable content links on your social media platforms and make that content interesting enough to be shared. Neil Patel, co-founder of KISSMetrics, Crazy Egg, and Quick Sprout, suggests the following six tactics:

- Post links to your article on every social network of which you are a member.
- Post your link to relevant LinkedIn groups that you're a member of.
- Submit your posts to Reddit.
- Submit your posts to StumbleUpon.
- Submit your posts to GrowthHackers.com.
- Send DMs to people whom you mention or link to in your post.

**5. Use guest blogging as a method to garner links.**

Building links through guest blogging on credible, authentic websites requires tactics similar to old-fashioned public relations efforts. Same goes for garnering links from conducting interviews.

**6. Create "natural" links, that is, links that are not attempting to manipulate the search engines.**

Remember, the reason you're building links is so people can find your site. Don't perform link building solely for the sake of building links. Instead, use links to build bridges between people and your website.

Setting forth a plan requires:

- ✔ Identifying influencers whose websites demonstrate high quality and authority
- ✔ Regularly creating and distributing quality content to those sources

✔ Reaching out to key influencers to share your content individually

✔ Building and fostering influencer communication and trust

✔ Focusing on generating great content first; backlinks will follow

## Sending social signals

Earlier you learned the importance of claiming your company pages. Building and maintaining company pages on social media networks enable consumer communication. Creating profiles on social media platforms helps your SEO efforts, too. Additionally, search engines may use the interactions of people with your social sites as social signals. To what degree search engines use this data is debatable. These social signals may contribute to your SEO because search engines view a high degree of interaction as a relationship and increased interaction as higher relevance. Then again, they may not. Google does index the links from social sites, so there is some SEO effect, even if very minor. Perhaps the greatest benefit is sharing content that is picked up and shared by an influencer who links to your content, creating an indirect benefit.

Some of the social signals I'm talking about include:

✔ Facebook Llikes and shares

✔ Twitter retweets

✔ LinkedIn posts and shares

✔ YouTube views

✔ Pinterest pins

✔ Google +1s

Time will tell whether or not social signals factor into your rankings and to what degree they do so. In the meantime, practice proper social media engagement by distributing valuable, consumable content that your readers love. By doing so, you're achieving your real goal, which is consumer engagement. If it happens to benefit your SEO efforts, that's a great bonus for you and your rankings.

## Things You Can Do Now

✔ Analyze your organic traffic by testing with free online tools.

✔ Check to ensure your website is responsive or mobile-friendly.

✔ Track your organic ranking history of your most important keywords.

# Chapter 16

# Attracting Visitors with Paid Search

*Y*our attraction factor is comprised of earned media, owned media, and paid media inputs. This chapter covers the basics of paid digital media, including Google and Bing/Yahoo! PPC. The purpose of this chapter is to develop an appreciation of paid digital media as an integral component to your inbound marketing strategy.

Some inbound campaigns do not need paid media; some do. Paid media, however, should at least be considered as part of your overall attraction efforts. Otherwise, you ignore a significant portion of your potential leads and possibly motivated buyers as well. At the two marketing firms I've owned, we've managed paid search campaigns ranging from $2,000/month to $500,000/month, even though one of the firms was founded on pure SEO. Why? Because paid search *works*. It contributes to your attraction factor, including increases in leads, customers, and a measurable positive ROI. In most cases, those paid search campaigns should be coordinated with other inbound marketing attraction inputs, like social media and SEO. Maybe paid search will work for you, too. This chapter shows you how. . .

# Rescuing the Reputation of PPC

Some inbound marketing purists dismiss paid digital media and PPC as somehow not being part of the inbound process. These practitioners draw a line between inbound marketing and paid search, treating them as two different disciplines entirely. I disagree.

Inbound marketing does not exist in a vacuum. Rather, as you've learned, it operates in a dynamic, fluid digital reality. Inbound marketing is a holistic system of connected parts. Still, a Marketing Sherpa study reports that only 48 percent of marketing professionals consider PPC a major part of their digital marketing tactics. Paid media is one of the attraction parts of inbound marketing and ignoring its contribution as a lead generation input is like ignoring Friday as a day of the week.

Paid media now often appear in your social media streams with ad content that's more relevant to users than their search-engine results. Your ad content for paid digital media should follow the same content guidelines as the content on your earned and owned media. Create your ads so they are timely, contextual, and, most importantly with paid search, relevant.

## Using paid media for attraction

Paid search is an input for your attraction factor. As such, it operates under your inbound attraction strategy. So, when is it appropriate to use paid search as part of your attraction efforts? Paid digital media makes sense when:

- ✔ You need to generate leads quickly.
- ✔ You want to bridge the time to rank organically with a supplemental lead generation source.
- ✔ You have specific target keywords whose difficulty makes it nearly impossible to rank on SERPs.
- ✔ Most of your target keywords are non-branded terms (not to imply that you don't buy branded terms. You do.).
- ✔ You want to test keyword conversions as part of your SEO strategy.
- ✔ Your ROI projections and results from paid search are financially beneficial.

Attracting visitors and leads through paid search is part of a holistic inbound marketing plan. The percentage of the total digital spend you invest on paid media depends on your company, your budget, and your business goals and objectives. Like all digital marketing attraction factors, you have to sift through the data and dig deeper, seeking information from multiple sources, including your own historical performance data.

# Learning paid search metrics

Whether you're measuring Google AdWords campaign or your Facebook display campaign, there are some basic measurement terms with which you should be familiar. As with everything inbound, it's best to examine these metrics holistically and interactively. No one metric tells the entire story of your customer's purchase path, which is usually a meandering cross-channel exercise in researching, shopping, and buying experience over time.

### Cost-per-thousand (CPM)

CPM is a hangover measurement from traditional media when detailed metrics further down the customer conversion paths simply didn't exist. CPM is a consumer awareness metric that measures your efficiency in reaching a particular audience via any given media vehicle. It is useful in comparing different media's efficiency in reaching people; however, it is far removed from any end action performed by a customer. As such, use it sparingly and only as a planning tool. Buying digital media off the impressions metric rarely makes sense.

### Click-through rates (CTRs)

CTR is simply the percentage of people who click on an ad as compared to how many times your ad was shown. It is expressed as (Clicks/ Impressions = CTR).

Figure 16-1 displays the CTRs by digital medium and by device. *CTR is not necessarily just a measurement of efficiency*, especially when considering PPC on Google and Bing/Yahoo! search results. Your ad's search position also affects your CTR (see Figure 16-2).

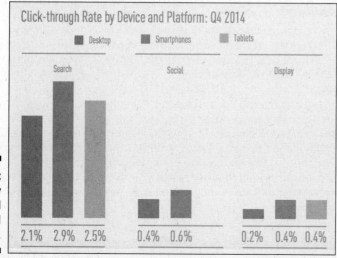

**Figure 16-1:** CTR by digital medium and device.

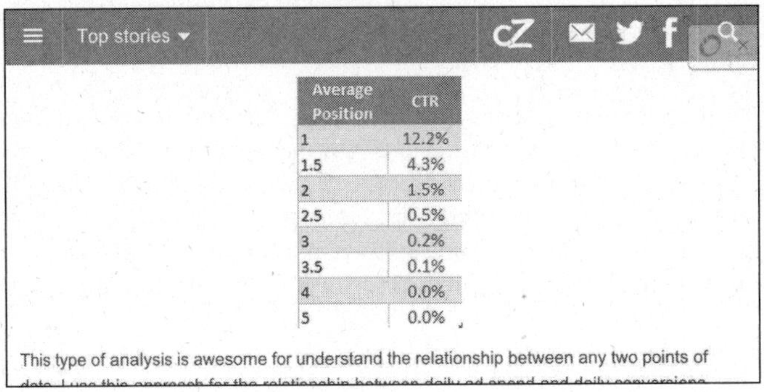

| Average Position | CTR |
|---|---|
| 1 | 12.2% |
| 1.5 | 4.3% |
| 2 | 1.5% |
| 2.5 | 0.5% |
| 3 | 0.2% |
| 3.5 | 0.1% |
| 4 | 0.0% |
| 5 | 0.0% |

This type of analysis is awesome for understand the relationship between any two points of

**Figure 16-2:** CTR by search position.

Other factors influencing your CTR are:

✔ Relevancy of your ad to the search result

✔ Niche industries with a relatively small total number of prospective customers

✔ Seasonality

✔ Day of week or time of day

✔ Buyer persona's propensity to click paid ads (higher with older demographics)

✔ Branded search as opposed to non-branded search

When projecting numbers for your Customer Conversion Chain, using your historical CTRs is a good place to start, then begin working on improving your CTR by segmenting the high-performing CTR channels and applying to your other inbound campaigns the known factors positively influencing your CTR.

### Conversion rates

*Conversion rate* is usually defined as the percentage of people who completed your desired action. In the broadest sense, conversion rate is the percentage of unique visitors who became customers. Figure 16-3 displays conversion rates by digital platform and device.

If you must set an overall conversion rate benchmark, first look at your historical data to set percentage increases from your current baseline conversion rate and work those into your Customer Conversion Chain model. If you don't have good historical data and insist on using a benchmark, target a 2 percent overall conversion rate objective and once you hit that, take it as high as you possibly can. In most cases, you shouldn't fall below an aggregate 1 percent conversion rate, but even that may be un-obtainable in many B2B business models.

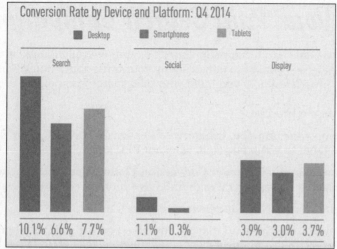

**Figure 16-3:**
Conversion
rate by
platform and
device.

## Cost-per-click (CPC)

CPC is the price you pay each time someone clicks on your ad, whether it's a display ad on a social media platform or search results on Bing or Google. Figure 16-4 displays CPC by digital platform and device.

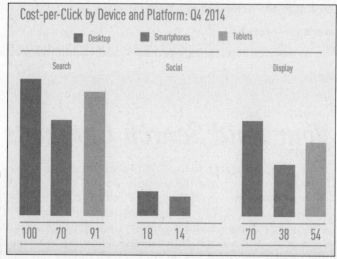

**Figure 16-4:**
CPC By
platform and
device.

# Building Your Paid Search Campaigns

Building a paid search campaign as part of your overall inbound market-ing campaigns is similar to constructing your other attraction components. Here's a process to help you build your paid search campaigns:

1. **Choose a product.**
2. **Group your targeted, categorized keywords into PPC campaigns and use them to write targeted, relevant PPC ads.**
3. **Hypothesize a Customer Conversion Chain from click to action, and include a target objective defined as a monetized end action.**
4. **Write custom text ads relevant to search terms.**
5. **Design attractive paid display ads based on the paid medium and the product you're featuring.**
6. **Create specific ad groups for targeted text PPC on search engines and for your product photo ads on Product Listing Ads (Google).**
7. **Link your ad groups to very specific landing pages based on the "4 P's of Inbound Marketing."**
8. **Connect your landing pages with an inbound campaign.**
9. **Monitor your PPC campaigns closely — as closely as you'd monitor a toddler near the deep end of a pool.**
10. **Measure your results.**
11. **Refine by testing, replicating successes, and eliminating failures.**
12. **Repeat.**

# Knowing Your Paid Search Channels

Looking at the great big search picture, paid search garners a mere 6 percent of total clicks. When you narrow the scope down to a typical SERP, the research numbers vary; however, it appears that click percentage for PPC to organic results on a typical SERP is approximately one click for PPC for every five clicks from organic results. Interestingly, a study by Catalyst Marketing Group published in 2014 notes that five of six clicks on a SERP occur on the area that immediately displays on your screen (above the "fold"). WordStream, a PPC software provider, published a report in 2012 stating that for keywords with high commercial intent (motivated buyers), searchers in the U.S. clicked on paid results at almost a two-to-one ratio over organic results. Bottom line: There's a lot of conflicting data out there that may or may not apply to your unique situation. Use the information as a loose guide, testing and retesting the ideal balance of digital media mix for *your* company.

# Setting up campaigns in Google and Bing/Yahoo!

Regardless of whether you're using Google or Bing/Yahoo! (the platforms are commonly bought together as one PPC campaign), planning your PPC campaign is the same:

1. **Define your business objective.**

   This should be easy if you've performed your diagnostic assessment, prescriptive strategy, and designed your inbound campaigns. Your PPC is an attraction tactic, so connecting to a specific campaign should be as simple as connecting any other attraction factor. If it's not, you're probably starting in the wrong place (such as using PPC as a quick fix to drive traffic rather than as an attraction input for your Customer Conversion Chain).

2. **Identify the people you wish to connect with your product.**

   Using your persona research, identify your most likely buyers and research further where they're consuming information and shopping online.

3. **Use your keywords.**

   You performed keyword research for a reason. Because keywords are stated consumer needs, it's easy to categorize and assign keywords based on your target persona's place in the purchase path. Load all your categorized keywords, and initiate your campaign closer to the action point (sale) in the Lifestyle Loop. Doing so with language suitable for the encouragement stage should increase your ROI while reducing the time to purchase.

4. **Write compelling ads.**

   Google uses Quality Score to grade your ads. Because Quality Score acts as a multiplier, a better score reduces your bid amount to rank higher. Why? Because Google wants to create the same thing for their organic and paid results as you do with your inbound content . . . relevancy.

5. **Connect your ads to relevant, contextual landing pages.**

   Use the landing page best practices I outline in Chapter 21 to create consistent messaging and comfort for people journeying toward purchasing.

6. **Test and monitor performance, detecting which keywords are attracting and which keywords should be taken out of your campaigns.**

   Don't forget to install tracking codes for your PPC campaigns. By tracking PPC keywords and campaigns, you may expand upon hardworking keywords by investigating long-tail forms. Add in negative keywords to specifically exclude words driving unqualified people. Invest more in the keywords that are driving quality traffic and less for those keywords that don't.

7. **Measure and report.**

   Look beyond PPC by comparing your paid efforts with your other inbound marketing attraction inputs like SEO and social media. Measure how PPC contributes to your overall attraction and conversion and measure how efficiently it achieves each of these objectives.

## Organizing your paid search campaigns

When organizing your paid search campaign, it makes sense to integrate your inbound diagnosis and strategy into the process. Your inbound campaign flows and the segmented keywords associated with different entry points facilitate the easy setup of your PPC campaigns. The process is similar for Google and Bing; they just use a different language. Google's campaign wizard is easy to follow, and Bing allows you to import your data from Google. The following steps show you how to organize your PPC campaigns in Google:

1. **Use your keyword categorization study to populate ad groups. Each of your ad groups should be based on the "4 P's of Inbound Marketing."**

2. **Create a campaign in Google AdWords (`www.adwords.google.com`). Each account may have up to 10,000 different campaigns associated with it.**

3. **Associate your ad groups with your newly created campaign. Each campaign can have up to 20,000 ad groups.**

4. **Write PPC text ads according to best practices (see the section, "Creating great PPC ads," later in this chapter).**

   Write as many ads as it takes to be relevant to each AdWord group. In some cases, you may have a slightly different ad for each keyword in order to provide relevancy. Google will need to approve your ads before the campaign launches which usually takes 24–48 hours maximum.

5. **Set your budgets by assigning a daily budget for each ad group and by inputting bids on individual keywords.**

6. **Choose settings for distribution of your messaging including geography, languages, and where in the Google Network you wish your advertising to be displayed.**

7. **Turn your campaign on, preferably starting with a single, most promising bottom-of-the funnel ad group first and rolling out your campaign slowly.**

8. **Monitor and adjust keyword performance in AdWords by drilling down to keyword status.**

## Creating great PPC ads

You don't just write great PPC ads to be fun and clever. Writing great ads generates better CTRs at a lower cost. Google grades your ad copy with a Quality Score. There is a simple formula for this:

Ad Rank = CPC Bid * Quality Score

A better Quality Score achieves much for your paid inbound attraction, including:

✔ Higher ranking in results.

✔ Higher CTRs, creating more unique visitors and more lead opportunities.

✔ Lower CPCs so you can generate traffic more efficiently, reinvesting the difference for increased PPC campaign exposure.

✔ Lower CPA because you've influenced activity all the way down the Customer Conversion Chain.

Figure 16-5 is another WordStream graphic demonstrating how a higher quality score creates a more efficient CPC through a combination of ranking higher and paying less for each click. Why would Google do this? Quality Score is related to Google's algorithm defining relevance. The more relevant your ad to the searcher, the more it will be displayed, even if it's at a lower CPC. Relevant content is important.

**Figure 16-5:**
Effect of
Quality
Score on
CPC.

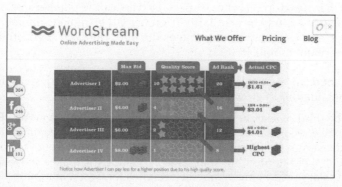

### Writing a great PPC Ad

Looking to mirror those high CTRs and low CPCs of the top performing paid search accounts? Keep it simple. Don't overthink and don't be too cute. Include the following when writing a PPC ad for search engine paid search:

- ✔ **Relevant headline:** You have a 25-character limit for headlines, so make every word count. Use your targeted keyword in your headline so the searcher and search engines recognize your ad as relevant.

- ✔ **Description:** Your description text is two lines, each consisting of a maximum of 35 characters. Be concise, use keywords (keywords appear in boldface when they're the search term being used), be specific, and include a (very) short CTA wording in your copy, such as "Order now."

- ✔ **URL:** Direct the featured link in your ad to the URL of a relevant landing page specific to the offer and campaign. For instance, if your CTA is "Order now" do not send your visitor to your home page. Instead, link to a purchase page featuring the product and a shopping cart.

Great ads create great results because they satisfy customers and search engines. Happy ad writing!

### Creating paid listing ads

*Paid listing ads (PLA)* are product image ads on Google. PLAs are a great option for e-commerce sites to promote product-specific marketing. The corresponding product for Bing is their Merchant store, which enables you to upload products and connect with a paid search campaign. The bidding process is similar to that of your regular PPC advertising; however, your CTR and conversion rates should be higher because people are searching at the shopping phase of the purchase path.

### Using mobile for PPC

Mobile searches now make up over half of all Internet searches, surpassing desktop searches for the first time ever in 2014. CTR rates may be higher than desktop searches, especially true for the number one position. According to a study by seoClarity (October 2014), ranking number one in mobile searches results in three times the CTR. Here are some other interesting facts about mobile PPC:

- ✔ 33 percent of Google searches originate from mobile devices. Expect that number to grow.

- ✔ One-third of searches are local searches conducive to mobile PPC. A Google study states that 78 percent of local searches on mobile devices move on to make a purchase offline. Although these conversions are difficult if not impossible to measure, this statistic makes sense when you consider the volume of mobile searches for, say, restaurants.

✔ Mobile searchers are more likely to click on an ad with a phone number; they have up to a 70 percent click-to-call rate.

✔ Including a click-to-call option with tracking helps accurately track mobile conversions.

✔ Mobile PPC searchers are three times more likely to convert. I believe this is for three reasons, two of them good:

- Mobile searchers are closer to performing an action at the bottom of the funnel, so encouragement messaging results in conversions.

- Mobile provides timeliness through immediacy. A searcher doesn't have to think to connect. They simply need to click right at the tipping point from shopping to buying.

- "Fat thumb syndrome": Your searcher didn't mean to click, but that screen is so damn small compared to the size of the average person's thumb. This is the negative reason because it is an accidental click, resulting in a bounce.

## Using paid search on social platforms

Social media engagement expands well beyond organic conversations. Each of the major social media platforms have increasingly added paid advertising into their business models, which means you may now expand your paid search efforts beyond the search engines onto social media platforms. Some of these, like Facebook and Twitter, are relatively affordable. Others choose to limit advertiser access to brands with huge budgets, like Instagram whose introductory ad pricing entry point listed hundreds of thousands of dollars. When purchasing paid advertising in a social environment, it is even more important to appreciate context so you don't inadvertently upset the delicate balance of social communications and obnoxiously intrusive sales messaging. Because paid social-media-user demographics are so easy to segment, you may now reach a highly targeted, highly responsive audience with a highly relevant and highly contextual message. You may pay more for CPCs, but if you have targeted the correct audience, your conversion rate should increase.

The following list offers some advice about paid search on the most popular social-media platforms:

✔ **Facebook (www.facebook.com/business/):** Facebook has developed the most comprehensive, helpful advertising guide of all the social media paid platforms. It's a particularly useful platform for business-to-consumer companies. Your ability to create campaigns based on your objectives is coupled with targeting ability based on demographics, geographic and psychographic. Using your customer list, enables you to privately and securely cross-tabulate that information with FB users, targeting current customers for messaging or excluding current customers for specific new promotional offers.

Facebook's advertising platform offers highly targeted advertising campaigns ripe for consumer interactivity, provided you create engaging content.

Facebook Marketplace ads appear on the side column of the Facebook news feed, much like a banner ad (See Figure 16-6).

**Figure 16-6:**
Facebook
advertising
options.

You may also advertise in desktop and mobile FB newsfeeds.

A promoted post is a way to promote your Facebook page to your FB fans and friends of fans, allowing you to reach more people than if you simply posted in your regular feed. This is kind of a "birds of a feather" mentality.

Sponsored stories appear in your FB feed, simply showing a person's interaction with your brand to their friends and a larger group of FB users. This is a good tactic to implement when you've created a mini-campaign directed towards your Lifestylers because they are, by definition, positive influencers for your brand.

Facebook Exchange (FBX) is a form of retargeting. FBX tracks a person's browsing so you can serve up a product an individual viewed previously on your website.

✔ **Twitter (www.ads.twitter.com):** Depending on your advertising's aim, there are a few ways to use Twitter for paid promotion including:

  • *Promoted Tweets* is a paid method to expand your reach into additional people's feeds.

- *Promoted Accounts* is an option if you're actively using Twitter and want to expand your Follower base. Using Promoted Accounts increases your frequency of populating "Who to Follow" in people's Twitter accounts, so it's a way to build your Follower base.

- *Promoted Trends* is a Twitter amplification mechanism. You create a custom hashtag (`#InboundMarketingForDummies` is probably too long), and it's featured in the hashtag trends bar. The aim here is to increase awareness and retweets to expand your message.

✓ **YouTube** (`www.youtube.com/yt/advertise/`): YouTube is part of the Google marketing network. YouTube is all about videos; it offers paid solutions for both video and banner content. Other YouTube options include:

- *In-Stream:* YouTube In-Stream features your 30-second video as pre-roll before people view their desired video (see Figure 16-7), so it's a bit more like disruptive traditional advertising unless you planned a highly targeted campaign with contextual video. Applying a URL overlay with links to your mobile site or your brand's YouTube channel increases consumer interactivity, and you only pay when people watch.

**Figure 16-7:** An example of YouTube 30-second ad.

- *Display Ads:* You can pay per impression or pay-per-click with display ads. Display ads are a more typical branding banner ad, but it's clickable to your website or relevant video from your company. Targeting by demographic, topic, or geography creates context. In-video overlays your messaging directly over the video being viewed, providing another option to display ads.

- *YouTube Mobile:* Banner ads and mobile page roadblocks to reach mobile users. Another option is mobile in-stream video ads, featuring your :15-second video.

- *YouTube Home Page Road Block:* With a rate card price of around $500,000, you can "roadblock" YouTube's home page, meaning you're the only advertiser featured for 24 hours, reaching the 70M visitors to YouTube's home page. Obviously, this is an option only for multinational brands and enterprise-level advertisers.

✔ **Pinterest (`http://help.pinterest.com/en/articles/how-to-promote-a-pin`):** Pinterest introduced paid CPC advertising in 2014 with Promoted Pins. What I like about Pinterest's philosophy is their desire to limit traditional billboard-type messaging, preferring contextual messaging instead. Bought Pins is currently only available to a few select advertisers; however, expect it to be rolled out more fully in the future.

✔ **Tumblr (`www.tumblr.com/business`):** You can advertise on Tumblr's "Radar" for a minimum rate of $25,000. Advertising with sponsored blogs, sponsored posts, and sponsored videos complete your advertising options for Tumblr.

✔ **Instagram (`http://business.instagram.com/advertising`):** Instagram features sponsored posts and a carousel advertising feature, allowing up to four images and a link.

✔ **BuzzFeed (`www.buzzfeed.com/advertise`):** Advertise on sponsored content, choosing from several options of contextual ad and video content.

## Paid display

Paid display advertising is a visual ad, much like a newspaper or magazine ad (but smaller and simpler), that displays digital across content networks. Paid display advertising is more akin to traditional advertising and it's often purchased much like you would purchase newspaper or magazine advertising. This often means purchasing on a CPM basis. Paid display is best for brand advertising, though providing clickthrough opportunities is key to the inbound measurement process. Click-through rates are much lower than other digital forms of advertising so, if you choose to use paid display beyond branding use the following guidelines:

✔ Create a simple action-oriented headline.

✔ Describe the payoff benefit for clicking.

✔ Make your ad clickable with a well-designed CTA.

✔ Use tracking codes to measure CTR and conversion rates as compared to your other inbound marketing attraction factors.

Paid display advertising may take on several different forms. Here are a couple variations of paid display advertising:

✔ **Portal roadblocks:** If you're a large brand with a large budget, road blocking a major platform's portal creates immense reach. It's also expensive, often costing hundreds of thousands of dollars for road blocking on sites like AOL or *Forbes* magazine (not included in Google's ad network). The fact is, most of you won't use road blocking unless you work for a company with extremely large digital ad budgets or you discover targeted niche sites whose visitors match your target personas.

✔ **Banner ads:** Paid banner ads display image-based advertising on the top, bottom, or side of a page. CTRs are lower than other targeted digital marketing tactics so track carefully when including banner ads into your attraction mix. Banner ads *might* make sense if you're planning to reach very specific, targeted niche customer groups. You're achieving context and relevance, but they're probably not the best place for you to start your paid attraction for inbound marketing.

Google Display network distributes your ads across a vast content network including Google-owned YouTube, Gmail, and Blogger. Ads may be text and video in addition to image-based display ads.

## Retargeting

Retargeting is different than remarketing. In fact, it may be your most efficient means of paid customer engagement. Because retargeting means communicating with your previous website visitors, it exploits the visitor's familiarity with your company, which, more often than not, makes it easier to reattract. True, some visitors exited your site because they didn't find what they wanted. But a certain percentage of your visitors are qualified and not yet ready to buy. Retargeting with links to engagement and education content loops visitors back into the purchase path.

Figure 16-8 is an example of a Facebook retargeted ad from Hotels.com. The ad populated my feed after I had searched for hotels in Antigua, Guatemala (relevant). In fact, the ad displays one of the hotels I had recently researched (timely), offering an encouragement CTA to "Book Now."

**Figure 16-8:**
A Facebook
retargeting
example.

Retargeting is fairly simple to set up in Google AdWords. You may choose to retarget all visitors or just visitors to a specific website page. Make sure you follow the inbound content rules, creating meaningful communications in the process. In addition to Google and Bing retargeting, check out the following companies (listed alphabetically) who perform retargeting:

- AdRoll (www.adroll.com)
- Chango (www.chango.com)
- ReTargeter (www.retargeter.com)

Don't forget to track your retargeting campaigns with Universal Event Tags (UET) to measure your results, comparing them to your other attraction inputs.

## Things You Can Do Now

- Analyze your past PPC campaigns by applying your historical Customer Conversion Chain metrics.
- Build your new PPC campaign based on your categorized keyword research.
- Build your new paid social campaign based on your categorized keyword research.

# Chapter 17

# Attracting Visitors with Social Media Sharing

*W*ith over two billion activated accounts worldwide, social media is the modern means by which people connect. Whether its Facebook, Twitter, or LinkedIn, social media has revolutionized the way we communicate. Social media platforms make it easy for people to find a date, share restaurant recommendations, and collaborate to plan a vacation. For business-to-consumer companies, social media platforms enable businesses to connect with people on a deeper, more meaningful level. Participating in social media engages your company with people based on lifestyle, creating brand connections on an emotional level. But social media isn't just for business-to-consumer companies. Business-to-business companies benefit from social media networking, too. This chapter examines social media as a contributing factor in your inbound attraction efforts

## Learning the Benefits of Social Media

Now that you've produced your content, it's time to share it with others and attract people to your company. Social media is a great place to share. The benefits of incorporating social media into your inbound marketing plan include:

✔ It increases your company's prospects and offers customer engagement with two-way communications.

✔ It cements customer loyalty.

- ✔ It improves brand interaction at every point in the Lifestyle Loop customer purchase path.
- ✔ It increases your traffic and the number of leads, using content to attract.
- ✔ It improves customer service.
- ✔ It improves your organic search-engine rankings.
- ✔ It provides consumer trend insights.
- ✔ It grows business partnerships.

Knowing your target personas makes it easier to understand which social media platforms they are most likely to use. For example, Pinterest participation is flooded with younger females, and LinkedIn is an obvious platform for any business-to-business company.

By sharing links to your content on social media to create easily accessible avenues, you'll attract more visitors. You're helping people arrive at a relevant, comfortable place by building social media "homes" and stimulating conversations and content sharing with these social media platforms. That helps increase onsite conversions.

But social media can be a dangerous game of wasted time and energy if you're not careful. To the corporate "suits" it may sometimes seem like social media is a game. Trust me, your customers don't view it as a game. People may rant and rave about your company, and if you're not listening and responding to conversations on social media, you're not fully playing the game of *business*.

From a marketing standpoint, social media may be used for quite a few purposes, including:

- ✔ Content sharing
- ✔ Thought leadership
- ✔ Lead generation
- ✔ Meaningful brand interaction
- ✔ Surveys
- ✔ Customer reviews
- ✔ Customer service
- ✔ Reputation monitoring and enhancement

If you're considering social media purely as a sales mechanism, however, you may want to reconsider. According to Experience: The Blog, fewer than 0.25 percent of the customers of "prestige" brands were acquired from Facebook and fewer than 0.01 percent from Twitter. Having said that, Social Media Examiner's (`www.socialmediaexaminer.com`) 2015 Social Media Marketing Industry Report states that 51 percent of experienced social media marketers report improved sales from social media. That number jumps to 73 percent for companies who invest more than six hours per week. I suggest you manage your expectations accordingly. Although your company may want to use social media to sell directly, more often it is better for communicating at the education level, linking to engagement content or reengaging customers and Lifestylers.

In most cases, it's hard to draw a direct correlation between your social media and the end customer action, especially if you're not using marketing automation software. This problem compounds when marketers view social media purely as a reach medium rather than as an engagement mechanism. But social-media metrics and rewards are mostly based around sharing information and rewarding good content with Likes, shares, pins, and retweets. Bridging that gap requires direct links to content so you can accurately track sourcing and measure social media against your other attraction inputs.

## Attracting visitors to your website

The goal of social media marketing is consumer and customer engagement through attraction and reattraction. Creating connective content and sharing that content in the proper contextual social media settings encourages consumer dialogue. As an inbound marketer, you engage by creating online relationships. By creating an online relationship that results in an end-of-the funnel action, you are using social media to successfully complete the first major conversion path of the Lifestyle Loop.

## Creating off-site visibility

Social media occurs off-site. Often, social media leans toward modern-day branding because it is often a long distance from the desired action — a sale. This is as true for the business-to-consumer global brand creating a cute, shareable video as it is for the business-to-business company demonstrating thought leadership by posting blogs and comments on LinkedIn. It doesn't have to be this way. You can move your social media messaging further down the customer purchase path. Building alternative connective platforms like a Facebook page, a Google+ page or hangout, or a LinkedIn forum creates alternative ways to engage.

# *Matching Your Message with the Medium*

Matching your content message with social media platforms just makes sense. It's contextual content marketing. With some content distribution channels, it's easy to make this match because the medium is the message. For example, when you produce video, you're probably going to post it on YouTube and Vimeo. But the distribution path isn't always so clear. Video uploads on Facebook now surpass video uploads on YouTube. Be creative in the types of content you share and always build links to your content and make your content shareable.

Over time, measure sources of social media visitors, and where those leads, customers, and repeat customers enter your website. You use this data to make better decisions about where to promote your content on social media. If you discover that you generated 100 visits from Twitter and only three from LinkedIn, you can promote more on Twitter to increase visits. If, however, you learn that all three LinkedIn visitors became customers and 0/100 of your Twitter visitors became customers, you may reconsider. Creating source reporting is imperative for accurate inbound reporting. The best option for this is a comprehensive marketing automation software tool because it automates the reporting for you. Alternatively, you can cobble together your own reporting system by attaching tracking codes (ask your developer) and combining manual reports with any automated reporting to which you have access.

In this case, using a free service like Bitly (`https://bitly.com`), create short links for your content. Make sure you create different short links for each social medium, even if it's for the same content, so you can track which platforms are driving the most engagement.

By attaching metrics to your messaging, you:

- ✓ Easily determine sources of your social media traffic
- ✓ Identify which traffic is most qualified
- ✓ Know which of your social media is best at attracting and converting
- ✓ Understand what types of content resonate with your target persona

Twitter is limited to 140 characters (120-125 if you want to leave room for effective retweets) so on that platform you'd better keep things short and simple. People on Facebook share everything from their kid's graduation picture to the taco they had for lunch. In addition to being an online networking medium, LinkedIn is a wealth of business information shared through posts and industry-specific forums. Each social medium serves a purpose. Effective social media attraction means knowing which platform(s) your prospective customers and clients are using, participating in those media by sharing valuable content and creating meaningful messages adopted to the social media platform on which you're sharing. (In other words, don't share your taco on LinkedIn!)

# Building a Following on Social Media

Social media is about engagement and sharing. It can be a tool for engagement, or it can be a deep distraction. Engaging on social media requires people on your end to have real conversations. Still, the 2015 Social Media Marketing Industry Report, which included some enterprise-level marketers, shows that only five percent of companies spend more than 40 hours per week on social media. So even though social media is potentially a very powerful tool for sales and customer service, consider carefully the amount of time, energy, and money you're willing to invest. Here's a basic guide:

- ✔ **Small companies:** You're the owner, so you're responsible for everything, including marketing:

  - • If you are a business-to-consumer company, use Facebook. Consider promoting your content that links to your Facebook page or blog posts.

  - • If you're a business-to-business company, use LinkedIn. Consider posting content that links to your website.

- ✔ **Medium companies:** You're a small marketing team. Maybe you're the sole marketing employee:

  - • If you are business-to-consumer, use Facebook and Twitter or Pinterest. Consider using posts to link to your website from these sources and YouTube, if you feature video. Add in one additional social media platform only if you have time to dedicate to engagement.

  - • If you are business-to-business, use LinkedIn and Twitter and Google+. Consider sharing information in industry forums and when permitted using those forums and other sources like SlideShare to link to your website content. Add in one additional social media platform only if you have time to dedicate to engagement.

✔ **Enterprise-level companies:** You have a large marketing team with at least one person devoted to social media:

- • If you are a business-to-consumer company, use Facebook, Twitter, Pinterest, YouTube, and interactive customer portals. Consider additional social media platforms based on your content strategy. Also, consider building your own branded interactive customer-centric online social media platform.

- • If you are a business-to-business company, use LinkedIn, Twitter, Google+, SlideShare, and industry forums to drive website traffic. Consider building your own industry-specific forums. Leverage your expertise and assets by building partnerships within industry-vertical publications and websites.

Use these ideas for social media participation by size as rule-of-thumb. If your target customer base is more likely to consume video content, by all means, use YouTube and the other video platforms. Be aware that many marketers underestimate social media's time commitment, resulting in little to no engagement. Social media is a marketing discipline, and lack of a social media plan is usually the culprit for anemic social media, regardless of size. After the novelty wears off, social media posts become fewer and further between. Although you can leverage multiple social media platforms by creating shareable content and simply providing links from each of these platforms, make sure you leave enough time to communicate with people.

# Segmenting Followers Based on Customer Conversion Path

Are you using social media to educate, engage, or encourage? The easiest way to answer this question is to refer to your content strategy. Certain social media platforms like Twitter and Instagram are designed around immediacy. Others, like Facebook, provide direct image links to purchase product. Most of your content shared on social media is going to be middle-of-the-funnel engagement. Exceptions to this include posting on social media directly after purchase and discount/coupon offers from companies like Groupon.

Tracking social media conversion paths may be difficult for the average marketer. Measuring Likes and retweets is fine, but investing in marketing automation software that measures your social media sourcing is better. The former demonstrates influence and some rewards in terms of visibility, but the latter is closely connected to the Customer Conversion Chain.

Analyze your social media channel sources by looking for those that deliver quality visitors who convert into customers over time. You do this simply by creating content, sharing links to it on social media and tagging with unique tracking codes, and then measuring the flow down the purchase path.

# Sharing Your Content on Social Media

In business, social media may be the most misused medium, and it may derive from a simple classification. Facebook and Twitter are each classified as social media in much the same way radio and TV are each considered broadcast media. It's clear in each of these cases, however, that the user-bases, capabilities, and communication mechanisms for each type of medium are much different. Understanding user intent and behavior helps you create meaningful engaging content. When marketers lump all social media together, treating them as similar and equal platforms, they have failed at social media before they have made a single post. So, let's look at each platform as a social *channel* instead:

- **Facebook:** Currently worldwide, there are nearly 1.4 billion Facebook monthly active users generating 4.5 billion Likes every day.

  Use Facebook for business-to-consumer prospect engagement and customer reengagement. Business-to-business companies may find more value in sticking to retargeting/remarketing efforts on Facebook. Begin by creating a company Facebook page (`www.facebook.com/pages/create`) as a hub so your fans have a place to go. The key to higher Facebook engagement is creating and sharing content that is new, clever, or unusual. Doing so stimulates content sharing that results in additional new visits.

  Facebook fans are your fans for a reason . . . they already like you. So, your primary engagement mechanism is to stimulate your fans to share with their friends, building your social network from trusted advocates. This may be particularly effective when your Lifestylers share content. Examine your Facebook fans to mine for potential brand Lifestylers. So whether you choose to feature product in your posts or to post content indirectly related to a sale, do so with the intent of creating amplification through sharing from your fan base. In other words, unless your product is so unique that people say, "Wow!" when they first view it, you probably want to post content that's earlier in the Customer Conversion Chain.

- **Twitter:** Currently, Twitter has over 300 million active monthly users tweeting 500 million times every day. Around 100 million log in daily with 80 percent logging in via mobile devices. With a half a billion tweets disseminated among the "Twitterverse" every day, choosing the best method for your company to use Twitter can be daunting.

First, create your account on Twitter (`www.twitter.com/signup`), using a Twitter "handle," which is your chosen name preceded by the "@" symbol (so mine is `@Tuxmiller`).

Twitter is an amplification medium designed for short messaging of 140 characters or less, so much of the Twitter activity is interpersonal communication. For a company to successfully use Twitter requires building followers. People tend to follow your Twitter account because they either liked the content you posted or because you followed them.

Participating on Twitter for engagement purposes absolutely requires publishing quality content on a regular basis. That shouldn't be a problem for you since content generation is at the heart of inbound marketing. Consider using Twitter for special promotions and new product launches. Twitter is also a good tool to monitor consumer sentiment about your brand, your competitors, and specific products. Larger companies may use Twitter as a customer-service mechanism. And just because you are a business-to-business company doesn't mean you can't participate on Twitter.

✔ **Google+:** Participating in Google+ makes sense for both business-to-business and business-to-consumer companies. Currently, there over 365 million users, and the +1 button (Google's equivalent of Facebook's Like) is hit five billion times each day. So, though Google+ was late to the social-media game, it's a serious platform for prospect engagement.

Start by setting up your company Google+ page (`www.google.com/+/brands`) so you have a hub for your activity. Next, publish content on a regular basis (say, at least once per week) with links to your website content.

✔ **LinkedIn:** LinkedIn has 364 million members, approximately one-third of which originate in the U.S. Creating a company page on LinkedIn provides a hub for linking your content. Creating a profile and a LinkedIn company page facilitates online business networking. By joining LinkedIn groups related to your industry, products, or customer base, you can create and share content to those people most likely to be interested. By posting thoughtful comments on other members' posts, you may attract additional followers with whom you can communicate further. LinkedIn is *the* hub of B2B online connectivity and relationship building.

✔ **YouTube:** YouTube sees over three billion video views *per day*! So if you have video content to share, consider creating your own YouTube account/channel (`https://www.youtube.com/create_channel`). Video is one of the most shared forms of content, so if you have the capabilities to produce videos designed for engagement, consider YouTube participation as mandatory.

Technically, your channel consists of the videos you choose to make public under your account name, but essentially the account and channel is the same thing for the inbound marketer. It's best to create your account name as a branded name so that your video content can easily be searched and found. Embed a code when you want a particular video to be viewed on your website rather than redirecting people away from your website to YouTube. Provide links from other social media, such as Twitter and Facebook, making your videos easily accessible. Don't forget to include social share buttons with your videos, too.

✔ **Pinterest:** Pinterest is a visual social medium in which nearly 73 million users (85 percent are women) post and share pictures. By creating a Pinterest business account, (www.pinterest.com/business/create) you may begin sharing interesting photos. Pinterest users scan different lifestyle categories and "pin" photos they like. Product photos are okay to share, but they'll probably only be "pinned" if they're interesting or unusual. Most of your social activity is going to occur offsite; however, it's possible on Pinterest to create links to meaningful content on your website. When doing so, ensure you are linking to visual content that is based more on imagery than sales messaging. The goal is not necessarily to make an immediate sale, but to create enough awareness and interest that people want to share your pictures.

✔ **Instagram:** Instagram consists of over 300 million users sharing over 70 million photos and videos every day. Businesses engage by creating an account (http://business.instagram.com) and sharing visual images with fellow users. Consider Instagram when connecting with younger demographics. Over half of Instagram's users are age 18-29.

Creating interesting visual imagery is the key to Instagram engagement. This is a social medium platform geared toward the initial stages of a relationship, so appearing too sales-oriented will probably turn off users. Sharing cool product? Okay. Pushing a sales event? Not cool. Instagram may be challenging for small- and medium-sized businesses because its format facilitates a consumer branding message over direct response messaging. Many medium and small companies cannot afford to implement a pure branding message campaign. If, however, you have the skill and tools for visual brand storytelling . . . go for it!

Regardless of which social media you choose, always make sure your content is shareable on at least Facebook and Twitter (and LinkedIn for business-to-business). Use short links to connect people to your content and tracking codes to determine the source of the resulting visits. Provide social share buttons on your home page, inside your blog posts, and within your engagement content, enabling social "word of mouth" sharing that sometimes leads to an electronic grass roots movement around your products.

# *Automating Content Distribution*

Creating content takes time. So does posting links to all that great content you have created. Automating your content distribution by planning social media content posting and linking around your content calendar creates scalable content distribution. Marketing automation software makes the inbound marketer's content distribution job much easier. In addition, check out these content automation platforms (some paid, some free) to help you target, distribute, amplify, and track your content message:

- ✔ **Bitly** (`https://bitly.com`): Shortlinks and tracking
- ✔ **Buffer** (`https://buffer.com`): Automated content distribution
- ✔ **Hootsuite** (`https://hootsuite.com/`): Automated content distribution
- ✔ **OnlyWire** (`https://onlywire.com`): Social content distribution
- ✔ **Outbrain** (`http://www.outbrain.com`): Headline distribution
- ✔ **SimpleReach** (`http://www.simplereach.com`): Targeted content
- ✔ **StumbleUpon** (`http://www.stumbleupon.com`): Social content distribution
- ✔ **TubeMogul** (`http://www.tubemogul.com`): Video distribution
- ✔ **Zemanta** (`http://www.zemanta.com`): Link distribution

# *Things You Can Do Now*

- ✔ Document what social media you're currently using, creating accounts and building page hubs for those you wish to add.
- ✔ Assess whether each of your social media platforms is reaching your target profile.
- ✔ Determine whether your social media outreach efforts are spamming or engaging.

# Chapter 18

# Using Email to Attract and Reattract

*L*ike all digital marketing, email marketing continues to evolve for the inbound marketer. The move from broadcasted email blasts to highly segmented individualized emails shows the progression to the inbound way. Rather than disrupting people's lives with unwanted spam, create valuable content with which consumers elect to interact.

Today, more than ever, practicing considerate, thoughtful email marketing is important. People and email service providers are applying filters for unwanted emails. Knowing what content to email and understanding the frequency of messaging desired by your target customers improves communication and increases email open rates! This chapter covers email marketing and automated email workflows as applied to your overall inbound marketing efforts.

## Knowing Where to Start

Have you ever suffered from "inbox overload?" It's that oppressive feeling when you look at your email inbox and realize there's no possible way you can manage the sheer volume of emails, much less read them all. If you've had this experience, just think about your prospective customers. So many emails are sent every day that there are thousands of apps to help people manage their email. Google changed their Gmail inbox by adding two new tabs to separate personal communications and promotions. Think about the negative effect on email open rates with just that one change.

# Writing Emails That Attract and Convert

There is a formula for writing emails that work. By quickly creating a connection with a reader in your email subject line and copy, you increase your email open rates and clickthrough rates. Writing attractive email requires:

- ✔ Using a short, interesting subject line to increase the open rate
- ✔ Creating short, written email copy so a reader may quickly decide whether to act
- ✔ Identifying with your reader's needs and concisely addressing those needs by providing a link to your possible solution
- ✔ Connecting your reader to your website by providing interesting content and conveying the value of that content
- ✔ Giving clear direction as to the next action the reader should take

Some factors affecting your success as an inbound email marketer are beyond your control. When Google introduced their new tabs segmenting emails, open rates dropped by 24 percent. You can't control that. Creating shorter messaging using language that's proven to work while writing connective copy with a clear CTAs increases open rates. You *can* control that. Read on.

## Creating effective subject lines

The goal of your email subject line is to get your reader to open the email. Period. Tell the reader what's in the email so they may determine if it's relevant to them. Set a clear, simple expectation of what's inside the email. For maximum open rates, use action verbs like "download" in your subject line and keep it shorter than 50 characters.

Of course, other factors affect your email open rate including list quality, prior connection, and permission to send. Table 18-1 shows email open rate by company size from a study performed by email company MailChimp.

| Table 18-1 | Email Stats by Company Size | | | | | |
|---|---|---|---|---|---|---|
| Company Size | Open Rate | Click Rate | Soft Rate | Hard Rate | Abuse Rate | Unsub Rate |
| 1 to 10 | 22.30% | 3.11% | 0.78% | 0.62% | 0.04% | 0.31% |
| 11 to 25 | 21.28% | 2.76% | 0.73% | 0.58% | 0.03% | 0.25% |
| 26 to 50 | 21.99% | 3.09% | 0.49% | 0.37% | 0.02% | 0.18% |
| 50+ | 23.65% | 3.01% | 0.72% | 0.65% | 0.03% | 0.21% |

Check your email open rates and CTRs against companies of similar size to yours to see how your email marketing is performing. Additionally, check out Figure 18-1 to see further findings from the MailChimp study, noting the different lengths of keywords that correlate with higher clickthrough rates. Your subject line lengths affect email open rates. Have you ever heard of the subject line "dead zone"? Apparently, subject lines with lengths between 60 and 70 characters have dreadful open rates. Who knew?

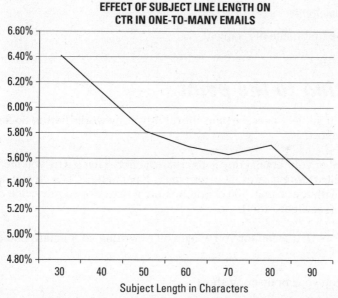

**Figure 18-1:** Clickthrough-rates with respect to subject-line length.

Even more interesting is a study by Adestra that found subject lines with fewer than ten characters had an astounding open rate of 58 percent! In fact, Adestra has a cool subject line keyword checker tool (http://subject-line-checker.adestra.com). (See Figure 18-2.)

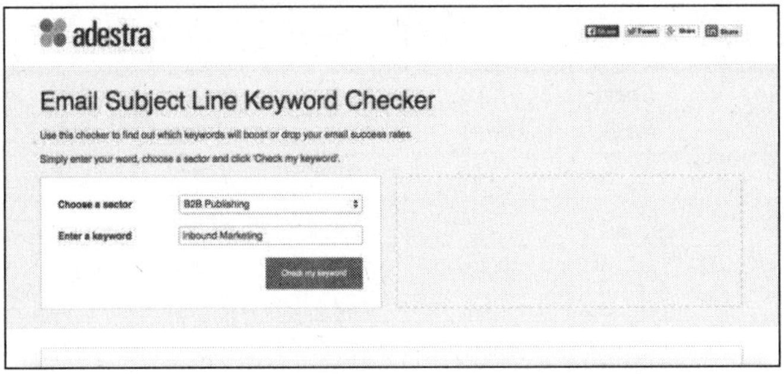

**Figure 18-2:**
Results from
Adestra's
Subject Line
Checker.

In addition to creating short, clear, directive subject lines, a 2014 study by HubSpot and Litmus discovered using the following words in your subject line increases open rates for one-to-one emails:

- ✔ *You*
- ✔ *Thank*
- ✔ *Tomorrow*
- ✔ *Download*
- ✔ The first name of recipient

## Getting to the point

Like your subject lines, writing short body copy works better. So keep your emails short.

The goal of your email copy is to create a click. That's why you measure email clickthrough rates. Shorter emails have better CTRs. In fact, although emails with fewer than 500 characters have better open rates, 360 characters is ideal (see Figure 18-3).

What does that mean for you when you're writing your emails and email templates?

- ✔ Keep your body copy short
- ✔ Be clear and directive as to the intent you wish the reader to take
- ✔ Provide an obvious CTA, linking to relevant content

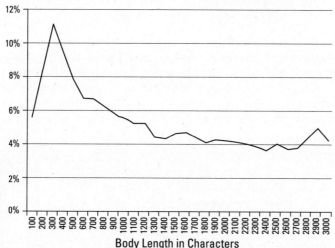

EFFECT OF BODY LENGTH ON CTR IN ONE-TO-MANY EMAILS

Body Length in Characters

**Figure 18-3:**
Effect of
body length
on CTR.

The 2014 HubSpot/Litmus study discovered that people said they were more likely to click on an email with an image. The actual data, however, culled from millions of sent emails, showed differently. In other words, people like images, but they don't increase CTR. In fact, images can actually *lower* your CTR. Does that mean you shouldn't use images in your email? Not necessarily. It does mean you should A/B test your email CTRs with and without images. If you do use images in your email copy, smaller images are better than large images, generally speaking.

## Empathizing with your personas' needs

When you performed a persona study during the diagnostic phase, you learned some things about your target customers. The persona studies identified pain points and needs. Because most of your inbound emails are follow-up emails to people who have performed some type of onsite conversion, you may have learned even more about those customers. For instance, if you're a roofing company and you followed-up with a customer who downloaded information about a metal roof, your follow-up emails would specifically address that information, so you'd have a record of it.

It may seem hard to write an empathetic email while keeping it short so here's a simple process for communicating effectively:

1. Acknowledge the reader.

2. Identify the desired action.

3. State a benefit for performing that action.

4. Provide an obvious CTA.

Figure 18-4 displays one of my own follow-up emails. Note the email's brevity. The subject line is short (16 characters). The body copy is fewer than 500 characters, and follows the procedure above. The link displays in bright orange, making it clear this is the next action to take and nurturing the lead towards the next logical conversion point, which is taking an inbound assessment survey.

**Figure 18-4:** An example follow-up email.

# Emailing Individuals Instead of the Masses

There is a difference between personalizing and individualizing your emails. Personalizing means includes messaging like, "Dear (INSERT NAME HERE)." This is fine for automated one-to-one emails and for emails sent to people who have engaged in some meaningful way with you. On the other hand, using this tactic in broadcast emails or even some workflow emails may backfire since creating personalization where none exists may come off as insincere and inauthentic.

Individualization means sending emails that correspond to a person's activity. One form of this is product personalization in which email messaging is based on prior product engagement purchase habits, or even your recent website activity. Segmenting your lists based on purchase path history makes it easier to individualize your emails and makes your ensuing email communications more meaningful. For instance, if I'm a Guitar Center customer and I've been identified as a guitar player, not a drummer, how likely do you think it would be for me to open an email about a sale on drumsticks? The drumsticks may be on sale at a great price, but if I have no use for them, why would I engage further? Answer: I wouldn't.

## Broadcast emails

*Broadcast emails* are messages sent to a large quantity of addresses obtained from a business partner or from a purchased list. Purchased lists may or may not include addresses from people who agreed to share their data this way, so be careful if you're conducting email marketing from this source. Lists obtained from business partners should have addresses that were collected knowingly by the recipients. If a company's expressed written policy includes a promise not to share the customer data they've collected, ask the business partner who originally cultivated the list to broadcast your message on your behalf, or, alternatively, send a co-branded message that's supported by you and your partner company. Broadcast emails from purchased lists with no recipient opt-ins are not based on permission marketing and therefore are inconsistent with inbound marketing practices.

## Workflow emails

Email *workflows* are series of emails designed to send individualized emails to segmented lists created by previous onsite actions. In other words, the type of email you send is dependent on:

- ✔ Who the email recipient is
- ✔ Which product purchase path the prospect is currently navigating
- ✔ What actions the recipient performed on your website
- ✔ Where your recipient is in the Lifestyle Loop
- ✔ The order of each email in your workflow series

Workflow emails may be sent during the nurturing stages of engagement and encouragement, so it's appropriate to form workflows for both marketing qualified leads (MQLs) and sales qualified leads (SQLs)

# Customer relationship management (CRM) emails

Prewritten CRM emails create efficiency for your sales team. Additionally, by prepopulating follow-up email templates with relevant sales information and accompanying links, your company creates consistent brand messaging.

It's easy to create prewritten email templates in CRMs like Salesforce so your sales team need only point and click to send out a follow-up email. In this instance, it's usually fine to personalize your follow-up messages, since prior contact has been established. A study by the McKinsey Global Institute found the average office worker spent over two-and-a-half hours per day writing emails! The time saved by not having to start each new email from scratch greatly impacts your sales team's follow-up capacity. As an inbound marketer, consider writing these template emails and populating them within your company's sales CRM. When you collaborate with your sales department, the content will be more meaningful, engaging, and representative of your brand. These email templates are editable so individual sales people can add in a couple of personalized lines in the email copy.

## Personalized emails

Personalized emails are the most engaging type of email you can send, and they're also the most likely to be opened and clicked by the recipient — because they're, well, *personal*. When email recipients know and trust you, they're more likely to open your email and respond. Knowing when to begin communicating personally with emails is important for two reasons:

- ✔ It builds a more trusting relationship, encouraging two-way communicating.
- ✔ It provides more relevant messaging, allowing you to accommodate an individual's needs

# Creating an Email Workflow

Email workflows are an automated series of emails designed for reattracting prior website visitors. Creating an email workflow requires email automation software or marketing automation software with email capabilities. Sending a series of progressive emails helps you follow up with leads that are higher in the Purchase Funnel and further away from a purchase. Email workflows are a reengagement mechanism designed to loop former visitors back into your website. So, using these workflows is an important, inexpensive method of increasing your lead conversion rates.

These emails reconnect and reengage with leads and MQLs, and customers. Generally speaking you want your sales team to follow up with SQLs so those individuals are not usually part of a workflow until they either become a customer or fall out of the SQL designation. Automated email workflows are a proven method of staying in touch with a prospect, following up with email content relative to their individual activity on your website and causing a reengagement.

## Designing emails for reaction and reentry

Your emails are designed to create website reentry to cause a reaction inside the Lifestyle Loop. Effective emails complete the loop, connecting a lost visitor who's exited your site in the past with a current website reentry resulting from that lost visitor opening your email and clicking through to your website content. Design workflow emails with CTAs linking back to appropriate website reentry points

## Understanding recency and frequency

*Recency* refers to how quickly you communicate with a customer after an action or event and how close in time each email in a workflow is sent. For instance, sending a "Thank You" email within seconds of someone downloading content from your website demonstrates a high recency.

*Frequency* is how often you communicate with your customers. Frequency is how often you send emails. Sending too many emails too quickly is perceived as spammy. If you don't send emails frequently enough, however, you may lose connection.

The key is to build your workflow series with enough time in between emails that you're seen as being communicative but not abusive. MailChimp discovered that 60 percent of emails are opened within the first 36 hours of receipt, after which time the open rate tails off dramatically. (See Figure 18-5.)

Using this as a rule of thumb, a workflow series sending an email every two-to-four days seems acceptable. If your sales cycle is very short, you may send emails daily, but do not send multiple automated emails within a 24-hour period (with the exception of "Thank You" emails). For example, the typical sales cycle to purchase an automobile is 72 hours after a consumer demonstrates interest, so your entire workflow needs to be built within that timeframe.

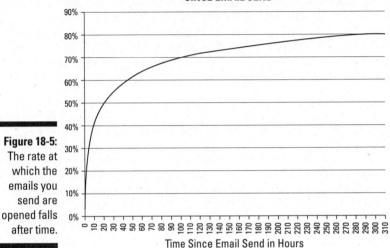

**CUMULATIVE EMAIL OPEN RATES BY TIME ELAPSED SINCE EMAIL SEND**

**Figure 18-5:**
The rate at which the emails you send are opened falls after time.

Time Since Email Send in Hours

# Building an email workflow series

Designing and building email workflows requires preplanning. Segmenting email delivery by associating an automated system of email deliveries creates reattraction and reengagement opportunities. Marketing automation software and email delivery software help automate this process, and I highly recommend using those tools to help with your inbound email marketing efforts. Here are some guidelines:

- Create workflows based on your product pyramid.

- Write email content based on the "4 P's of Inbound Marketing."

- Create workflow rules so recipients receive the most important emails; emails that are relevant or in the most recent product purchase path.

- Deliver your emails in a timely and meaningful manner.

- For prospects with multiple conversions, create a workflow hierarchy, suppressing inclusion in less important email workflows, thereby avoiding inbox overload for your recipients.

Figure 18-6 shows an example of a simple automated email workflow compared to the complex automated workflow in Figure 18-7. Downloading an e-book is a middle-of-the-funnel conversion that requires some demonstrated interest, but not a lot. This new lead may or may not be an MQL, but it's certainly not an SQL. As such, it requires nurturing toward the next conversion.

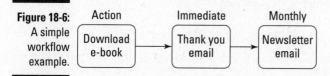

**Figure 18-6:** A simple workflow example.

The complex workflow consists of five emails sent over an eight-day period. Upon completion of the survey, the lead is considered an SQL and receives a follow-up sales call. This workflow series includes an immediate "Thank You" email and periodic follow-ups.

Completing the survey requires more commitment, implying greater demonstrated interest. That's why this workflow has more frequency than the simple workflow. The recency of the complex workflow is coordinated with the follow-up procedure with your sales department, which consists of telephone follow-up immediately and on Days 1, 2, 4, and 6. By integrating the automated workflows with the sales process, the workflow avoids potential conflict and over-communication by sending too many emails.

## Creating email workflow rules

The workflow examples in Figure 18-7 show you how workflow can become complicated very quickly. Overloading a prospect's inbox with emails is not conducive to inbound marketing best practices!

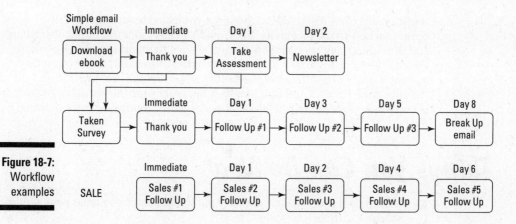

**Figure 18-7:** Workflow examples

Here are some basic rules for workflows:

- Clearly define the difference between MQLs and SQLs.

- Understand your sales team's follow-up procedure and build workflows around it.

- Create workflows for each product purchase path.

- Design a hierarchy of workflow rules so that prospects receive emails from only one product workflow, *unless the prospect specifically requests to receive additional emails* by opting-in to additional product workflows.

- Design your workflows according to the recency and frequency that makes sense for *your* target customers and *your* product purchase cycle length.

- Suppress individual recipients out of less important (further from desired action) workflow emails.

## Knowing when to stop

Email workflows aren't designed to deliver emails forever. If the customer purchase cycle is one year, it may be fine to send an email once per month, but don't overload someone's inbox by sending daily emails. You'll want to periodically cleanse your list of non-qualified recipients, bounced email addresses, and, perhaps, those who haven't opened up an email for a designated time, signaling disinterest. In that case, either keep them in your newsletter or remove them from your email lists.

Additionally, the CAN-SPAM Act requires you provide an "Unsubscribe" option on non-personal emails. Do provide an easy method of unsubscribing and don't be tricky about it. If someone wishes to unsubscribe, why would you still attempt to push your message to that individual? As an inbound marketer practicing attractive marketing, you wouldn't. So, provide an "Unsubscribe" option and don't make it necessary for the recipient to click several more times with unclear buttons or tricky multiple choice options.

## Things You Can Do Now

- Take inventory of your current email templates. If you have zero, you're starting with a clean slate!

- Ask your sales department which emails seem to "work" (get a response) and when they send each of these emails. Document their answers to create personalized automated emails for your salespeople.

- Look for opportunities to automate follow-up emails.

# Part VI
# Understanding the Power of Conversion

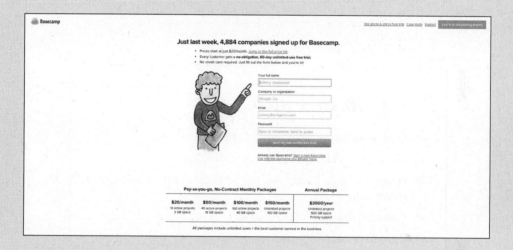

For an explanation of the key points of the Customer Conversion Chain, see www.dummies.com/extras/inboundmarketing.

# In this part. . .

- ✔ Understanding the definition of a conversion.
- ✔ Breaking down the Customer Conversion Chain.
- ✔ Learning multiple conversion steps that occur before the ultimate conversion.
- ✔ Collecting customer data properly.
- ✔ Using data responsibly and respectfully.
- ✔ Reconnecting with customers with conversion data.

# Chapter 19

# Knowing Your Conversion Types

A customer's path to purchase is a meandering series of steps, crowded with distractions and disturbances. As an inbound marketer, you cannot control the purchase decision but you can influence it by paving the path with stepping stones of conversions.

Upon attracting visitors to your website, you want to engage them. This requires conveying a certain degree of trust. The deeper the engagement, the deeper your need to communicate and demonstrate trust. Conveying trust in a valuable product causes a conversion. A conversion, as you may recall, is defined as an exchange in which a visitor shares his or her personal data, such as name, address, phone number, and email address, in exchange for something of perceived value.

The first conversion for each lead sets off a chain of follow-up reactions, opportunities for the inbound marketer to engage more deeply with the prospect to encourage an action such as a sale or donation. This series of conversions is called the Customer Conversion Chain. Each link in the Customer Conversion Chain is a measurable and influential factor affecting your ability to achieve your overall goal: to create customers, repeat customers, and, eventually, brand advocates known as a Lifestylers.

You can't measure what you don't know. In this chapter, you'll learn about different inbound conversion types helping you identify key points along the customer purchase path. Your inbound marketing influences each of these conversion points. By understanding the importance of each conversion link in the Customer Conversion Chain, and by communicating at each of those conversion points while measuring the results, you close the reporting loop of customer attraction, conversion, action, reattraction, and reaction.

# Knowing Your Conversion Types

The Customer Conversion Chain (see Figure 19-1) consists of a series of measurable, meaningful points along a customer's conversion path to purchase. Note that the chain may appear backward to the traditional marketer because it starts at the end point, your Customer Lifetime Value (LTV). Because inbound marketing focuses on customers and on desired business outcomes, this reversal makes sense. Asking, "How do I create a customer for life?" is the inbound way. Assigning a value to the purchases over the life of your customer relationship means you're thinking about long-term customer relationships rather than on a single transaction. Knowing your end game provides comfort and confidence when executing your inbound marketing plan. Reverse-engineering that plan based on known conversion data provides a more statistically confident marketing model. Eventually, your business outcomes become more predictable.

**Figure 19-1:**
The
Customer
Conversion
Chain.

Traditional marketers measure media impressions as their primary marketing campaign metric. Although this is a factor to consider in the Customer Conversion Chain, the media-impressions metric is far removed from the ultimate action, customer-creation. Its impact on the outcome may therefore have less impact than other influencing factors.

The links in the Customer Conversion Chain form a series of inter-connected conversion points, linking a person with your product. All of these points are measurable, and allow you to wield some influence over them. Here are the links in the Customer Conversion Chain:

- ✔ **Customer LTV:** What is the value of your average customer over the life of your typical business relationship? Multiply the number of transactions for you average customer by the average dollar amount per transaction. This is your Customer LTV. For instance, if you're a subscription-based company with a $100/month fee and your average person remains a customer for 36 months, your LTV is $3,600. Now that you know your Customer LTV, you can ask, "What am I willing to invest to obtain one new customer?"

- ✔ **Customers:** The first sale creates a new customer. When a person showing demonstrated interest in your product actually makes a purchase, they are a customer. Populate your "Customers" link in the

Customer Conversion Chain with the average amount of your typical first transaction. This may vary by product and product category. Knowing this number for each of your product Purchase Funnels helps determine which products to support with inbound marketing. Allocating funds to those product campaigns that are the most profitable or the highest converting generates higher ROI.

✔ **Demonstrated Interest:** The definition of "demonstrated interest" is different for every company. Demonstrated Interest is the step closest to a Customer purchase. Demonstrated Interest may be:

- Contract sent for a business-to-business company (this may also be classified as an "opportunity" because it's so close to a purchase)

- Onsite shopping cart population for e-commerce

- Free 30-day trial

- Requests for proposals (RFP)

- Sales presentations

✔ **Sales Qualified Leads (SQLs):** SQLs are those leads who match your buyer profile model, either in demographics, location in the purchase path, or onsite activity. SQLs are higher quality leads than MQLs, primarily because they're closer to a purchase action. SQLs may be determined by a person in your organization, through automation, or both. The basic criteria for SQL classification is a led who has demonstrated need, intent, timeline to purchase, and an established budget.

✔ **Marketing Qualified Leads (MQLs):** MQLs are leads that have passed some criteria that elevates them above being an everyday lead. Perhaps they mirrored a proven customer profile or performed multiple actions further down the purchase path. You can communicate with MQLs through automated email workflows, creating opportunities for reengagement.

This means your organization may determine MQLs via a judgment call based on a prospect's phone call with your internal team, through indicators signifying a qualified buyer as interpreted from answers in form fields, or through automated lead scoring. Collaborating with your sales team to determine your company's definition of an MQL standardizes the procedure of delivering higher quality leads to your sales department. Close ratios and sales revenues elevate correspondingly.

✔ **Leads:** Your *leads* are the people who performed a first conversion by engaging with you on your website or on the phone. Some refer to leads as *contacts*; however, this may be confusing when you're sharing your CRM with your sales team. Contacts are the people in your database. Leads are those who performed an action that included sharing data, thereby connecting them with your company.

✔ **Visits:** Visits are easy to track. This is your website traffic. Breaking your traffic down by sorting your website's *unique* visitors from total traffic and by examining the number of first-time visitors usually provides more actionable data.

✔ **Impressions:** Your different digital media will reach different numbers of people. Impressions measure how many people saw your message. When observed alone, impressions don't provide much value to the inbound marketer other than the relative reach of your messaging, measured as the number of impressions gained by each digital medium. The main functions of measuring impressions is to compare initial efficiencies of each digital medium in reaching your target audience by digital medium and to use impressions as a factor in the Customer Conversion Chain, looking at how many visitors you attract compared to your total impressions. Typically, the impressions metric is expressed as cost-per-thousand (CPM) to reach any given audience, with a lower number signaling a higher efficiency.

# Understanding the Customer Conversion Chain

After you've successfully attracted people to your website, nothing meaningful occurs until the first conversion. Nothing. So, to see what's going on, let's walk through the purchase path in the order your customers do.

## Calculating cost-per-click (CPC)

Imagine you own an online music store that sells musical instruments. Sam is a stranger searching for a guitar online and sees your cleverly written, keyword-targeted paid search ad promoting your custom-built guitar line and decides to click on it. Your cost for that click is $1. What have you learned? You've learned that your cost-per-click (CPC) for that visitor was $1; nothing more and nothing less. Yet . . .

Many digital marketers, inbound or not, use CPC as an efficiency metric and you should, too. CPC is not, however, the primary inbound marketing metric. Nor is it the sole metric. Because inbound marketing is holistic in nature, all conversion points are interconnected. Your CPC metric is relative to other factors like:

✔ The CPC for the keyword term clicked as compared to the CPC for other terms clicked; or as compared to the CPC for other digital media you're using (or could be using) to attract visitors

✔ The profitability of the product purchase path to which the keyword is associated

✔ The quality of traffic attracted by that keyword term, which you can only determine further down the Customer Conversion Chain

## *Figuring cost-per-lead (CPL)*

Measuring CPC makes sense when considering a particular digital medium's contribution to and efficiency in attracting new website visitors. Even though CPC is an inbound *attraction* metric, it's good business practice to connect that information with your *conversion* metrics, too. This is where cost-per-lead comes into play

After clicking on your paid search ad, Sam is now your visitor. He pokes around your site, researching electric guitars. He's interested in guitars, but he doesn't know much about them. Suddenly he spots an image of a slick, custom-designed electric guitar. He imagines how cool he would look wielding that musical ax. He notices your offer for a free e-book explaining the benefits of custom-built electric guitars over stock guitars. Wanting to learn more, he gives his name and email address in exchange for the download. As you now know, this is your first onsite conversion. Sam is now a lead. Your relationship has begun, and you may now begin to figure CPL.

Everything you've invested in time and money can be applied to your leads to determine how efficiently you're creating first conversions. This is your cost-per-lead (CPL). Most people only use the dollars invested (not time invested) when calculating on the tactical level. You should calculate and report your CPL on a monthly, quarterly, and annual basis. Here's the formula:

CPL = Dollars Invested / Leads

For our online music-store example, this calculation would go as follows: This month you invested $10,000 in digital media to drive traffic to your online music store's website. Your efforts generated 10,000 visitors of which 6,000 were unique (average CPC of $1.67 based on *unique* visitors), one of whom was Sam. Additionally, Sam was one of the 200 visitors who became a lead this month. Your CPL for the month, then, is $50.

Monthly Digital Investment in Digital Media = $10,000

Monthly Number of Leads = 200

CPL = $10,000/200 = $50

It only cost you a dollar for Sam to become a lead so why wasn't your CPL $1? Sam was one of 6,000 unique visitors and 200 of those people converted to lead status. Of those 6,000 unique visitors, 5,800 visited your website and did not convert. Now you can glimpse how analyzing metrics beyond CPC and CPL may create marketing efficiencies downstream while generating increased revenues: What if you can reattract some of those 5,800 visitors back to your website through retargeting? Do you think the conversion rate would be higher?

# Defining an MQL

After reading your very cool e-book on custom electric guitars, Sam notices your CTA button, your onsite tool that allows people to choose the features of their ideal electric guitar. Sam clicks onto the tool's landing page, noticing the headline: "Let's Build Your Custom Electric Guitar, Sam!" (The headline was tailored for Sam by using the information Sam entered into your form— yes, you really can individualize the experience like this.) The onsite tool has an additional form field (optional) asking for a budget range. Sam fills in his budget of $2,000 and accesses your guitar customization tool. By submitting this information and clicking through to the tool, Sam reengaged, taking one step closer to your desired action. By sharing his budget, Sam reconverted, in this case triggering a reclassification as an MQL.

At this point, Sam has shown enough interest to increase his lead score as he migrates closer to an action. Additional actions will increase his lead score until he becomes an SQL or falls off the purchase path.

The Electric Guitar Customization tool your marketing team built is awesome, and Sam creates a left-handed six-string guitar with a rosewood body, ivory inlays up the neck, and gold tuning pegs. The problem is, the price for these features adds up to $6,000! Even though your developers created the tool so it displays the custom-built guitars three-dimensionally with the customer's name inlaid on the face of the guitar, it's beyond Sam's budget. Sam has a desire to purchase but doesn't have the budget for that product. He signs off his computer to go to sleep.

# Scoring leads to create SQLs

Over the next week, Sam returns to your tool four times, each time tweaking the components of his custom-built guitar, but he's never able to build one that's within his budget. Each time Sam revisits, his Lead Score increases, eventually triggering an automated reengagement email asking him if he'd like to have a short, five-minute conversation with one of your in-house luthiers about guitar components and features. The payoff for Sam is a set of three personalized guitar suggestions from a pro, all of which are closer to his budget range. He clicks the link to request some suggestions, fills out a form, submitting his phone number as part of his request. He is now one step closer to purchase and, based on your predetermined classification rules, he's now defined as an SQL.

## Defining demonstrated interest

Your pro connects with Sam, conducting a discovery call, learning Sam's guitar preferences, confirming his budget and intent. Sam is now viewed as an opportunity because he has now demonstrated interest.

After the call, Sam enters an email workflow, receiving emails displaying images of the three guitar options at or near his budget. Your promotional message is a free custom nameplate if Sam purchases in the next 30 days. The third email arrives right after Sam receives his tax refund check. He clicks on his favorite guitar's "Purchase Now" CTA button, puts it in his shopping cart, fills out the form fields, and completes the purchase. Your email content was timely, relevant, and contextual to Sam's needs. He bought a $2,000 guitar and is now your customer.

## Figuring cost-per-acquisition (CPA)

Out of the 200 total leads, Sam's purchase this month makes him one of 50 who completed the journey to becoming first-time customers. The average sale was $1,000.

Cost-per-Acquisition (CPA) = $200

CPA = $10,000 marketing investment/50 Customers = $200

Measuring cost-per-acquisition is very important. Knowing the acquisition cost for your average customer, for an individual product, and for key segmentations has a significant impact on choosing your future marketing tactics. Analyzing CPA by key segments helps you make smarter business decisions. For instance, what if you discovered that 5 of the 50 customers who bought from you (10 percent) averaged a $5000 purchase and represented 50 percent of your sales? You might respond by modeling those customer groups and designing campaigns geared toward attracting more of the them. If that customer market size is big enough and consistent enough, your CPA could be five times the average and still be performing.

## Calculating budget and ROI

Here are a couple of other simple metrics, based on the example above:

Advertising Budget = $10,000 Budget / $50,000 Sales = 20 percent

ROI = $50,000 Sales / $10,000 Budget = 500 percent

If those ratios work for this business model — that is, if the result is an acceptable profit margin and net income — you may now begin to test opportunity budgeting. Opportunity budgeting is investing in potential based on historical data and trends until you reach an unacceptable point of diminishing returns.

So if you could invest $20,000 and generate $100,000 in profitable sales, would you do it? Yes.

If you invested $200,000 and you knew with certainty that it would generate $1 million in profitable sales? You would — unless you didn't have the capacity to produce and fulfill that volume, or unless your cash flow after the investment wouldn't be sufficient to bridge the purchase cycle gap. That is, unless you wouldn't have enough funds left over to cover the non-revenue producing time between first contact and first contract. Barring either of these two circumstances, you'd proceed. The problem is nothing in business is ever certain. Rather than risking it all, you should incrementally increase your opportunity budget to test the boundaries of your ROI.

# Collecting Customer Data

Collecting customer data can be tricky. Many times you're asking for information that people don't want to readily hand over. That's why you create and deliver valuable content and rewards to exchange for the customer data.

Here are some inbound marketing rules-of-thumb when collecting customer data via your website conversion forms:

- ✔ **Give some information away for free.** It builds trust early in the customer research stage.

- ✔ **Don't give *all* your content away for free.** Allow access to some valuable content only after a visitor exchanges data.

- ✔ **Create conversion opportunities other than just "Contact Us."** You'll connect earlier in the purchase process, creating some influence on the purchasing decision.

- ✔ **Provide additional conversion access without being disruptive.** You can do this with an unobtrusive customer service chat box, for example, as opposed to a giant pop-up.

- ✔ **Imagine your visitors' perceived value of the benefit gained from handing over their contact information.** Design original form fields with that perceived value in mind. In other words, only ask for information that enables your marketing messaging and sales follow up to communicate effectively in satisfying a potential customer's needs.

- ✔ **If you're a business-to-business company, it's usually okay to ask for more contact information than a typical business-to-consumer company.** Again, this may vary based on your personas' perceived value.

✔ **Create trust signals at the proper conversion points.** This means, say, adding the Better Business Bureau logo for product requests and secure pay icons at your shopping cart checkout, but not at earlier conversion points.

✔ **Assure consumer privacy.**

✔ **Provide opt-in/opt-out opportunities at point of form completion.**

Eventually, the value gained from a product purchase makes exchanging more personal data — including credit card data, name, address, phone number, email address and so on — worthwhile for the customer. Most of us exchange personal data with companies every day. We hand over our data because we trust the company and because we believe we will derive enough value and satisfaction from the transaction to make it worth our while. Your visitors, leads, and customers act the same way.

# Implementing Lead Scoring

*Lead scoring* is an automated method of quantifying the quality of a lead. It is performed with marketing automation software. The intent of lead scoring is to identify which leads possess the greatest propensity to buy, increase marketing focus to those prospects, and hand off higher quality leads from marketing to sales. When you perfect your lead scoring model, your close rate of new business elevates, providing self-stimulated growth. Leads are scored based on a few criteria, including the following:

✔ Time spent on-site

✔ Pages visited

✔ Number of online engagements

✔ Place in the purchase path

✔ Demonstrated interest

✔ Modeled customer types

✔ Modeled purchase paths

When first instituting your lead scoring, you're scoring behavior is based on input from sales and educated guesses as to which behaviors signal buying signs. Initially, use rough estimates as to what score value associates with which behavior. Over time, refine your lead scoring system by monitoring customer conversion path trends. Note which activities seem to be more likely to result in a sale and assign a higher score for a lead who performs that action. Eventually, you may wish to analyze an aggregate of actual customer purchase paths, refining your lead scoring and possibly even create quicker conversions by directing future leads down those proven conversion paths.

Table 19-1 shows a hypothetical example. The rule here is that a lead becomes an SQL at 100 points, resulting in a follow-up call from your sales department.

| Table 19-1 | Hypothetical Scores for Lead Actions |
|---|---|
| *Lead Action* | *Score* |
| Completes "Contact Us" form | 100 points |
| Completes "Perform Demo" form | 100 points |
| Attends webinar | 60 points |
| Completes "Product Specs" form | 50 points |
| Completes form on high converting landing page | 50 points |
| Downloads encouragement e-book | 40 points |
| Downloads embrace-level e-book | 20 points |
| Visits a new website page | 1 point/page |

After you've honed your lead scoring for new leads, you may wish to implement lead scoring for returning customers and Lifestylers, too. Be sure to continually monitor lead scoring to form associations or disassociations between behavior onsite and purchase action. Over time, customers and their purchasing considerations change. By observing changes in conversion behavior while it's happening, you facilitate proactive lead scoring changes in real time, not only when leads are weak and sales are down.

# Organizing Your Data for Future Conversions

You've successfully attracted visitors to your website and they're converting into leads. What do you do with customer data? Perform lead and customer segmentation. Segment your customers by looking at:

- ✔ Products they purchase
- ✔ Persona behavior on-site
- ✔ Top 20 percent average ticket
- ✔ Top 20 percent of volume of purchases
- ✔ Highest conversion percentages for each Customer Conversion Chain metric

- ✔ Lowest 20 percent CPL
- ✔ Lowest 20 percent CPA
- ✔ Customers who bought vs. non-purchasers
- ✔ Qualified lead sources vs. unqualified lead sources
- ✔ Lifestylers behavior vs. everyone else's
- ✔ Shortest time from first contact to first contract

Of course, you want to look at your big-picture aggregate statistics. For the most part, you're using that data as a reference to identify overperforming segments and underperforming segments compared to the norm. Segmenting your data to identify unusually high performing traits usually pays off bigger than reporting the aggregate historical statistics. The former shows proactive insight in solving problems. The latter make everyone else's eyes glaze over as they reach for another donut.

# Knowing What To Do with Contact and Customer Data

Collecting visitor and customer information comes with great responsibility. There are two macro-issues here: Abiding by the law and respecting other human beings.

## Respecting your relationships

You're collecting visitor and customer data for a reason, and it's not to disrespect these people. Use the Inbound Marketer's Golden Rule: *Market unto others as you would want to be marketed to . . . or may you suffer a torrential thunderstorm of spam to your personal email inbox for all eternity.*

Using a few communication guidelines to communicate with people after a conversion goes a long way. Be respectful by:

- ✔ Not overcommunicating
- ✔ Using polite language
- ✔ Unsubscribing immediately upon request
- ✔ Using attractive marketing language instead of pushy sales language
- ✔ Being considerate in your telephone follow-ups
- ✔ Using common business etiquette when performing a webinar
- ✔ Sending communications that are relevant and targeted

## *Using collected data responsibly*

Collecting data responsibly means:

- ✔ Providing something of real value when asking for customer data
- ✔ Adhering to laws and regulations for data collection
- ✔ Knowing the laws for data collection/cookies/privacy in the country/ state/province/territory in which you're operating
- ✔ Understanding any regulations regarding data collection/cookies/ privacy for the industry in which you're marketing (such as with U.S. healthcare and its associated HIPAA compliance)
- ✔ Knowing the laws and security standards for customer data privacy and security

I'm not a lawyer and you probably aren't either, so seek legal counsel if you have any doubt about whether any of your inbound marketing efforts break the law, even if only unintentionally.

One last pet peeve: All those full-screen pop-ups must convert pretty well for all you SEO/CRO/PPC/content marketers out there because I ran into, I don't know, a couple thousand of them while researching this book. Please stop it. You're giving our industry a bad name!

# *Things You Can Do Now*

- ✔ Estimate the number of your website pages that offer CTAs, using 90 percent as your success benchmark.
- ✔ Compare current lead data collection processes against important/ optimal collection and set a minimum standard to engage with sales, establishing your criteria for a MQL.
- ✔ Check to ensure that you are using your data responsibly and legally.

# Chapter 20

# Increasing Website Conversions

· · · · · · · · · · · · · · · · · · · · · · · · · · · · · · · · · · · · · · · · · · · · · · · · · · · · · · · · ·

## In This Chapter

▶ Discovering different methods of increasing conversions

▶ Measuring and sharing conversion data

▶ Tweaking CTAs for increased conversions

▶ Learning which conversions matter

▶ Replicating successful conversion paths

· · · · · · · · · · · · · · · · · · · · · · · · · · · · · · · · · · · · · · · · · · · · · · · · · · · · · · · · ·

*N*ow that you know about the different conversion types comprising the Customer Conversion Chain, the next logical discussion is how to increase your conversions.

In this chapter, I discuss evaluating your Customer Conversion Chain so you can begin implementing changes. Using a fictional software-as-a-service (SaaS) company as an example, I explain how to look for opportunities to increase conversions. Applying this knowledge to your own situation requires three things:

✔ A functioning website designed on conversion architecture

✔ Access to business numbers and digital marketing analytics

✔ Some form of automation software, even if it's basic

If you don't like numbers or math, skip this chapter so you can spend time memorizing the components of the conversion chain and researching a CRO expert to help you. It's okay, really . . .

# Applying the Customer Conversion Chain

Now that you've populated your own Customer Conversion Chain based on what you learned in Chapter 19, analyzing your numbers and applying improvements will help you identify opportunities to increase conversions and grow your revenues. This is your first step in conversion rate optimization (CRO). There are some basic guidelines to consider when performing CRO. They are:

✔ Know why you're measuring each of your conversion points.

✔ Associate your conversion metrics with revenue outcomes.

✔ Measure what's important to your company; don't use popular or misguided (often the same) metrics.

✔ Measure for the sake of creating actionable initiatives, not for the sake of producing beautiful dashboard reports.

✔ Value trends over anomalies.

✔ For best CRO results, segment your data and focus on key segments; don't use aggregate data.

To illustrate this process, consider the example of Moira, a popular (fictional) business-to-business software-as-a-service (SaaS) entrepreneur whose model is based on annual software subscriptions of $6,000 per year ($500/month). Figure 20-1 shows Moira's conversion chain. I introduce it early in the chapter for a reference point. Fact is, you can apply this base knowledge for any organization, from billion dollar business-to-business manufacturing companies to business-to-consumer e-commerce sites and to just about any situation that includes connecting digital marketing with business results. Measuring, analyzing, and applying Customer Conversion Chain metrics works for chief marketing officers, business owners, multinational marketing departments, and small businesses, and it will work for your company, too. All you need is access to numbers and a desire to grow your business.

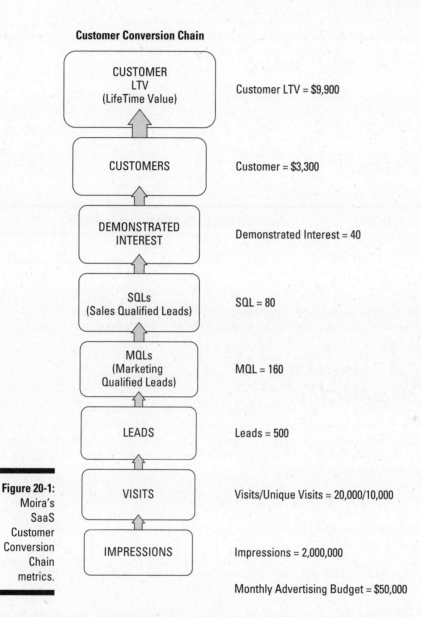

**Customer Conversion Chain**

| | |
|---|---|
| CUSTOMER LTV (LifeTime Value) | Customer LTV = $9,900 |
| CUSTOMERS | Customer = $3,300 |
| DEMONSTRATED INTEREST | Demonstrated Interest = 40 |
| SQLs (Sales Qualified Leads) | SQL = 80 |
| MQLs (Marketing Qualified Leads) | MQL = 160 |
| LEADS | Leads = 500 |
| VISITS | Visits/Unique Visits = 20,000/10,000 |
| IMPRESSIONS | Impressions = 2,000,000 |
| | Monthly Advertising Budget = $50,000 |

**Figure 20-1:** Moira's SaaS Customer Conversion Chain metrics.

# Analyzing the Links in Your Customer Conversion Chain

Moira is an entrepreneur who bootstrapped a startup SaaS company several years ago. She knows that her annual subscription rate is $6,000. The vast majority (90 percent) of her customers need only one annual subscription per company. The remaining 10 percent of customers purchase two subscriptions, so the average purchase for this second minority group is $12,000.

When combining the two client-types, the average sale for a customer's first purchase is $6,600. The average customer maintains a subscription for three years.

Under Moira's current business model, her Customer Conversion Chain looks like Table 20-1.

| Table 20-1 | | | Moira's Customer Conversion Chain | | | | | |
|---|---|---|---|---|---|---|---|---|
| *LTV* | *Cust.* | *DI* | *SQLs* | *MQLs* | *Leads* | *UV* | *V* | *Imp.* |
| $9900 | 10 | 40 | 80 | 160 | 500 | 10k | 20k | 2M |

The next few sections examine Moira's Customer Conversion Chain to determine current inbound marketing metrics, from impressions through to LTV.

## Customer LTV

Now, it's time to take a look at each link in Moira's Customer Conversion Chain. I've added a few initial observations for each link so you can see how you might approach a real-life situation. First, is an overview of the lifetime value of Moira's customers.

Customer LTV = $6,600 Avg. Purchase × 3 years = $19,800

**Cost-per-acquisition:** Based on current data, CPA is: $50,000 ad spend / 10 customers = $5,000.

CPA seems high. It will take nine months ($5,000 CPA / $550 per month) to recover Moira's costs to acquire each customer.

Action point: Moira should consider a pricing test offering a 10 percent price discount for prepaying the annual subscription resulting in recouping your CPA right away, affording her company some working capital to invest in additional customer acquisition or to apply to the bottom line.

**Cost-per-lead:** Based on current data, CPL is: $50,000 ad spend / 500 leads = $100.

CPL seems to be in line with the industry average, but who wants to be average? A bigger issue seems to be the gap between the average CPL and the high CPA. This may signal a problem with onsite conversions.

Action points: Moira should drill deeper on the attraction source inputs to see if there are clear winners and losers for CPL. Move down the Customer Conversion Chain metrics to further examine onsite conversion metrics.

**ROI:** We know that Moira's company is investing $50k/month to generate about $198k in new revenues, but this revenue won't be recognized all at once. Additionally, we ask Moira for her gross profit margin and she says 70 percent, which is fairly typical for a SaaS company. Investing $50k for $70k gross profit is the true ROI for LTV.

Revenue ROI = $198,000 LTV / $50,000 Ad spend = 396 percent

Gross Profit ROI: LTV =($198,000 × 70 percent, or $138,600) / $50k ad spend = 277 percent

Note: Now that we know the gross profit margin, the actual time to recapture her CPA is 13 months:

$550 per month × 70 percent = $358 gross profit

$5,000 CPA / $385 = 12.99 months

This suggests Moira has more than a marketing problem. She has a business problem. Under Moira's current business model, she'll need enough cash reserves to cover the time between customer acquisition and breaking even on her CPA. And, that doesn't even take into account a 30-day sales cycle and the 30-day Free Trial period. That's two more months added on to the total purchase cycle.

So to bridge the gap and sustain her company during the time she's recouping her original investment, Moira needs 14 months × $50,000, or $700,000. Growth through new customer acquisition may seem like the obvious solution, but, ironically, taking this path only exaggerates the problem under the current situation. Obtaining more customers by spending more increases the dollars needed to sustain the company from the time between the marketing investment to attract visitor and the actual customer acquisitions from that original dollar investment. In this situation, the business will be in a negative cash position, possibly imploding as soon as growth stops. Do you see the problem here? Do you see why marketing matters?

Action points: Moira should seek efficient ways to acquire new customers or she should seek investors. Statistically speaking, that's the best she can do. Marketing can't perform miracles.

# Customer

When a lead makes an initial purchase that lead becomes a customer. It's important to know the average first transaction for your customers so you can figure out your marketing ROI. Here's a look at Moira's customers:

Customer = $6,600

Moira's customers come in two types: Type A, who need one annual subscription, and Type B, who need two. According to Moira, 90 percent of her customers are Type A.

Segmenting these customers, it's easy to see that one group (B) is worth twice as much on a dollar-per-transaction basis than the other group (A). Incrementally, it costs *no more* to acquire this lead or to communicate with this lead. In fact, Moira's operational costs are cut in half when performing a demo, setting up a free trial, and servicing this valuable customer.

Action points: Moira should research the Type B customer, looking specifically at comparative data for significant variances against Type A, including:

- Keywords used to enter site
- Pay-per-click and click-through-rate
- Source customer used to find site (social media/SEO/PPC)
- Cost-per-lead (this could be double for Group B and still be fine)
- Cost-per-acquisition (if it's the same, you may have just hit a gold mine — provided the market size for Group B is large enough)
- Return-on-ad spend (RAS)
- Onsite activity including time on site, page views, and pages visited
- Lead-to-customer ratio

In short, if the market size for Group B is large enough and conversion ratios are acceptably promising, Moira should perform a specific Customer Conversion Chain analysis just for Group B to hypothesize growth.

# Demonstrated Interest

Moira defines demonstrated interest as a prospect who signs up for a 30-day free trial of her software. Of the people who sign up for the free 30-day trial, 25 percent become a customer. Out of 40 people who show demonstrated interest, ten become customers. The close ratio is 25 percent.

Maybe there's an internal process that could increase Moira's close ratio, but other than recommending that human beings follow up with the non-subscribers, there's little you can do about that. So the question to ponder is this: Is there something Moira can do in any of these situations to have a positive influence on either the number or the quality of people who use the software on the 30-day Free Trial?

Action points: In reality, this doesn't seem to be the primary issue, but the fact is, sales increase when you attract more qualified people with demonstrated interest to perform a product demo. That's probably going to happen farther upstream. I recommend examining the post-demo communications and CTRs for reattraction to see if Moira's efforts to reattract are underperforming.

# SQLs

Moira defines SQLs as people who have successfully completed a software demonstration with a sales consultant. Of the people who complete a sales demo, 50 percent move on to demonstrated interest by signing up for a free 30-day trial.

In this case, Moira researched the close ratios and 50 percent is a pretty darn good number for her industry. So, unless there is a reporting problem any inefficiency in the conversion chain is probably not from the SQL link, and marketing influence here may be limited anyway.

Action points: I advise Moira to check her marketing communications to see if improving any of the following would have a meaningful impact:

- ✓ **Predemo engagement:** Is Moira's company sending automated meeting reminders to reduce no-shows? Is her marketing team creating content that asks plenty of qualifying questions prior to the software demonstration?
- ✓ **Product demo:** Has marketing looked at the presentation to ensure that it's written in language that "speaks" to each target persona?
- ✓ **Post-demo:** Is she sending a workflow series of emails that are both reattractive for reengagement or encouragement for a sale?

# MQLs

Moira defines her MQLs as individuals who have attended a webinar, completed a buyer survey, or filled out a "Contact Us" form. She also uses visitor onsite activities for lead scoring with a 100-point score elevating a lead to MQL status.

Big picture, 160 of the 500 total monthly leads are considered a MQL. Half of those connect with a salesperson for a product demo. That sounds good and it probably is, but Moira could test for improvements. Is there a big difference between the customer conversion paths taken by MQLs and SQLs?

Action points: I recommend looking at Moira's lead scoring to see if perhaps more people should be designated SQLs rather than MQLs. Because this designation would increase the number of follow-up calls for her sales team, she'd need to make sure Sales has capacity to handle the new workload. Also, because a percentage of these leads may be incrementally harder to encourage, the close ratio from SQL would probably go down.

Modeling the respective conversion paths for MQLs and SQLs and navigating MQLs toward any distinct, differentiating SQL path onsite may increase the percentage of leads who schedule and perform a demo, which would positively affect Moira's Demonstrated Interest and Customer numbers down the chain. Lastly, she should look at automated email messaging and consider A/B testing a promotional message with a CTA with an urgent deadline against the current CTA, in the hope of increasing demonstrated interest. (So, maybe a 60-day free trial for the first 10 people to schedule a demo?)

## Leads

Moira defines inbound leads as website visitors who contacted the company via web phone calls (tracked by a unique number on her website), onsite e-book downloads, or other onsite form conversions like "Contact Us."

Improving Moira's CPL of $500 seems possible. To achieve a more efficient CPL, she might consider two alternatives; either increasing the quality of the leads or reducing the ad spend by analyzing where the 52 percent of unqualified traffic is sourcing.

Action points: Moira should review the content strategy to retool the target keyword list as a starting point that has implications for both SEO and PPC. She should compare performing and non-performing keywords, see what words are attracting the most unqualified leads, and remove them from her plan. She should examine the engagement content that her customers consume and navigate some of the less qualified (but not least qualified) traffic to those conversion pages to determine whether the quality of the page is causing conversion or if she's simply attracting visitors who will never convert as a quality lead.

# Visits

According to Moira's Google Analytics, her website's monthly traffic is 20,000, 50 percent of which were returning visitors and 50 percent new visitors. Unique visitors equals 10,000 people per month.

So what? Because Moira's website attracts only 10,000 unique visitors per month (the other half are from people returning to the site one or more times), the conversion ratios are actually much higher than originally reported. In fact, they're twice as good. It's why I recommend using Unique Visitors as your baseline traffic numbers instead of overall traffic numbers. So, why did I use overall traffic in this example? To prove my point! It may not be as easy to increase your conversion ratios as it might first appear. Using flawed data to project future outcomes may end in disaster so beware the sources of your conversion metrics. In this case, use the number of unique visitors.

Action points: Moira has tremendous reattraction: 50 percent of her customers are returning to her site. Why isn't the other half reconverting? You'll always have unqualified traffic, sure, but I would look at the reattraction workflow campaigns, asking if the reconversion rate should be higher. If the answer is yes, she should take a look at the actual workflow, test the workflow and its components including email frequency and recency, CTAs, and reengagement content.

# Impressions

Moira's attraction marketing generates monthly traffic numbering 20,000 people each month, half of which are unique visitors. 10,000 visits are from people returning to the site.

Comparing the attraction sources and the amount invested into these initial attraction inputs and the amount invested and the resulting reattraction may suggest some answers to some important questions, including:

✔ Does the fact that 50 percent of visits were revisits signal that inbound remarketing and retargeting campaigns are performing well?

*or*

✔ Does the fact that only 50 percent of her site's visitors are new signal an inefficient initial attraction campaign?

Action points: Drilling deeper requires a CTR and a conversion ratio for the past month, and then comparing it to historical traffic and conversion data. Market anomalies, seasonality, or events may explain away spikes. I would particularly look at any reattraction, reaction, and reconversion campaigns to learn the source of the revisits. Lastly, checking the attraction source of the 50 percent of traffic designated as first time visitors, following those visitors down the conversion path, and segmenting them as buyers and non-buyers helps over-performing conversion sources. Identify those sources and invest more to see if you produce similar results.

# Everything Inbound Is Connected

Every conversion point is a link in the Customer Conversion Chain. Each conversion link influences the other links. One damaged conversion link can break the chain. To demonstrate the relationship, I created the table shown in Table 20-2, changing just one conversion point at a time, increasing the tweaked variable by 10 percent. The tweaked conversion point is shown underlined and in boldface; other affected conversion points are also in boldface (no underline).

**Table 20-2   Conversion Points in Relation to the Conversion Chain**

| LTV | Cust | D.I. | SQL | MQL | Lead | U.V | V | Imp |
|---|---|---|---|---|---|---|---|---|
| $99,000 | 10 | 40 | 80 | 160 | 500 | 10k | 20k | 2M |
| $108,900 | **11** | 40 | 80 | 160 | 500 | 10k | 20k | 2M |
| $108,900 | 11 | **44** | 80 | 160 | 500 | 10k | 20k | 2M |
| $108,900 | 11 | 44 | **88** | 160 | 500 | 10k | 20k | 2M |
| $108,900 | 11 | 44 | 88 | **176** | 500 | 10k | 20k | 2M |
| $108,900 | 11 | 44 | 88 | 176 | **550** | 10k | 20k | 2M |
| $108,900 | 11 | 44 | 88 | 176 | 550 | **11k** | 20k | 2M |
| $108,900 | 11 | 44 | 88 | 176 | 550 | 11k | **40k** | 2M |
| $108,900 | 11 | 44 | 88 | 176 | 550 | 11k | 40k | **2.2M** |

Observe the many different methods of achieving the same results. Note that, everything remaining equal, it will cost an extra 10 percent or $5,000/month to generate more impressions via the same sources. You may be able to achieve the same result at no cost with a tweak closer to the sale. In reality, you'll be tweaking multiple conversion points, dialing up and dialing down. This is the fine-tuning of your Conversion Machine.

# Understanding the Value of Your Conversions

All conversions are not created equal. A sale is more valuable than a visit, but you can't make sales from inbound marketing without visitors. Your inbound marketing plan becomes a constantly fluid system requiring constant planning, monitoring, measuring, analyzing, and tweaking. Just realize that tweaking some points in the Customer Conversion Chain wield greater influence than others.

## Determining the value of your customer segments

Inbound marketers are as guilty as anyone else in the business world in compiling reams of meaningless data reports. Marketers tend to look at aggregate data, which explains the "what" but not the "what if," or the "why." Asking "what if" all along the customer purchase path results is the road to improved marketing and business outcomes. If you take nothing else away from this book, remember to ask "why" and "what if." Answering the "why" with insightful solutions is rewarding and fun, I promise!

With that in mind: What if you segmented your data into more meaningful groups? Using Moira's two customer groups as an example, let's segment and analyze.

Customer Group A represents 90 percent of customers and 82 percent of revenues. Customer Group B represents 10 percent of customers and 18 percent of revenues.

Total revenues are $66,000 per month.

What if you replaced one customer from Group A with two from Group B?

Customer Group "A" now represents 80 percent of customers and 67 percent of revenues. Customer Group "B" now represents 20 percent of customers and 33 percent of revenues.

Total revenues are now $72,000 per month.

What if you replaced two customers from Group A with two from Group B?

Customer Group "A" now represents 70 percent of customers and 54 percent of revenues. Customer Group "B" now represents 20 percent of customers and 46 percent of revenues.

Total revenues are now $78,000 per month.

If you, as an inbound marketer, determine how to replace three valuable customers with three even more valuable customers, you increase your marketing efficiencies while increasing sales. Sounds like a winner to me.

But wait, there's more. By replacing just two customers from one segment with another, you've also increased the LTV each month from $198,000 to $234,000, an increase of $36,000. Over the course of the next 12 months, you've just created enough customers to generate $432,000 in incremental revenue over the next three years!

## Replicating successful conversion paths

Let's keep this short. When you discover a successful conversion path for one segment, replicate the working parts by testing and applying your actionable findings to other product pyramids, inbound campaigns, and conversion paths.

Remember what my buddy, business partner, and inbound marketing expert, Nate Davidson says: "Do more of what works. Do less of what doesn't."

## Things You Can Do Now

- ✔ Determine your Customer Lifetime Value (LTV).
- ✔ Populate the Customer Conversion Chain with your organization's data.
- ✔ Examine your strong and weak links in the chain. Be honest.

# Chapter 21

# Building Effective Landing Pages

*L*anding pages are the crucial point between your website visitors' expressing interest and performing a desired conversion action. As such, landing pages are an important bridge in the conversion process. Building landing pages as connective bridges and constructing your landing pages with proven conversion components will increase your onsite conversion rates.

In this chapter, you'll learn what a landing page is, how to build landing pages that convert, and see some examples of good landing page design.

## Defining a Landing Page

Landing pages are crucial to your inbound success because they are the main onsite conversion point. Landing pages are where visitors become leads. They are the genesis of the conversion process. But landing pages are misunderstood and misused, especially with respect to inbound marketing principles and best practices.

A *landing page* is a web page that acts as a conversion hub to which you direct onsite and inbound traffic. A landing page's primary function is a single conversion. (See Figure 21-1). Landing pages are sometimes made non-crawlable to search engines for SEO purposes, though you can certainly link to landing pages from the SERPs.

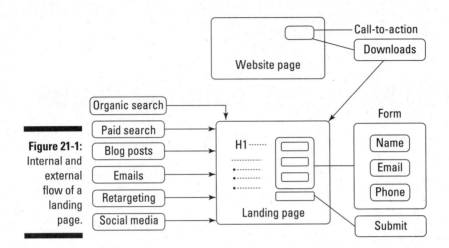

**Figure 21-1:**
Internal and
external
flow of a
landing
page.

Unless you have a one-page website or you're a company like Groupon, your home page should not be a conversion page. Your home page should serve as a navigational page for website visitors, making it easy for visitors to get where they're going. If you're directing all your inbound traffic to your home page, you're not practicing inbound marketing. You're executing traditional digital marketing. That's not good.

Landing pages are side door entry points to your website (although they may also be accessed from inside your website). A well-designed, well-connected landing page (accessible both externally and internally) will outperform your typical web page, in terms of conversions.

# Improving Your Conversion Success Rate with Landing Pages

Increasing your overall conversion rate is the quickest path to growth yet most companies focus on increasing website traffic and ignore conversion rate optimization. This applies to increasing the conversion rate of landing pages, too.

Building a landing page used to be a difficult, time-consuming task but marketing automation software and landing page design software has simplified it tremendously. Creating landing pages for each of your campaigns, and for each conversion point, creates content consistency for your visitors, so it's just a good inbound practice. HubSpot reports that businesses with more than 40 landing pages demonstrate a conversion rate that's over 12 times that of businesses with five or fewer landing pages. That's bad news for the average small business, whose website averages only three landing pages, for which 85 percent of the traffic goes to only one. How many landing pages do you have?

Looking at your historical conversion rates and recording that information before improving your landing page design helps you measure your future progress. There is no magic conversion percentage because it varies by industry, landing page components, offer type, number of visitors, and visitor source. HubSpot says the average landing page conversion rate is 5 to 15 percent. Look at your historical conversion percentages for your first comparisons. If you're business-to-business and want a benchmark, shoot for 20 percent conversion on your landing pages, but by all means keep improving your landing pages for even better conversion rates.

If you want to grade the landing pages for your Google AdWords PPC accounts, check out WordStream's Landing Page Grader at `www.wordstream.com/landing-page`.

## Knowing the components of an effective landing page

A landing page is designed to convert. Period. Building landing pages that convert means including the following:

- ✔ **A unique offer:** This is the most important contributor to increased conversion because it's the essence of why your visitor is on the landing page in the first place. Try to avoid offers that mimic other standard offers in your industry. Make yours stand out.

- ✔ **A directive headline:** Use a benefit statement to clearly state what the visitor should do to convert.

- ✔ **Focused copy with benefits summarized in a bulleted list**

- ✔ **Simple form fields:** Ask for only as much information as is warranted by the perceived value of the person downloading. Asking for too much information too early reduces conversion. Use auto-fill type, smart forms that remember prior form fields, drop-downs, and simple bubble choices if it makes it easier for the user to complete the form.

- ✔ **A graphic representation of the offer:** This may be a photo, a graphic representation of the downloadable, or a picture of the author or sales rep (depending on the offer).

- ✔ **Little-to-no site navigation:** Too many choices lead to nonconversions. The desired action is conversion. Make that the clear choice by eliminating your navigation menus from your landing page design.

✓ A simple proof point, such as a customer testimonial, customer reviews, or compelling statistic that reinforces the value of your deliverable

✓ A post-conversion "Thank You" email with an immediate reengagement opportunity

The landing page building and testing company, Unbounce, creates effective landing pages for themselves (as you would expect). Figure 21-2 shows the middle-of-the-funnel landing page to download an e-book. It features a simple headline, an illustration of the book, and concise form fields. It also has a unified brand-consistent look.

**Figure 21-2:** Unbounce's engagement landing page.

Similarly Unbounce's bottom-of-the-funnel landing page (see Figure 21-3) encourages a 30-day free trial. Several components make this a good landing page, including value creation via descending price points and a comparative features chart, additional side benefits, and clear suggestion to click for a 30-day free trial.

I consider shopping cart pages, purchase pages, and encouragement pages to be landing pages. Figure 21-4 displays Unbounce's purchase page linked to the 30-day free trial CTA button. Note the simplicity of the form and the testimonial references off to the side. What a great way to lessen buyer's remorse while creating higher confidence and, most probably, higher conversions.

## Building a better landing page

According to Marketing Sherpa (www.marketingsherpa.com), about 75 percent of companies have trouble optimizing their landing page copy.

Let me bring some clarity to the issue of building and optimizing better landing pages.

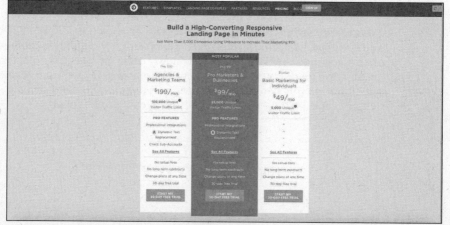

**Figure 21-3:** Unbounce's encouragement landing page.

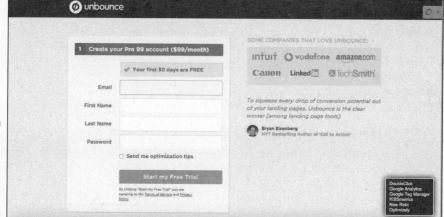

**Figure 21-4:** Unbounce's purchase landing page.

## Build simple landing pages

When building your landing pages, keep it simple. Drive your visitors toward one clear action, using only the necessary components to create engagement.

Groupon uses their home page as a landing page and asks only for an email address. The page includes a geographically personalized benefit statement ("Save 50% to 90% in St. Louis") that creates immediate engagement. After you fill out the form, a second form field asks for your zip code to enable more relevant offer delivery, and — *voila!* — you're immediately directed to the current local offers for St. Louis. You can't get much simpler than that.

### Reinforce the desired action

Using well-known company logos with testimonial statements reinforces the visitor's engagement as a positive action. As shown in Figure 21-5, Basecamp does a good job with this concept. Basecamp's encouragement landing page has a headline that tells users how many other people just completed the same form fields the visitor is about to complete. There's perceived safety in numbers, so this headline reassures users that filling out the form is a safe choice. This landing page also features clean graphic design.

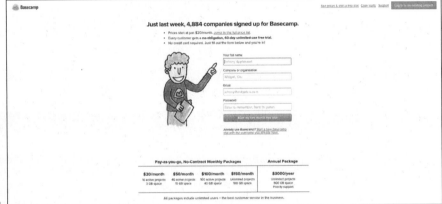

**Figure 21-5:**
Basecamp's
landing
page.

### Build landing pages for deeper engagement

Shutterstock provides stock photography online. They have very cleverly turned their home page into a deep engagement page by creating a one field form that is essentially a search bar for the image you desire. (See Figure 21-6.) With a library of over 50 million stock photo images and 50,000 more images added daily, they're probably going to have an image that matches your search. Shutterstock also reverses the shopping process by introducing price only after you've found what you desire. Brilliant!

### Build mobile-friendly landing pages

As mobile Internet access continues to skyrocket, your landing pages must be responsive. Building mobile-friendly landing pages with simple graphics and big, easy-to-click CTAs facilitates conversion from any device. In the case of Uber, the industry-disrupting ride-on-demand driving service, many of their new customers will convert from mobile. Think about it, when you need a ride, you use your mobile phone. Uber's sign-up conversion page is basically just a form (see Figure 21-7). No bells. No whistles. Just a quick way to convert at a time when the new customer needs quick access and action. By using this simple form, Uber is using mobile landing pages to serve their customers' needs. Your prospects may not need the simplicity of Uber's landing page, but you should build and test your landing pages to display for optimal mobile conversion.

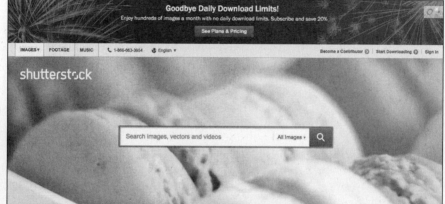

**Figure 21-6:**
Shutter-
stock's
landing
page.

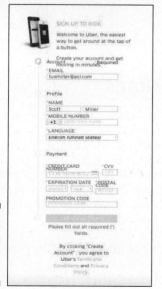

**Figure 21-7:**
Uber's
mobile land-
ing page.

### Build with bold, directive graphics

WebDAM's landing page (see Figure 21-8) to download their guide on choosing digital asset management (DAM) software succeeds graphically. The contemporary color choices of blue and orange work in highlighting the two most important graphics on the page, which are a graphic representation of the downloadable book and the CTA button that clearly states, "Download Guide." The form fields clearly state the information needed, and each field is supported by a graphic representation — very cool. The CTA is clear and the privacy statement builds confidence for visitors to exchange their data. But, the best graphical element is actually the arrow-shaped form, subtly designed to suggest the download to the visitor. Well done!

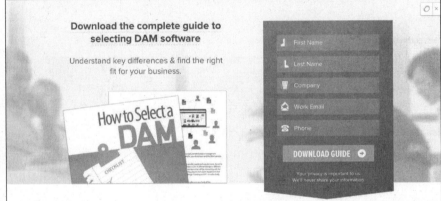

**Figure 21-8:** WebDAM's landing page.

## Testing your landing pages

Rarely do you hit a conversion home run when building your first landing pages. In fact, it usually pays to A/B test your landing pages. In A/B landing page testing, you're testing two versions of a particular landing page with "A" being the original landing page and "B" being the new landing page. Test by sending roughly half of your visitors to the "A" page and the other half to the "B" page. By monitoring which landing page performs better for conversions over time, you can significantly increase this conversion input, achieving positive results on down the Customer Conversion Chain.

Here are some things to remember when testing your landing pages:

✔ **Test one thing only:** Only change one component at a time. So on each version of your landing page, change only the Headline, the form, or the benefit statements, not all three. The exception to this is when you're testing for page layout as a conversion fact. If you're A/B testing the overall graphic design, keep all the components, but arrange them differently or use a different color scheme.

- ✔ **Test the highest trafficked landing pages**
- ✔ **Test regularly**
- ✔ **Test with intent of specific conversion improvement**

WordStream (`www.wordstream.com`) performed a study for companies with 1,000 or more landing pages, and discovered that 80 percent of website traffic goes to only 10 percent of the landing pages. (See Figure 21-9.) Unless you're testing some drastic landing page changes, why test on the 90 percent of landing pages that have the least impact on your conversion rate? Focus instead on landing pages garnering the most traffic, and your conversion rate changes will be more pronounced.

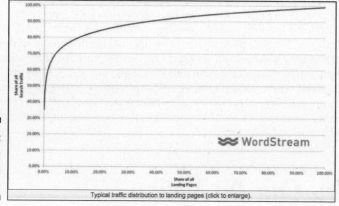

**Figure 21-9:** Landing-page traffic distribution.

Some marketing automation software platforms make building landing pages easy. Optimizely (`www.optimizely.com`) and Unbounce (`www.unbounce.com`) are some tools for building multiple variations of a landing page. Here are some other testing tools for the non-enterprise organization:

- ✔ **Convert (`www.convert.com`):** Offers A/B and multivariate testing for agencies and experts.
- ✔ **Google Analytics Experiment (`https://support.google.com/analytics/topic/1745146`):** Enables A/B testing integrated with your Google AdWords PPC.
- ✔ **Marketizator (`http://www.marketizator.com`):** Offers testing that connects with Google Experiments by creating an event.
- ✔ **Monetate (`www.monetate.com`):** Includes a robust set of tools, including A/B testing.
- ✔ **Nelio A/B Testing (`www.wp-abtesting.com`):** Offers WordPress A/B testing for landing pages and much more.

## *Replicating successful landing pages*

Discovering what works at each point of the Customer Conversion Chain is part of the fun of being an inbound marketer. Most websites have enough traffic; it's their conversion rate that is under-performing. Your landing page may be the most important link to conversion success because it's the direct catalyst for engagement and encouragement. Because of this, discovering which landing pages convert the best may be the quickest way for you to increase sales.

By testing one landing page in a chosen inbound campaign at a time, you discover which page derives a better response. After you've confirmed the conversion rate by allowing it to play out over time, it's time to apply your knowledge to other landing pages. Simply create a variation of the most successful landing page, as defined by conversion rate, and create a similar version for a landing page in another campaign. Create an A/B test for the redesigned landing page against the original landing page to determine whether the new page increases your conversion rate for that campaign, too. When you see a pattern, you can leverage your success by replicating the successful conversion pages for all your landing pages, resulting in an increase of your overall website conversion rate. You have now created scalable, measurable success with some seriously positive implications for your inbound marketing campaign.

# *Things You Can Do Now*

- ✔ Take inventory of your current landing pages, spot-checking to ensure they are optimized for conversion.
- ✔ Check to see that your landing pages relate to respective conversion path.
- ✔ A/B test one of your landing pages.

# Part VII
# Measuring Success
# with Analytics

For advice on choosing marketing automation software, check out
www.dummies.com/extras/inboundmarketing.

## In this part. . .

- ✔ Knowing the most important success metric of all.
- ✔ Using Google Analytics.
- ✔ Using Google Webmaster tools.
- ✔ Measuring with marketing automation software.
- ✔ Utilizing user testing.

# Chapter 22

# Measuring Your Inbound Marketing Results

**M**easuring your inbound marketing results is the final part of the inbound process. Good inbound strategy clearly defines success metrics and milestones. After hypothesizing outcomes based on your Customer Conversion Chain and applying inbound marketing tactics, it's time to measure your success.

This chapter covers very basic analytics reporting. More detailed custom reports are available, and I encourage you to build those reports around your custom needs. Using the basic reporting outlined here provides a foundation for you to expand your efforts. Be aware, however, of the common flaw of creating analytic reports only for the sake of creating more reports. The most important part of measuring your inbound marketing isn't what happened. You can't change that. The most important part is attempting to understand *why* things happened, and making adjustments and improvements backed by data and connected to business objectives. Keep this in mind before you create yet another report.

## Knowing Your Most Important Metric

If you can measure only one thing, make it your business outcomes. Reporting from there should move backwards down the customer purchase path in attempt to discover possible roadblocks to achieving those business outcomes. As you do this, ask yourself the following questions:

✔ Did you achieve revenue/unit sales goals and what does data tell you for future improvements?

✔ Did you achieve market share goals and what does data tell you for future improvements?

✔ Did you achieve your measurable brand awareness goals and what does data tell you for future improvements?

✔ Did you achieve your conversion goals and what does data tell you for future improvements?

✔ Which conversion points overperformed and which underperformed, and what does your data tell you for future improvements?

✔ Did you achieve your attraction goals, and what does data tell you for future improvements?

✔ Did your marketing efforts provide an acceptable ROI, as stated by your plan, and what does data tell you for future improvements?

Elevate your marketing metrics out of the grass and into the sky. The number of Facebook Likes, though important, is often a weak influencer, far removed from the desired consumer end action. That end action is usually a sale, and that conversion action should be your primary metric inbound. Everything else is secondary.

# Understanding Google Analytics

Google Analytics is a powerful free tool measuring your inbound hub — your website. In addition to providing a robust set of website data, Google Analytics allows you to connect your Google AdWords account, integrating your paid search metrics. Tagging your inbound campaigns facilitates additional measuring of your inbound marketing efforts. Google Analytics is the digital marketing's industry standard measure.

## Starting with Google Analytics

Starting off with the basics is usually the best with any new software and Google Analytics is no exception. So if you're that person who starts a project and reads the instructions later, resist the urge. Start off with the basics and build your analytics set in a step-by-step process at first, because you probably don't fully understand what you'll want to measure in the future.

My recommendation? Go slowly by internalizing the dashboard reports for a couple months then decide which custom reports, if any, make sense to measure. And even then be disciplined in the type and volume of reports you build. Just because you can measure something doesn't mean you should. Measure only those factors that contribute to your online marketing and business objectives.

Here's how to start with Google Analytics:

1. **Set up GA goals (start with simple goals) based on website activity you want to measure, which may include:**

    - E-commerce

    - Conversions

    - Specific marketing events/initiatives

2. **Install tracking codes on your website (or have your developer do it).**

3. **Review dashboard reports, identifying those metrics important to your marketing/business objectives and use as a baseline.**

4. **Link other appropriate Google accounts into your GA reporting metrics including:**

    - AdWords for your paid search on Google

    - E-commerce, if you are an online retailer

    - AdSense if you are an online content publisher and are a part of Google's network.

    - Google+ integration

5. **Review your keywords, optimizing for your paid search efforts and using (with much more limitations now) for SEO as much as the tool allows.**

6. **Tag your inbound campaigns.**

    This is important to you as an inbound marketer, especially if you choose not to implement marketing automation software with tracking. Tagging your email, paid search, and other initiatives creates sourcing information enabling you to evaluate where you visitors, leads, and customers originated.

7. **Consider setting up custom reports after you have familiarized and internalized the basic reports.**

## Learning the Google Analytics dashboard

The Google Analytics dashboard displays your website's key statistics and you should familiarize yourself with at least the basics. Knowing your website visitors' onsite behavior helps you make intelligent, data-driven decisions. In other words, instead of using speculation, intuition, or "common sense" (which is rarely "common" or "sensible"), to decide your future online marketing path, improve your future efforts by studying and acting upon behavioral data specific to people on your website.

On the Google Analytics dashboard (see Figure 22-1), you'll find the following:

**Figure 22-1:**
The Google
Analytics
dashboard.

✓ **Sessions:** This states how many times your website was accessed. It includes people who visited your site only one time and people who visited your website repeatedly.

✓ **Users:** These are the number of unique visitors to your website. Unique visitors (rather than website traffic) is a key factor in figuring accurate conversion rates.

✓ **Pageviews:** Looking at page views provides clues as to how engaged your average visitor is. The deeper someone ventures into your website, the more total page views. More page views means more user engagement.

✓ **Pages/Session:** This metric shows an average of how many pages were viewed each time a person visited your website. When visitors consume more pages per session it signals content consumption, which is a good thing.

✓ **Avg. Session Duration:** Measuring visitor's average session time. More time spent on site signals deeper engagement.

✓ **Bounce Rate:** A *bounce* occurs when a visitor visits only one page and exits your site. This is different than *exit rate,* which is a measurement of the percentage of people leaving your site from a particular page after viewing multiple pages.

✓ **% New Sessions:** Knowing the ratio of New Visitors to Returning Visitors illuminates the degree to which your inbound tactics are attracting and reattracting. Applying a filter in "Segments" may shine light on different paths to conversion and nonconversion, providing clues as to where on your website you can navigate traffic to pave a frictionless path toward conversion.

## Knowing why you are measuring

You are analyzing two different areas of performance in Google Analytics:

- Users' onsite behavior
- Technical website performance

Of the reports listed below, site download speed is the only one that is a directly technical issue. You may be able to detect other technical issues by seeing symptoms in your other reports. For instance, other metrics, such as a high bounce rate, could be a function of a website's technical deficiencies (such as a 404 "Page Not Found" error) or it could be a function of something else, such as poor content or poor navigation.

# Choosing Your Reports

The number of reports you can create in Google Analytics is limited only by your imagination. In the following sections, however, I've listed only the most basic inbound-marketing reports. Even if you're outsourcing your digital initiatives to multiple outside experts and practitioners, gaining a grasp on your overall performance helps you understand what's occurring on your website and improves communications with your marketing team.

## Source report

Setting up goals is important, so it makes sense to set up reports based on the goals and objectives you set forth in your inbound marketing plan. To keep it simple, my goal examples below are based on one goal, "Contact Us."

Figure 22-2 displays a source report for my website. The source report shows which are attracting your visitors. Note that a couple of studies, including one performed by Google, determined that Google underreports organic traffic, designating it as "referrals." Currently, it's possible that up to 60 percent of your referral traffic is actually organic so consider manually applying that into your attraction source evaluation.

Notice how it ranks by attraction source and is easily compared for each of your important GA dashboard metrics. This is important because it provides relevance and should stimulate questions from the analyzer. Why is one source's bounce rate higher and one lower? Why do people from certain sources stay on the website longer? Why are some sources completing a goal at a rate seven times that of (in the example) other sources. At this point, you're not looking to fix any problems. Nor are you making any assumptions. You are simply playing Curious George, investigating possibilities.

**Figure 22-2:**
An example
Google
Analytics
source
report.

## *Location report*

The location report displays a world map and table featuring the geographic area of your visitors (see Figure 22-3). It's important to look at your visitors' geographic place of origin so you may filter out any countries, states, or cities you do not serve. Using location reporting to determine your percentage of traffic that is geographically qualified may provide clues as to how to better use local digital marketing. It's also helpful to filter out any areas you do not plan on servicing. For instance, much of my traffic from India (second-ranked geographic traffic) is from people researching our inbound marketing articles. We have generated only two quality leads from India over the past two years, so filtering out India and any other countries I don't service, paints a more accurate picture about my website traffic quality, defined geographically.

**Figure 22-3:**
A Google
Analytics
location
report.

## User flow

User flow is, in my opinion, one of the coolest features in Google Analytics. It displays an aggregate of where people enter your site and which pages they visit in sequential order (see Figure 22-4). Using this tool, you're able to look at onsite conversion flow.

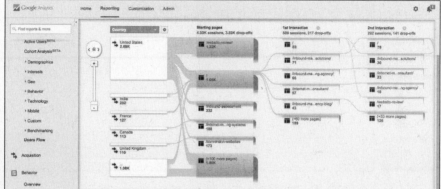

**Figure 22-4:** The Google Analytics User Flow report.

You can easily see and filter the visitor's country of origin and filter the results. For instance, if I only wanted to see user flow paths from U.S. visitors, I click on U.S. and choose one of two options:

- ✓ **Highlight Traffic Through Here** displays the traffic that originates from here, comparing it to total traffic for the subsequent pages in the user flow. In the example above, clicking Highlight Traffic Through Here shows you where people from the U.S. went as compared to other visitors. You can click on any pages in your user flow to highlight incoming and exiting traffic.

- ✓ **Explore Traffic Through Here** displays the visitors who visited the page you click. Using this feature helps you isolate segmented user flows, and determine how a particular set of people journey through your website. Using this feature by clicking Explore Traffic Through Here on an end conversion page provides a glimpse into conversion paths taken to reach this conversion page. Now you can look for pages that may act as roadblocks to a frictionless Buyer's Journey on your website.

## Site speed

Site speed affects UX and your SEO. It's a simple report (see Figure 22-5), providing download speed by page, ranking by your most-visited pages. Looking at the sample report shows that my page download speed, at over four seconds, is way too slow. Knowing this means it's time to get one of my developers to fix the issue. I'm shooting for a page load speed under one second, but certainly no more than two seconds. Fortunately, Google helped me discover this problem.

**Figure 22-5:** Google Analytics Site Speed report.

On the left hand menu, under Behavior, click Site Speed, then click Speed Suggestions. Enter the page URL into the pop-up (it's simplest to copy and paste it from the Google Analytics) and Google provides suggestions to improve your site speed on a tested page.

Site speed's influence on your organic rankings increased recently. Using this tool enhances your SEO and UX, which may affect your conversions positively.

## Mobile device report

Knowing your percentage of mobile visitors is as easy as pulling up the Mobile Device report (see Figure 22-6). Some website are heavily dependent on mobile. This report displays the percentage of people accessing your website from desktop, mobile, and tablet. Consider using this data by comparing mobile conversion paths to nonmobile conversion paths. Are your mobile visitors converting at the same rate as desktop users? Are you conversion pages mobile-friendly or are you seeing a large number of mobile user exits from any given page?

Figure 22-6:
Google
Analytics
Mobile
Device
report.

# Landing Page report

Conversion is half of the inbound marketing equation and landing pages
are your main conversion mechanisms (see Figure 22-7). Under Behavior,
click Site Content, then click Landing Pages. Because landing pages are your
conversion points and the goal of inbound marketing is conversion, using
this tool provides meaningful data a couple ways:

✔ Compare relative conversion performance for each of your most
important landing pages.

✔ Use the landing page report to determine which pages you want to examine in User Flow report. Look for any similarities of customer purchase
paths for high performing landing pages while looking for purchase path
roadblocks (and on-page) for under-performing landing pages.

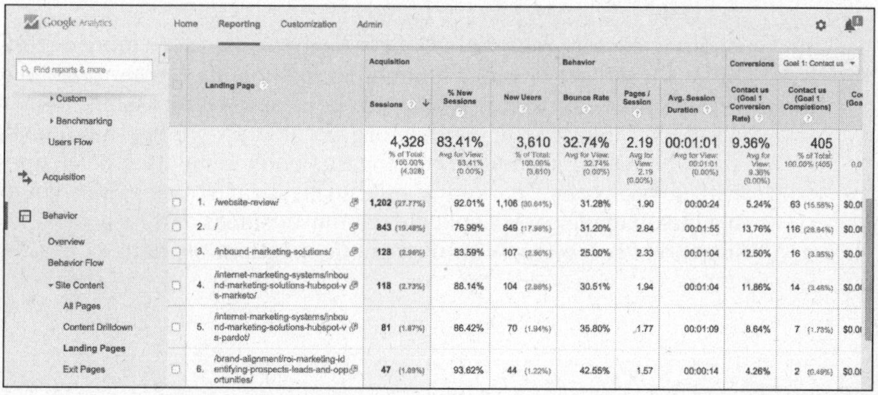

Figure 22-7:
Google
Analytics
Landing
Page report.

## In-page analytics report

Knowing where people are clicking on each of your website pages . . . and where they're not . . . is the key to improving your conversion rates. In-page analytics (see Figure 22-8) reports onsite analytics on your website instead of inside Google Analytics. It displays the percentage of clicks a link from your page is getting. The percentage displayed is for the link, not necessarily the image, button, or text link. This is important to note because providing multiple links to the same page results in the same percentage click for each link. So, unless there's only one link to a path, the report is not telling you exactly where your visitor clicked on the page. So, you can't determine which component was clicked but you can determine which pages people are clicking through to on your website as a percentage of total clicks on the particular page being measured.

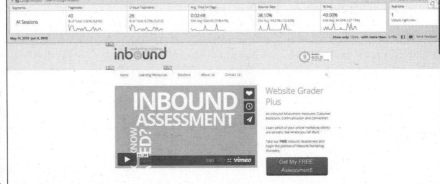

**Figure 22-8:** Google In-Page Analytics report.

# Custom Reports

Building custom reports in Google Analytics measure more accurately the KPIs you set forth in your inbound marketing plan. When building these reports it's best to start where this book started by asking, "Why do you have a website?" Hopefully, you're more adept at answering that question than you were when you began reading this book. Using that basic question along with several other marketing and business questions guides you in building meaningful reports specific to your business and its goals and objective instead of compiling brontobytes of nonactionable data.

## Google Conversion Funnel

It's possible to match up your customer purchase path along the Lifestyle Loop with Google Analytics. Building a custom Conversion Funnel report in GA that matches your key conversion KPIs enables a visual data report (see Figure 22-9). In an attempt to isolate individuals, your custom conversion funnel report treats multiple page views as one unique view (see Figure 22-10), so your conversion numbers are not skewed.

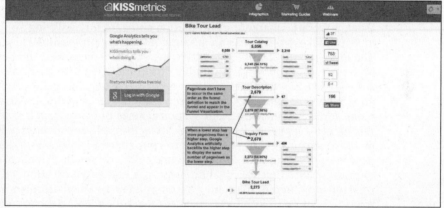

**Figure 22-9:** Google Analytics Conversion Funnel.

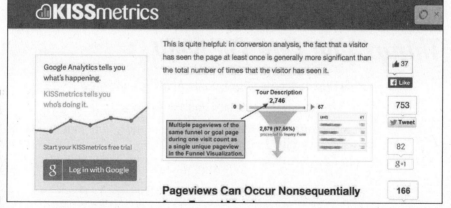

**Figure 22-10:** Multiple page views treated as one unique view.

Reporting your conversion funnel in GA is limited to onsite activity. So, if you're e-commerce, you can easily tag, track, and monitor your ROI and track the customer conversion path to purchase. By examining your ensuing reports, you may discover insights to facilitate a more frictionless purchase process. Of course, most businesses' ultimate action conversion occurs offsite, which means the GA Conversion Funnel is valuable but limited when analyzing the entire inbound process.

## Marketing Automation Software Reports

Using integrated marketing automation software for analyzing your customer journey makes your life as an inbound marketing professional much easier. The more points of conversion KPIs the software measures, the better. Many MAS platforms connect ROI numbers by connecting with custom relationship software like Salesforce.com. Integrating marketing automation software into your analytics reporting does not replace Google Analytics; it enhances it. Using additional measurement systems closes the loop from initial attraction through engagement, conversion, reattraction, and reconversion. Focusing on only measuring KPIs significant to your success, automating the reporting process, and using your findings to make data-driven decisions all contribute to making more time for ideation, testing, and content creation. I regularly recommend different marketing automation software platforms for clients, regardless of size. Not doing so causes marketing inefficiencies and, in my opinion, is sometimes even irresponsible. It's kind of like a pilot flying during a thunderstorm in the dark with no instruments.

## Things You Can Do Now

- ✔ Set up *or* access your Google Analytics account.
- ✔ Perform your dashboard analytics check.
- ✔ Make sure your website is mobile-friendly and your site load speed is quick.

# Chapter 23

# Understanding User Testing

*E*arlier in this book I mentioned that if something's worth doing, it's worth measuring. Now I submit to you that if something's worth measuring, it's worth testing. By purposefully testing your key success metrics and acting on your discoveries, you may intelligently affect your outcomes. Increasing the positive impact of any given inbound marketing factor results in an increase in the overall successful outcome of your inbound marketing initiatives. Testing factors that affect your key metrics provides insight into incremental improvements you may discover and implement for every point in the Customer Conversion Chain.

This chapter is not a thorough examination of extremely sophisticated or technical testing methods. I'll hire a mathematician for that. As an inbound marketer, you need simpler behavioral tests, the findings of which may have a more immediate impact on your marketing results. My main focus is on split testing because it's the most manageable for the typical inbound marketer. This chapter covers sound testing principles for basic testing techniques. The intent is to teach a simple and quick means of discovering which parts of your digital marketing work best, and leveraging that knowledge in positive business outcomes.

## Gaining Insight from User Testing

When performing user-testing, it's helpful to know the difference between attitudinal testing and behavioral testing. Attitudinal testing is what users *say* they do. Behavioral testing is what they *actually* do. Inbound marketing's goal is to increase attraction and conversion. So, measuring *behavior* is your primary objective. To quickly increase your conversions remember this: ABABT or Always Be A/B Testing. Focusing on A/B testing means measuring actual behaviors, assessing the impact of format changes, and applying actionable positive influence on the end result. Other attitudinal testing is valuable for understanding the psychology of communicating with your customer personas, and if you have access to that research, by all means, use it! For purposes of testing the Customer Conversion Chain, I want to limit the conversation to testing that you, as an inbound marketer, can control, measure, and implement on your own. Most certainly, A/B split testing and possibly multivariate testing fit into this category.

If you choose to test beyond A/B testing, use the chart that digital marketer Christian Rohrer designed because it's a good starting point. (See Figure 23-1.) Understanding which questions you want answered molds the type of testing you should perform. Use this list to help you decide on a test type:

✔ If you want to know what people do, use behavioral testing (like A/B testing).

✔ If you want to answer "how many?" or "how much?" use quantitative testing.

✔ If you want to know the answers to why something is happening and how to fix it, use qualitative testing.

✔ If you want to know what people say, use attitudinal testing.

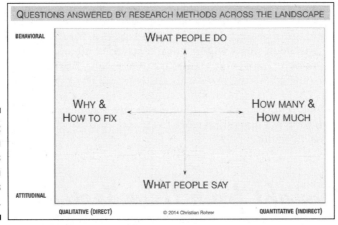

**Figure 23-1:** Christian Rohrer's research methods chart.

Christian created another, more detailed chart that I feature later in this chapter to help you choose the actual style of research testing.

# Knowing What to Test

Because of the complexity of inbound marketing, the things you could test are infinite. So start off simply, testing those points of attraction and conversion that contribute the greatest to your successful outcome. That way, any positive changes you learn by testing may be applied with more impact.

The fact is, you can test anything that you know or suspect may have a meaningful impact on your inbound marketing efforts. I recommend you begin by testing input factors that are closest to the desired consumer action you're seeking. So, if you're e-commerce, consider starting your testing on your shopping cart page and work backwards down the customer conversion path. The exception is if A/B testing that close to a purchase would have a profoundly negative impact on sales. Alternatively, you may consider testing the weakest link in your company's Customer Conversion Chain.

If you're serious about inbound marketing, invest in marketing automation software or conversion optimization software. And, remember: ABABT!

# Knowing Your Minimum Sample Size

Garnering meaningful data is only as good as the validity of the test you're performing. Maybe you're not so great at manually formulating statistical degrees of confidence. Neither am I, actually. Check out Figure 23-2 and meet your new A/B testing best friend, the Sample Size Calculator from Optimizely (www.optimizely.com/resources/sample-size-calculator/).

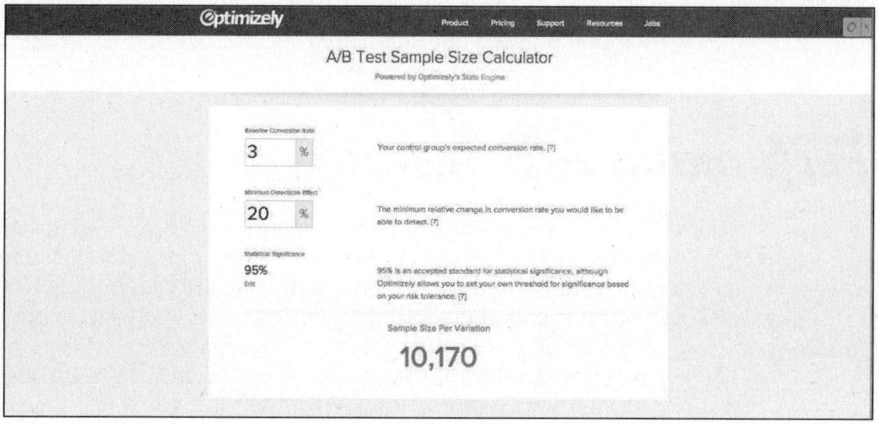

**Figure 23-2:** The Optimizely Sample Size Calculator.

Simply fill in your current conversion rate (it defaults to three percent). Next, input your minimum detectable effect. This is the amount of "lift" or increase over the original control you want your test to be able to detect. The lower you make this number, the more respondents you'll need. With a lower number, then, the test will take longer, but it will provide finer results. The statistical significance box autofills with the recommended 95 percent — this is recommended for a reason. Unless you possess the serious chops of an experienced marketing researcher, leave this value alone so you don't get into trouble. The tool is built to help provide some testing parameters, but in the end it is you that performs the test, not the tool.

Statistical significance alone does not equate to validity. You must give your tests time to work themselves out. You otherwise risk getting an early "false read" that may show one of your test subjects overperforming. If you stop the test and apply the changes immediately, you risk applying false assumptions that will not carry through down the Customer Conversion Chain. To avoid this, make sure you test the minimum amount to achieve statistical significance and then keep testing. For instance, if you're A/B testing two landing pages for a couple days, generating huge traffic and one out-converts the other . . . do not stop!

Keep testing through two business cycles, as defined by your industry's purchase cycle. This may be an extremely long time for business-to-business companies. To be safe, run your test for at least 30 days to account for unforeseen time anomalies. To create higher confidence in your results, make sure you're generating at least 250 testable actions per version. Lastly, make sure your number of conversion itself is big enough to draw meaningful data and project future performance more accurately. If you had tons of traffic to each of two landing pages you were testing, and for the first page one person converted and for the second, two people, you've learned nothing that can be applied. Assuming the second page will convert 200 percent better than the first page is a fallacy that will get you in trouble, so be careful and don't get into testing that's over your head.

# Performing A/B Testing

Today, inbound markcting offers more control over your advertising message than ever before. With access to complex data points, it's possible to know more about who is visiting your site, how they are responding to your message, what drives them to action, and what is and what is not working.

The key is refining your approach. One effective method is through A/B testing, also known as split testing. With the right software, A/B testing costs next to nothing to implement. Split testing works by examining a "control" (A) against one single changed variable, also known as your "treatment" (B). It allows you to identify what brings a better response rate.

A/B testing individual components of your marketing approach is a great way to understand and identify what is working. It allows you to refine your message, drive more traffic to your site, and generate more leads from the traffic you are getting. Ultimately, your inbound marketing drives more revenue opportunities.

If you decide to try testing yourself, here are several guidelines and best practices to consider before getting started.

- ✔ **Keep it simple. Only conduct one test at a time.** For example, if you're testing a new on-page CTA button directing visitors to a landing page you're also testing at the same time, the results can easily become cloudy. What's performing better, the CTA or the landing page? You have no way of verifying what caused a specific effect. Do not conduct multiple overlapping split tests at the same time.

- ✔ **Test only one variable at a time.** To determine how effective an element is, you need to isolate that variable in your A/B testing. Whether it is a page element or graphic, a call-to-action or an email campaign, only test one variable at a time. By focusing your testing on an entire page, email, or CTA as the variable, you can often achieve dramatic results.

- ✔ **Small changes may have big results.** While big sweeping changes can often increase lead generation numbers, small changes can be just as important. When developing your tests, remember that even something as simple as changing your headline, your image, your form field size, or the color of your CTA button may offer significant results. Sometimes small changes are easier to measure than big ones.

- ✔ **Consider testing one larger variable such as an entire landing page.** While you can test the color of a CTA button as a variable, you might wish to test an entire landing page, unique promotional offer, or full email as a variable. Instead of testing a single design element like a headline or image, consider creating two separate landing pages as variable and test them against each other. In this case, you're testing the overall design layout rather than the individual components making up the landing page or email. This is a higher level of testing and can result in dramatic results so you'll learn which page performs better, but not which component, or combination of components, is causing that lift.

- ✔ **Start by measuring closer to the desired end action, usually a sale.** I've stated this before, and I'll state it again: Testing closer to the Action in the Lifestyle Loop will create the opportunity for more influence. Just be aware that impact may be a positive or negative impact! Your testing can have a positive impact on your conversion rate, but how is it affecting your sales numbers? Applying what you've learned from A/B testing results can affect your bottom line. You may find that while your conversion rate may drop, leads may be more qualified and result in higher sales numbers. As you create your tests, consider metrics like click-through rates, leads, traffic, conversion rates, and demo requests.

# Setting Up User Testing

User testing can tell you a lot about your website and inbound marketing campaigns in a very short time. Have you ever written content, any content, and had it proofread by a couple people only to discover there's a glaring typo that somehow is glaringly obvious after your content is published? I have, and it's embarrassing and frustrating. The same can be said about UI and UX. What seems like a logical onsite navigation path and obvious CTA choices to you and your developer when you initially chart it out on paper may not work as you intended. Even after you've reviewed your website on an interactive demo site, test its usability before you launch it live to the public. Why? UX navigation mistakes aren't as obvious as a typo in your content. Visitor activity is invisible, and people who bounce aren't going to tell you why they left. I perform user testing to spot unintentional design dead-ends, roadblocks, and friction on the customer conversion path and I urge you to do the same. Performing user testing prelaunch helps maximize consumer action, which is exactly what you want out of your inbound marketing.

## Testing a single factor

Similar to your split A/B testing, it makes sense for you to choose only one thing to test when performing user testing. (Are you sensing a testing trend here?) Testing a workflow, a conversion campaign, or a website navigation sequence make sense any time you're creating a new version of each. Wouldn't you rather learn your conversion roadblocks before you launch new inbound initiatives so you're not fixing things on the fly? Trust me, the answer is "Yes!"

## Testing with click-tracking

Tracking user clicks through click recording software is an effective method of testing where your users are going on your website pages. By collecting and aggregating this information and then displaying it as a heat map, you get a clear picture if people are clicking in the places in the manner in which you designed any particular page. This is particularly effective for observing and reporting which CTAs are being clicked and which are not being clicked. There are too many options for me to cover in this book; however, here are four paid click-tracking options, listed alphabetically:

- Crazy Egg (www.crazyegg.com)
- Inspectlet (www.inspectlet.com)
- Lucky Orange (www.luckyorange.com)
- Mouseflow (http://mouseflow.com)

Researching with click-tracking and analyzing the resulting heat map reports instigates better website page UI design. That's good for your visiting customers, which means it's good for you.

## *Testing with screencasting*

One method of easily spotting obvious navigation roadblocks is hiring paid testers to perform onsite actions and tasks. Two paid services that deliver are UserTesting (`www.usertesting.com`) and TechSmith's Morae (`www.techsmith.com/morae`). Each of these record the activities of actual users interacting with the subject of your test. For instance, by providing your prelaunch working prototype of your soon-to-be launched website, you pay for users to perform specific activities, like shopping and checking out or navigating through a workflow.

UserTesting uses professional testers who screencast and narrate their onsite activity. So you see the tester's mouse move toward a CTA button, for instance, while the tester says, "Now I'm going to click here to see where this takes me." You name your number of testers, and you receive recorded sessions quickly, sometimes under an hour. Morae is capable of recording test subjects' facial expressions, eye movements, and mouse-click behavior. If accessing historical report data is important, you can archive results digitally. Either way, you'll know where your UI roadblocks are very quickly.

Regardless of whether you choose one of the two research tools above or an alternative, your process is the same:

1. **Define your research scope.**
2. **Create the scenario.**
3. **Define the user task.**
4. **Observe and notate key positive or negative interactions.**
5. **Formulate a summary.**
6. **Make recommended changes.**
7. **Retest to see if identified roadblocks have been eliminated from the customer purchase path.**

In my consulting experience, I've learned that showing clients, developers, and IT users interacting with our collective digital marketing efforts proves far more powerful than telling them what the problems are. When you record users stumbling around a web page, not knowing where to go next, it's usually obvious to all which components need to be fixed. It can be a humbling experience, but the reason I'm an inbound marketer is to build up sales, not my ego.

## Reporting results

Reporting and documenting your test results, regardless of the testing performed, is good inbound marketing practice. Knowing which past testing factors succeeded and which failed builds a shareable knowledge base from which you can draw upon to make successively better decisions in the future. Documenting the intent, timing, observations, and action points helps you and your inbound marketing team leverage your collective knowledge to maximize conversions.

Testing is an ongoing process. Creating a testing culture within your organization stimulates continual raising of your success bar. I like the Usabilla graphic in Figure 23-3, because it demonstrates the testing process as continuous. There is no beginning and no end.

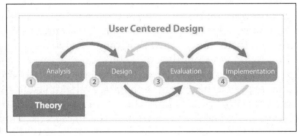

**Figure 23-3:**
Usabilla
testing
process.

Commit to a culture of measuring, testing, and reporting. Not every marketing initiative will work. It's valuable to know about those failures so your organization doesn't repeat past mistakes. Likewise, documenting your testing history provides a resource from which you can replicate successes resulting in an overall lift in CTR and sales while lowering your cost-per-lead and cost-per-acquisition.

## Things You Can Do Now

✔ Test a CTA button with an A/B test.

✔ Test a landing page with an A/B test.

✔ Perform a screencasted UX navigation test.

# Part VIII
## The Part of Tens

the part of tens

Enjoy an additional Part of Tens chapter online at www.dummies.com/extras/inboundmarketing.

## In this part. . .

- ✔ Learning how to systematically start your inbound marketing.
- ✔ Understanding key business metrics to measure.

# Chapter 24

# Ten Steps to Implementing Inbound Marketing

• • • • • • • • • • • • • • • • • • • • • • • • • • • • • • • • • • • • • • • • • • • • • • •

Getting started with inbound marketing doesn't have to be a monumental task. By taking a logical calculated approach, you can be up and running with your inbound marketing within 90 days.

In order to begin inbound marketing, you need the basics of your Conversion Machine to be in place. You need a functional website that is both attractive and conversion-oriented. Your goals and objectives should be very clear and manageable. Lastly, assessing your current digital marketing position and defining your problems in business terms rather than in marketing terms increases your conversion rates and your success rate.

## Determining Whether Your Organization Is Open to Change

The first step in implementing inbound marketing into your organization is company acceptance, of a new method of marketing. Basing your inbound marketing on customer-centric, attractive marketing that pulls customers into a relationship with your company is much different than interruptive "push" marketing methods. By expressing your marketing initiatives with positive business outcomes, key decision-making people within your organization are more likely to comprehend what you're trying to achieve with inbound marketing and embrace it.

Leading your company's evolution into inbound marketing requires commitment, communication, and coordination. For those with the foresight and fortitude, the payoff is great. Here's how to determine if your company is ready for inbound marketing:

1. **Assess your current marketing to determine if there is a measurable link between your marketing initiatives and your business outcomes.**

2. **Identify gaps in your current marketing plan and your desired inbound marketing to determine your marketing initiatives priorities.**

3. **Paint a picture of the positive business outcomes by writing down several "What if?" questions that include not only the marketing department, but also the sales department, customer service, billing, and so on.**

4. **Share your ideal outcomes with colleagues to see who on your team has the most to gain by implementing inbound marketing, then seek their support.**

5. **Research investment costs of implementing inbound marketing, including the costs of paid assessment, marketing automation software, expert consultant fees, content creation, paid search, SEO, PPC, and social media, then break down those costs into manageable pieces with a timeline.**

6. **Create a presentation for the *business* case for implementing inbound marketing.**

7. **Seek budget approval.**

# Discussing Internal and External Goals with Other Departments or Colleagues

Knowing your company's goals and objectives is paramount to implementing inbound marketing and its associated philosophy and methodology. One of your jobs as a marketer is to help the companies achieve those goals and objectives. To do this, you need information. Interview others inside your company, starting with people in different departments that are on the same level as you, and then moving as high up the management chain as is permissible or as you feel comfortable. Some of the people in other departments that it may make sense for you to visit include:

✔ Your boss (to get her permission and feedback before proceeding with others)

✔ Sales team/management

✔ IT

- ✔ Customer service
- ✔ Accounting
- ✔ Distribution/logistics
- ✔ Owners/top management

Don't act nosy, suspicious, or like a know-it-all. Rather, be candid by explaining that you're looking at ways marketing can help the company, including each respective department. You'll quickly realize who is open to change and who may be a barrier to it. No matter. This isn't for you to judge; instead, it's important for you to see where you can make the greatest impact within your organization in the shortest timeline possible.

# Formulating Your Company's Customer Conversion Chain

The quickest way to build a business case for inbound marketing is to formulate a Customer Conversion Chain for one of your best products or services. You may need help with this, but you can surely get started by looking at analytics to determine your current monthly numbers for the following:

- ✔ Impressions by attraction source (PPC, SEO, social media, and so on)
- ✔ Website sessions/unique visits
- ✔ Leads/contacts
- ✔ Quality leads
- ✔ Demonstrated interest (presentations/demos/trials)
- ✔ Customers
- ✔ Average purchase (in dollars)
- ✔ Repeat customers
- ✔ Average repeat purchase (in dollars)

# Determining Budget of Time, Energy, and Money to Achieve Goals

After performing your initial Customer Conversion Chain assessment, evaluate the resources you'll need (in terms of time, energy, and money) to begin inbound marketing. Every company operates with limited resources so how you choose to allocate yours eventually will determine an optimal allocation of your marketing resources.

Answer the following questions about your marketing budget:

- ✔ What is my current marketing budget?
- ✔ Is my marketing allocation enough to achieve stated business goals and objectives?
- ✔ Which budgeted items are fixed spending (such as annual software subscriptions, media contracts, and so on) and which are flexible spending items?
- ✔ Which marketing initiatives measurably contribute to stated goals and objectives, which are less measurable, and which are not contributing or are non-measurable?
- ✔ Of the company products you're currently marketing, which are the highest volume and which are the most profitable?
- ✔ Which products offer the greatest opportunity for growth and what is the associated budgeted dollar amount with those products?
- ✔ Which areas of marketing would benefit the most from either reallocating marketing budgets or creating new budget line items?

Money is one thing, but timelines are another. You may have a highly profitable product line with a very long sales cycle, which means your marketing investments will take longer to pay off. When considering time allocation into your inbound marketing equation, answer the following questions:

- ✔ Which of your target customer personas are the heaviest users of digital media?
- ✔ Which products have the shortest purchase path timeline?
- ✔ Which products have the longest?
- ✔ Which of your products currently has the most content associated with each point in the purchase path?
- ✔ If you could devote time to only one product, which one would it be?
- ✔ Which of your products are most conducive to digital marketing as defined by search volume?
- ✔ Which of your current marketing efforts could easily be replaced by efficiently reallocating time devoted to those efforts into inbound marketing?

Your collective internal energy is an oft-overlooked factor in determining budget. Consider the following questions and then decide where to reallocate your budgets and time both internally among your marketing team and externally with marketing partners:

- ✔ Which areas of digital marketing does your internal marketing team possess expertise?

- ✔ Which of your current external marketing vendor partners contribute the least to your business goals and objectives?

- ✔ Who on your internal team has experience in digital marketing, who can learn, and who needs to be replaced with internal experts?

- ✔ Can you achieve your marketing and business goals with your current team or do you need to add seats and/or hire experts?

- ✔ What combination of internal marketing team and external marketing partners will help you implement inbound marketing strategy and tactics the quickest?

Both energy and time are consumed in a steep learning curve when you and your team have to simultaneously learn inbound best practices, inbound terminology, and then actually perform the inbound marketing. That's why sometimes it pays to add internal and external experts onto your marketing team.

# Performing an Inbound Marketing Assessment

Find a consultant or marketing firm and invest in a paid inbound marketing assessment. This is your starting point to frame your future initiatives, regardless of who performs those initiatives. Keep an open mind as to what you may discover and who might be best suited to perform future inbound marketing tactics. Your IMA outlines a series of prioritized inbound initiatives some of which you may be able to deliver with your current internal marketing team and some that may require help from external marketing partners. You won't know this until after you perform your IMA.

Remember, starting with tactics to solve your problem is a dangerous endeavor, especially the tactics touted by ad agencies promoting only the services they're selling (SEO, content, social media, PPC, and so on) as the end-all fix. Those agencies may be experts in those areas, but what they're selling may not be the optimal tactic to achieve your business objectives. Instead, use your IMA to determine which inbound marketing tactical inputs are most likely to contribute to better outcomes and then seek experts in those specific areas — not vice-versa.

Should you choose to invest in an outside firm to perform your IMA, make sure of the following:

✔ The firm has performed other IMAs.

✔ The firm provides an objective report on gaps between your current marketing and best practices.

✔ The firm does not require you to utilize any further services in tactical implementation. You should be able to use your IMA report for internal execution, application with another marketing firm, or the firm that performed the IMA, if you choose.

✔ The IMA reports inbound marketing priorities so it's clear which tactics you need to focus on first.

# Writing Your Inbound Marketing Strategy

Writing a strategy is no small undertaking; however, your strategy is your inbound marketing roadmap so it's important to your success. After introducing the findings of your IMA to your internal team members, and outlining gaps, opportunities, and priorities, begin writing your strategy.

Often, because of the company knowledge of budgets, key initiatives, and general inner workings of your organization, marketing strategy is written internally. Because inbound is a newer concept to marketers and their companies, inbound marketing strategy is more likely to require help from an outside expert. Should you choose this route, you'll still need to be intimately involved in providing internal company information because of the aforementioned reasons.

By performing an IMA first, followed by a written inbound marketing strategy, you're setting the state for success. You can learn more about inbound marketing strategy in Chapter 4.

# Assigning In-House and Outsourced Inbound Marketing Responsibilities

After creating the framework for the inbound marketing work to be done, you'll need to apply your discoveries by assigning marketing initiatives and tactics. I've covered some basic methods of determining the allocation of time, money, and energy. Here are some additional questions to ask when considering whether to perform your inbound marketing internally versus outsourcing:

- ✔ Do you have the time and expertise to build a conversion-based website in-house?

- ✔ Do you have the time and expertise to set up analytics, create meaningful attraction and conversion dashboard reports, and recommend future action points?

- ✔ Do you have internal competency in content creation?

- ✔ Do you have internal SEO competency?

- ✔ Do you have PPC/paid-search competency?

- ✔ Do you have social-media competency?

- ✔ Do you have competency in conversion optimization?

- ✔ Can your internal team build out complete campaigns that include blogs, content pages, landing pages, CTAs, and automated email workflows?

- ✔ For any of the questions you answered "yes," which, if any, benefit from additional outside help?

- ✔ Will you achieve you objectives more quickly with an internal marketing team, an external marketing firm, or a combination of the two?

You may be able to implement all your inbound marketing efforts internally. It depends on your internal marketing team's base of knowledge and how quickly you wish to achieve your objectives.

# Retooling or Rebuilding Your Website

You now know that your website is the engine in your Customer Conversion Machine. If your website isn't built upon conversion architecture, it doesn't make sense to attract additional traffic. Budget for a conversion-based website build now. In that budget, consider adding in marketing automation software from the get-go.

Because your website is the hub of your online attraction and conversion activity, your first initiative in applied inbound is to retool or rebuild your website. Sometimes, it makes sense to do a quick retool in order to increase conversions while redesigning an entire rebuild or your website. At the very least, create a basic CTA Map, add in CTA buttons and forms, and build out conversion-based landing pages so you can increase conversion with your current website traffic.

# *Writing Your First Shared Strategic Blueprint*

As part of your strategy, break down objectives and initiatives into three month marketing sprints with clear marketing goals. These marketing conversion goals are based on your Customer Conversion Chain and are formulated by populating our digital media inputs into that formula.

Chapter 5 provides a simple sample of a Shared Strategic Blueprint (SSB). Chances are, your first SSB projections will be way off. Don't worry. Start with conservative milestones, learn as you go, examine trends, and prepare to be flexible when populating your second SSB. The important thing is to begin forming a habit of planning and accountability. There is no right or wrong answers and there is no magic bullet. An SSB helps you and your company be cognizant of the daily, weekly, and quarterly marketing inputs that contribute to achieving your business goals.

Outline which campaigns you plan on building and the timeframe in which they'll be completed. Remember to include build-out time for the campaign so that you're not including inadvertent falsely high attraction and conversion numbers. Add those numbers into your SSB only after your estimated campaign completion date. Be willing to change your input numbers should you not achieve your campaign build-out timelines.

# *Beginning Content Creation*

Creating content is so important to your inbound marketing that you'll probably want to start creating product campaign content while you're rebuilding or retooling your website. In your strategy, you'll have outlined your content assets, your content gaps based on the Lifestyle Loop purchase path, and your content needs. Consider creating content in the following ways:

- On-page website content
- Encouragement content ("Contact Us" forms, product with pricing, coupons SKUs, and so on)
- Engagement downloadable content such as ebooks and white papers
- Landing-page content
- Email content

If you have the resources, it's possible to create all this content simultaneously.

# Chapter 25

# Ten Important Inbound Marketing Metrics

• • • • • • • • • • • • • • • • • • • • • • • • • • • • • • • • • • • • • • • • • • • • •

*O*ne of the goals of inbound marketing is to create avid fans of your company's brand and products. These loyal repeat customers, known as Lifestylers, live your brand and advocate for your products. Knowing the value of your customers and defining their dollar value over the lifetime of your relationship helps you calculate a return on your marketing investment. So, in this chapter I outline the ten important inbound conversion metrics for you to populate your Customer Conversion Chain, enabling you to reverse-engineer a plan. Calculate the numbers for each metric, beginning with the end in mind (LTV) so you can make more educated decisions when allocating your marketing resources.

## Lifetime Value Of Your Customer (LTV)

Your customers are worth more than one purchase. Their value to your company can be defined in influence and in dollars over the course of your business relationship with them. For purposes of calculating ROI, you can simply use the lifetime value of your customer (LTV). Using historical sales data, you can figure it in two different ways. The first one is this:

**Average Transaction Purchase Amount ($) × Average Number of Purchases = LTV**

For this first formula, let's use the example of an online education company whose average course fee is $30. If this company analyzes its data to discover that an average student will take ten courses, the lifetime value of its customer is $300. ($30/course × 10 courses = $300)

The second way LTV can be calculated is this:

**Average Annual Purchase Amount ($) × Average Length of Customer Engagement = LTV**

For this second formula, let's say you're a mobile-phone carrier whose average customer has a two-phone plan at $60 per month per phone, and the average customer remains active with you for three years (36 months). Furthermore, let's assume that you have data that shows that the first year's purchase will also include two mobile phones and setup fees totaling $1,004.

First year total revenues (mobile phones, setup, and 12 months of service) = $2000

Second 24 months of contract revenues = $(2 \times \$60) \times 24 = \$120 \times 24 = \$2,880$

$2,000 (Year 1) + $2,880 (Year 2 and 3) = $4,880 LTV

To obtain an even more accurate LTV number, you could apply revenue "erosion," which arises from contract cancellations and non-fulfillment; however, I have not done so here.

# *First Action Value (Purchase)*

Because it takes time to realize your customers' LTV, you may sometimes want a quicker view of your marketing ROI. Knowing the initial value of the first action makes it easy for you to calculate your initial ROI.

Using the example of the mobile-phone provider from the previous section, let's presume that there is an initial phone purchase that averages $330 and a setup fee of $22 per phone. Let's also assume that, for these numbers, there is a one-year contract commitment required.

Because the average customer purchases two units, the phone hardware cost is $660 ($2 \times \$330$) and the initial setup cost is $44 ($2 \times \$22$).

The first-year contract for two phones amounts to $(2 \times \$60) \times 12 = \$1,440$. Let's also assume the data shows that your customers who don't fulfill their contracts reduce this amount to, on average, 90 percent of the total first-year contract fees, lowering your average first year to $1,296 ($1,440 − $144 = $1,296).

From this you can calculate your first action value — in this case, the purchase of mobile phones, setup, and one-year service — by adding these three values: $660 + $44 + $1,296, or $2,000.

Your customer's average first action value purchase, then, is $2,000.

As you become a more sophisticated inbound marketer, you can segment buying groups based on groups who have higher LTVs and focus on attracting more of the same while facilitating their purchase path toward conversion. Likewise, you'll eventually be able to identify patterns in those who cancel and attract fewer of those types of customers.

# Cost-Per-Acquisition

Measuring your cost-per-acquisition (CPA) helps you define your marketing ROI. To quickly achieve this, simply take your attraction marketing budget and divide it by the number of first-action purchases. In our mobile phone example, let's assume your marketing budget was $100,000/month, and that this historically generated an average of 250 customers per month.

CPA = Budget / Number of Customers

$100,000/250 = $400 cost-per-acquisition

If $400 CPA has traditionally been an acceptable number to acquire new customers (meaning it's a profitable equation for your company), you may now begin to formulate predictive models to project future business.

If you invested $200,000 at $400 CPA, you'll generate 500 new customers per month.

Does that mean an investment of $1,000,000 might result in 2,500 new customers per month? Nobody knows, so it's best to adjust your investment in small increments until you reach a point of diminishing returns. If, however, you knew with 100 percent certainty that your million-dollar investment would result in 2,500 new customers, you would certainly invest that much in marketing. There are only two reasons you wouldn't:

- ✔ You lack the capacity to produce and serve that number of customers.
- ✔ You lack the cash flow to sustain the marketing budget for the time between first contact and first contract.

Too often, we focus on efficiencies rather than on opportunities because efficiencies are immediately and tangibly defined as expense savings. Opportunities, on the other hand, are speculative and therefore more unpredictable. This is not to say you should shy away from opportunity budgeting. Rather, you should proceed with cautious conservatism and care.

# Return-On-Investment (ROI) Cost-Per-Lead/Cost-Per-Acquisition

Now that you've broken down your marketing budget by assigning your marketing initiative inputs to product pyramids, you can easily figure your ROI. Here's how it's calculated:

(LTV × Number of Customers) / Marketing Budget = Total ROI

In the case of our mobile phone company, that looks like this:

250 customers per month × $4,880 = $1,220,000

$1,220,000 / $100,000 marketing budget = 12.2 × return or 12,200 percent

Your marketing budget was 8.2 percent of sales ($100,000/$1,220,000). Just remember you're not realizing your full return all at once. Rather, in this example, it requires three full years to capture the full return on your marketing investment.

For your more immediate ROI, simply replace the LTV number in your equation with the first action value. This is expressed as:

(First Action Value × Number of Customers) / Marketing Budget = Immediate ROI

In the case of our mobile phone company, that looks like this:

($2,000 × 250) / $100,000 = $500,000 / $100,000 = 5 × (500 percent return)

In this scenario, your marketing budget is 20 percent of sales.

# Presentation-to-Purchase Close Ratio

Your sales department is responsible for creating sales. As such, your organization should measure the percentage of the people who demonstrated an interest in your product who become customers, also known as your *close ratio*. "Demonstrated interest," in this sense, may refer to the people who attended a sales presentation, a product demo, trial offer, or any other promotion that involves your sales department. A closed sale is your "first contract." The close ratio may vary wildly by industry and company. There is no standard definition of a good close ratio, so you'll have to look internally at historical data to see what your company's close ratio is and evaluate it accordingly. Some factors that will affect your evaluation of your company close ratio include:

- Number of leads delivered
- Quality of leads delivered
- Which product is being sold
- Price
- Your sales department's ability to sell appropriately
- Seasonality of product purchase
- The profile or persona of the customer making the actual purchase
- The complexity of the buying parameters (is it a quick, simple low-dollar transaction or a long, complex buying cycle?)
- The competitive nature of the market

To figure your close ratio, simply divide the number of people who became customers by the number of people who demonstrated an interest (as this term was mutually defined and agreed upon by your marketing and sales departments).

So, if one person from every three presentations becomes a customer, your close ratio is 33 percent (1/3).

If you gained 6 customers for every 10 product demonstrations, your close ratio is 60 percent (6/10).

If you close one customer for every 100 product trials, your close ratio is 1 percent (1/100).

As an inbound marketer, you should not be held accountable for the close ratio because it is a function of sales. It's an important metric for you to track, however, because your conversion links earlier on in the Customer Conversion Chain, especially the quality of leads you're able to deliver, can influence the close ratio.

# MQLs-to-SQLs Ratio

It's your job as an inbound marketer to attract and measure leads; your responsibility to understand lead quality. This is another simple conversion ratio to calculate. Simply divide sales qualified leads (SQLs) by marketing qualified leads (MQLs).

A sales qualified lead (SQL) is a lead that expressed interest, passively or actively, in at least one of your product offerings.

A prospect who downloads several engagement content pieces, filling out multiple forms and sharing potential buying signs along the way, may be considered an MQL. Someone who completes a "Contact Us" form has expressed an active need and may be further down the purchase path but may still be designated as an MQL to be passed on to sales. In a business-to-business model, your salespeople determine SQLs through personal interaction by determining whether the prospect possesses need, intent, timeline, and budget.

There are a couple different ways to track SQL conversion rates; by comparing either SQLs to MQLs or comparing SQLs to total leads. Each is a measure of lead quality, however, they are two different metrics reporting from a different base. The formulas, respectively, are:

- **SQL / MQL:** This ratio provides clues as to the quality of leads your marketing department is nurturing and then handing off to sales. Examining the SQLs conversion path from MQL to SQL helps you improve or shorten the customer conversion path.

- **SQL / Total Leads:** This ratio tells you the lead quality from a lead's initial conversion. Knowing the SQLs to their original attraction source (SEO, PPC, etc.) helps you improve your conversion efforts by identifying those sources attracting a better initial lead allocating more marketing efforts towards those sources.

# Contact-Conversions-to-MQL Ratio

The number of your contacts that become marketing qualified leads (MQLs) is the first measurement of lead quality. Upon conversion, the marketing department designates each lead as one of the following:

- Ideal customer matches or "A" leads.

- Prospective leads who appear to be good matches, either by the engagement information they provided, their onsite activity, or their status as buyer decision-makers; also known as "B" leads.

- Prospective leads who provided information, but whose onsite activity, information given, or other factors caused the marketing department to view them as questionable. These are "C" leads.

- Contact Leads who are not good prospects. Classify these leads as "unqualified".

This is a simplified classification system, and you can certainly develop more sophisticated designations based on lead scoring, product pyramids, or sub-categories/classifications.

As with some other conversion ratios, the contact-conversions-to-MQL ratio is a simple formula: MQL / Total Leads.

# Unique-Visitors-to-Lead Ratio

Increasing your traffic does not necessarily mean you'll see a proportionate spike in your contacts/leads. In fact, if your marketing is driving unqualified traffic to your website, your lead conversion ratios may actually go down. In other words, increasing your number of visitors may look like you're gaining traction but it doesn't always translate to an increase in sales. The inbound marketer understands that they have a meaningful influence on the business outcomes. You are best served to understand your role in that process, increasing positive marketing inputs that in turn result in positive results.

As such, you should monitor your website conversion ratio very closely. Understanding your onsite conversion and comparing each individual inbound campaign's conversion ratio helps you spot over-achieving campaigns. By identifying which marketing components are contributing to the increase in conversions, you can test and apply those high conversion points in your other inbound campaigns, often replicating your success. This in turn contributes to an increase in your overall conversion rate.

Figuring your unique visitors-to-lead conversion rate is easy. Do make sure you use unique visitors and not your total website traffic. The formula is: Number of Leads / Number of Unique Visitors

So if you have 10,000 visitors per month and 500 of them engage with you by providing contact information or by contacting you, your ratio is 500/10,000, or 5 percent.

Your overall conversion rate is a different number, figured by dividing the total number of customers by total number of unique visitors. It looks like this: Total Customers / Number of Unique Visitors

When you hear other marketers refer to a website's "conversion rate," this is frequently the formula to which they are referring.

# Cost-Per-Lead

Figuring your cost-per-lead is, again, a very simple ratio. Simply divide your marketing expenditures by the number of total leads.

In our hypothetical mobile phone company, the monthly budget is $100,000, resulting in 500 leads per month, so the cost-per-lead is $200. Note that your CPL will always be lower than your CPA because not every lead becomes an acquired customer.

One of the reasons you track CPL is so you can compare CPLs by source. If you, as the marketer for the mobile phone company, discovered that the CPL for SEO leads was $100 compared to $200 for PPC and $300 for social-media leads, you might begin investigating why. This doesn't necessarily mean you should put all your efforts into SEO because you haven't yet determined the quality of your leads from each source. For instance, if 90 percent of your social-media leads eventually became customers, you'd probably be willing to pay the CPL premium. Also, the volume of leads for any particular source may not generate enough customers to achieve your sales objectives. So, if the total volume of leads from your most efficient source (SEO, in this example) would provide only a maximum of 125 of the 250 total customers needed to achieve your sales objective for the month, you need a digital media mix. Examining CPL and CPL by source is a good comparative starting point in creating inbound marketing efficiencies.

# Buyer Purchase Path Sales Cycle Timeline

The time customers spend on any particular purchase path ranges from mere seconds to years. Factors that affect the average purchase time include price, commoditization of product, whether the customer is a business or an individual, and the buying decision-making norms for a given industry.

After you've discovered the average purchase cycle by product and applied the other metrics in the Customer Conversion Chain, you may now actually begin predictive inbound marketing techniques, which considers all of the factors above to formulate future ROI.

# Glossary

**A/B testing:** In marketing, a comparison of two ads, ad campaigns, landing pages, promotional offers, or websites to see which is more effective. In traditional A/B testing, the A version is usually the current design or the control and the B version is the variant, usually identical to the A except for a single change. This change can be as simple as changing a color in a call-to-action from red to blue or as complex as creating an entirely new ad or website. Testing each allows marketers to conclude which performs better to create more conversions.

**analytics:** The study of meaningful patterns of data in order to research trends or analyze performance. For web analytics, web platforms make finding this data easy. Marketers can use this knowledge to fine-tune and improve their marketing efforts.

**blogging:** From a marketing perspective, blogging means regularly publishing fresh content to your website. This content includes things such as articles, commentary, and visual content like infographics, photos, and videos. Blogging functions as an inbound attraction function, inviting new visitors to your site while promoting thought leadership.

**bounce rate:** The rate in which visitors leave the first page of your site they land on without visiting any other pages. A high bounce rate has a negative effect on search engine rankings.

**buyer persona:** See *persona*.

**Buyer's Journey (also known as the *sales funnel*):** This is a way of describing the buying process, and it's set up in three phases:

- ✔ *Top of the funnel (ToFu):* This refers to the first stage in the buying process; leads are in the first stage of researching a potential problem.

- ✔ *Middle of the funnel (MoFu):* In this phase, customers know they have a problem and are looking for more information. They may download a white paper or an e-book.

- ✔ *Bottom of the funnel (BoFu):* This is the stage of the buying process leads reach when they're just about to close as new customers. They've identified a problem, have shopped around for possible solutions, and are very close to buying. Typically, next steps for leads at this stage are a call from a sales rep, a demo, or a free consultation.

**call-to-action (CTA) button:** A call-to-action button is a button encoded with a web link that website visitors click to move to the next step in the sales funnel. It is usually located on a landing page or conversion page and shows this person is interested in learning more.

**Call-to-Action (CTA) Map:** A Call-to-Action Map is the internal structure of the website created strategically to guide web visitors through the buying process. It includes your website wireframe and site map and is designed as a blueprint to create a streamlined user interface. Users get to the next step, or the next landing page, by clicking a CTA.

**clickthrough rate (CTR):** The percentage of people who click on an ad with respect to the number of times your ad was shown (or click on an email with respect to the volume of emails sent). It is arrived at by dividing the number of clicks by the number of impressions.

**closed-loop marketing:** Holistic tracking goals and campaigns in order to show how marketing efforts have impacted an organization's business objectives, including the bottom line.

**content:** From a marketing perspective, content consists of articles, blogs, commentary, infographics, ideas, photos, or videos created to attract buyer personas. If created correctly, buyer personas will read it, engage with it, and share it.

**context:** The setting of a word or event. From a marketing perspective, context refers to placing the right type of content in front of the right people. It's important to ensure your content is created for the intended audience. Keep your buyer personas in mind when creating content, and make sure both the form and substance appeals to them.

**content management system (CMS):** A set of processes that enables the management of your website information from content creation through distribution.

**content relationship management (CRM):** A software platform that allows you to synchronize the marketing data you collect with your sales team.

**conversion:** The willing release of personal consumer data in exchange for something of perceived value, usually a downloadable piece of content. The ultimate conversion is a sale, donation, or subscription.

**Conversion Machine:** A high performance website is also known as a "Conversion Machine" because it is the hub of attraction and conversion.

**conversion path:** The strategically developed path or series of web pages that web visitors are guided through in order to create a conversion. To better assist them throughout your site's buying process, they are guided along this path with CTA buttons and offers that appear to the consumer as intuitive, logical next steps.

**conversion rate:** The percentage of people who completed your desired action. In the broadest sense, conversion rate is the percentage of unique visitors who became customers.

**cost-per-click (CPC):** The price you pay each time someone clicks on your ad, whether it's a display ad on a social media platform or search results on Bing or Google.

**cost-per-lead (CPL):** The price you pay for each lead you attract. CPL can be calculated by taking the total dollars spent in a given period of time to attract leads and dividing that by the number of leads you actually received. Digital Dollars Invested divided by the number of leads captured. Calculate on a monthly, quarterly, and annual basis.

**cost-per-thousand (CPM):** A consumer-awareness metric that measures your efficiency in reaching a particular audience via any given media vehicle.

**Customer Conversion Chain:** A series of metrics that measure key conversion points in the customer conversion path including impressions, visits, unique visits, leads, marketing-qualified leads, sales-qualified leads, opportunities, customers, and the lifetime value of a customer.

**Einstein Assessment:** A proprietary, all-encompassing website audit, which includes calculations and consulting, and acts as a roadmap to digital success.

**Facebook:** The largest social-media platform, on which people can find, like, and engage with your business.

**The 4 E's of Content Marketing:** *Educate, Engage, Encourage,* and *Embrace.*

**The 4 P's of Inbound Marketing:** The "new" 4 P's of Marketing, used for inbound marketing, are *profile/persona, product pyramid, place in purchase path/loop,* and *path to conversion.*

**The 4 P's of Marketing:** Typically used in the basics of marketing. The 4 P's are *product, place, price,* and *promotion.*

**Google+:** A social platform that allows users to create profiles and engage with business profiles.

**G.O.S.T.:** Acronym for *goals, objectives, strategy,* and *tactics.*

**HTML (Hypertext Markup Language):** The language and set of codes used to write web pages.

**inbound marketing:** A set of marketing processes and concepts designed to attract qualified leads digitally, rather than through the use of more traditional means of marketing, such as TV, radio, and print. By aligning your content with your buyer personas' needs, leads are naturally attracted to you, allowing them to convert and become your customer. At its core, inbound marketing consists of customer attraction and conversion.

**inbound marketing assessment:** A strategic way to grade your digital marketing with a holistic focus. Reports attraction and conversion statistics, while pinpointing pitfalls and opportunities.

**keywords:** The terms, phrases, subjects, and categories people use to search for you or your organization online. Choose keywords that aren't too difficult to rank for, making it easy for search engines, such as Google and Bing, to find you. Also be sure to choose keywords your buyer personas are searching for.

**landing page:** A landing page is a page on your website that includes a form designed to capture visitor contact information, making them a lead. In exchange for their information, the page offers an e-book, a webinar, or some other valuable offer.

**Lifestyle Loop:** An ongoing process allowing marketers to connect with individuals, rather than with the masses, in a continuous "loop" of interactivity that includes attraction, reattraction, engagement, and reengagement throughout a dynamic customer purchase path.

**Lifestyler:** A loyal customer advocate or brand evangelist.

**LinkedIn:** A social-networking site for professionals and businesses.

**marketing automation:** A software platform with associated tools and analytics designed to incorporate an automated attraction, lead-nurturing, conversion, and analytics reporting strategy with behavior-based workflows, triggered emails, and analytics.

**marketing qualified lead (MQL):** Leads who match your buyer profile model. Whether or not a lead fits your buyer profile is a judgement call, typically made by a human within your organization, so predetermined lead scoring may help to quantify.

**off-page optimization:** A type of SEO that refers visitors to other pages that share your content and creates incoming links. When you create useful, interesting content, people are more likely to share a link to it.

**on-page optimization:** A type of SEO that takes place on any particular website page to ensure search engines find you. This includes using a title tag, URL, image tags, and keywords.

**open rate:** The rate in which your sent emails are opened by the addressee.

**pay-per-click (PPC):** A digital advertising option for marketers to choose on an online platform, like Google or Facebook. When this option is selected, ads will show on their customers' screens, and marketers will pay only when someone clicks the ad. Opportunities exist to customize your target audience and analytics to show exactly how well it performed.

**persona (buyer persona):** A profile of your target customer. It includes demographics, psychographics, behaviors, wants, and needs. This helps you market and write content that helps or intrigues them because it is deemed valuable and attractive to the user.

**Pinterest:** A photo- and image-sharing social media platform.

**product pyramid:** A consumer conversion path with its own set of keywords, for each product.

**qualified lead:** A contact who requested additional information about a product or service and/or filled out a website form. Qualified leads have a need for your services/products.

**QR code:** A QR code (abbreviated from *quick-response code*) is a square barcode that looks pixelated and can be read by smart phones. It is encoded and, when scanned, directs a user to a URL.

**remarketing:** A digital marketing effort aimed at a known person who has previously engaged with you, whether it's the first conversion or the end action of your specific inbound marketing campaign.

**retargeting:** A digital marketing effort aimed at an unknown person who has not yet engaged with you but has visited your website.

**return on investment (ROI):** What you get back from the marketing effort investment you make.

**sales qualified lead (SQL):** A lead that has been scored and evaluated based on need, intent, budget, and timeline.

**search engine optimization (SEO):** Optimizing/enhancing your web page or website so that search engines can easily find it and place it at the top of the search results.

**search engine results pages (SERPs):** Pages that display from the search engine when you type in a particular keyword or phrase.

**Shared Strategic Blueprint (SSB):** A plan for business success in which you have a quarterly internal marketing meeting, collaborate with your team to create marketing goals and priorities, and make sure each objective is S.M.A.R.T. (specific, measureable, attainable, relevant, and time-bound).

**S.M.A.R.T.:** When creating internal objectives, make sure they are *specific, measureable, attainable, relevant,* and *time-bound.*

**spaghetti theory:** When you create a workflow for each of your products/services, your workflows can easily get intertwined and confusing, and can appear to be thoughtless, spammy emails to the customers you've worked so hard to gain — in other words, a big bowl of "workflow spaghetti." Thoughtfully consider and plan each workflow you build with a purpose.

**Twitter:** Twitter is a social-media platform on which users follow one another and provide short blurbs or "tweets" others can see and share.

**URL:** The direct address to a web page or piece of information on the web. Typically begins with www and ends with .com.

**website grader:** A tactical way to "grade" your website to see how you are doing with technological metrics and website statistics.

**workflow:** A set of triggered emails sent to a lead with the intent to nurture and guide him or her through the conversion path. These can be automated as well as behavior-based. A workflow is sometimes referred to as a *drip campaign.*

**YouTube:** A video-sharing website and social-media platform.

# Index

• K •

**• O •**

● Z ●

# About the Author

Inbound marketing strategist, speaker, and author **Scott Anderson Miller** fed his serial entrepreneurship with 13 start-ups (some winners and some losers) over the past 25 years. He entered marketing at age 14, selling ads for the family newspaper after a successful career as corner newsboy. Later he worked at several newspapers and TV stations before founding his current firm in 1996. He has owned two marketing firms, including one ranked in the 2014 *Inc.* 500 (*Inc.* magazine's list of the fastest-growing private companies in America). As owner of Marketing Matters Inbound, Anderson practices expertise in conversion optimization, creating the Customer Conversion Chain and the Lifestyle Loop in the process. He's an occasional mountain climber and enjoys world travel with his wife, Cindy, and their three grown children, Ian, Sam, and Mary Grace. He is also infatuated with monkeys.

# Author's Acknowledgments

Thank you to my business partner and colleague, Nathaniel C. Davidson.

This book would not have met deadline without the help of Sarah, Natalie, Jay, and Ben and the entire Marketing Matters Inbound team. Thank you.

Thanks to my mom and dad for encouraging me to take the road less traveled.

Thank you to Curious George for inspiring me every day.

# Dedication

This book is dedicated to my wife and soul mate, Cindy Luther Miller, whose undying support and hand-holding makes this life's journey together a treasured experience.

## Publisher's Acknowledgments

**Acquisitions Editor:** Amy Fandrei

**Project Editor:** Christopher Morris

**Copy Editor:** Christopher Morris

**Technical Editor:** Michelle Krasniak

**Editorial Assistant:** Claire Brock

**Sr. Editorial Assistant:** Cherie Case

**Project Coordinator:** Kumar Chellapa

**Cover Image:** Sergey Furtaev/Shutterstock